WITHDRAWN

HARVARD LIBRARY

WITHDRAWN

FROM REBUKE TO CONSOLATION

Program in Judaic Studies
Brown University
Box 1826
Providence, RI 02912

BROWN JUDAIC STUDIES

Edited by

David C. Jacobson
Ross S. Kraemer
Saul M. Olyan
Michael L. Satlow

Number 338

FROM REBUKE TO CONSOLATION
Exegesis and Theology in the Liturgical Anthology of the
Ninth of Av Season

by
Elsie R. Stern

From Rebuke to Consolation

Exegesis and Theology in the Liturgical Anthology of the Ninth of Av Season

Elsie R. Stern

Brown Judaic Studies
Providence, Rhode Island

© 2004 by Brown University. All rights reserved.

No part of this work may be reproduced or transmitted in any form or by any means, electronic or mechanical, including photocopying and recording, or by means of any information storage or retrieval system, except as may be expressly permitted by the 1976 Copyright Act or in writing from the publisher. Requests for permission should be addressed in writing to the Rights and Permissions Office, Program in Judaic Studies, Brown University, Box 1826, Providence, RI 02912, USA.

Copyediting, Design, and Typesetting: Abe Hendin / AH Prepress
http://ahprepress.com
Indexes: Nancy Zibman

Library of Congress Cataloging-in-Publication Data
Stern, Elsie R.
    From rebuke to consolation : exegesis and theology in the liturgical anthology of the Ninth of Av season / Elsie R. Stern
      p. cm. — (Brown Judaic Studies ; no. 338)
    Includes bibliographical references and index.
    ISBN 1-930675-21-6 (cloth binding : alk. paper)
    1. Ninth of Av—Liturgy. 2. Rabbinical literature—History and criticism. 3. Consolation (Judaism) I. Title. II. Series.

BM675.K5Z87 2004
296.4'539—dc22

2004024032
CIP

Printed in the United States of America
on acid-free paper

*To my parents, Jack Stern and Priscilla Rudin Stern (z"l),
with great love*

Contents

Acknowledgements ix
Abbreviations xi

1 • Introduction   1

Interaction of Non-Rabbinic and Rabbinic Culture in the Late Antique Palestinian Synagogue. 7
Synagogue and *Beit Midrash:* The Intended Audiences of Rabbinic Literature 8
The Theology of the Tisha b'Av Season in the Context of Late Antique Palestine 11
Exegesis and Theology in the Literature of the Tisha b'Av Season 12

2 • The Tisha b'Av Lectionary Cycle   17

The Synagogue Bible and Popular Jewish Theology 17
History of the Tisha b'Av Lectionary Cycle 20
Lectionary Poetics 24
    Identification 26
    Selection 27
    Correspondence 27
    Arrangement 28
Analysis of the Lectionary Cycle 28
    Lamentations 28
       Summary 39
    Haftarot of Rebuke and Consolation 39
    Haftarot of Rebuke 41

Sin-Punishment-Restoration	43
Measure-for-Measure Punishment	44
Reliability of the Prophetic Word	48
Summary	50
Haftarot of Consolation	51
Lamentations and the Haftarot of Consolation	51
The Dialogic Structure	58
The Dialogic Paradigm and the Theology of Intimacy	60
Redemptive Nature of Divine Love	69
Enactment of Divine Reconciliation	72
From Grief to Consolation	72
Exhortation and Efficacy	73
The Theology of Consolation in the Context of the Synagogue	74
Conclusion	76

3 • Pesikta de-Rav Kahana 13 and 22 — 79

Sitz im Leben	81
Poetics	83
Individual Units	83
Chapters	84
Analysis	87
Chapter 13	87
Unit 1	89
Units 9–11	91
Unit 10	94
Unit 15	96
Summary	97
Chapter 22	97
Unit 1	98
Unit 2	101
Unit 3	104
Unit 4	104
Unit 5	105
Summary	107
Theology of Consolation and the Culture of the Synagogue	108
Conclusion	110

4 • Eleazar Kallir's *Kedushtot* for the Sabbaths of Consolation — 113

Sitz im Leben	114
Piyyut as Prayer	116

Piyyut as Poetry	118
Kedushtot for the Sabbaths of Consolation by Eleazar Kallir	118
Rhyme	120
Allusion	121
Case Study 1: *Magen* for *Kedushta* to Shabbat *Naḥamu*	123
Rhyme Patterns	128
Allusion	130
Litany of Biblical Verses	134
Relationship to the *Kedushta* as a Whole	136
Summary	136
Case Study 2: *Magen* and *Meḥayeh* to Shabbat *Vatomar Tzion*	137
Rhyme Patterns	142
Allusion	144
Litany of Biblical Verses	149
Relationship to the *Kedushta* as a Whole	152
Summary	153
Poetry, Prayer, and the Synagogue Context	153

5 • Targum Jonathan's Translation of the Haftarot of Consolation   155

Targumic Function and Exegesis	157
Analysis of Targum Jonathan to Isaiah 40:1–23	159
The Romantic Trope: Isaiah 49:14–23; 50:1–3; 54:1–8; 62:1–5	163
Conclusion	167

6 • Conclusion: The Literature of the Tisha b'Av Season   169

Text, Ritual, and Communal Experience	171
The Propagation of Rabbinic Judaism in Late Antiquity	174

Bibliography	177
Index of Texts Cited	195
General Index	205

Acknowledgements

I could not have completed this project without the support, wise counsel and good humor of many teachers, friends and colleagues. This project began as my dissertation at the University of Chicago Divinity School, which I wrote under the direction of Michael Fishbane and the readership of Tikva Frymer-Kensky and John Collins. Through their teaching, these mentors taught me to develop my skills as a scholar; through their examples, they showed me how the best scholars ground their curiosity, passion, and engagement with contemporary concerns in rigorous scholarship. I am also grateful to Larry Hoffman, Ray Scheindlin, and David Stern, who were incredibly generous with their time and wisdom at various stages of this project.

I would also like to thank the administration of Fordham University and my former colleagues in the Theology department there. Fordham granted me the research leave that allowed me to revise this monograph for publication and my colleagues in the Theology department offered me vital counsel and support through the process. I am particularly grateful to my colleague, friend, and mentor, Harry Nasuti, whose relentless encouragement catalyzed the rebirth of this project. I would also like to thank David Ruderman, Director of the Center for Advanced Judaic Studies at the University of Pennsylvania, who has allowed and encouraged me to continue my scholarly research in my current professional home.

I owe many thanks to Saul Olyan at the Brown Judaic Studies series as well as Abe Hendin and Nancy Zibman. Their eagle-eyes and attention to detail have made this a much better book. In addition to the many teachers and colleagues who have provided guidance and support, I am deeply grateful to the family and friends who have supported me through the various iterations of this project. I am especially grateful to my parents, Jack Stern and Priscilla Stern (*z"l*), my brothers, Jonathan and David Stern, my sisters-in-law, Nancy Kasten and Jamie Gardner, and my friends and comrades-in-arms, Rachel Anisfeld, Beth Berkowitz, Natalie Dohrmann, Connie Furey, Tim Lytton, Julie Schonfeld, Bradley Solmsen. Without their emotional, intellectual, and technical support, this book would not have come to be.

Finally, I am most grateful to my husband, Steve Cohen. We met when I was putting the vowels in the manuscript of the dissertation, married when that manuscript was hibernating in a drawer, and welcomed our daughter Sarah into the world as I was revising the manuscript for publication. Through our life together, I have been blessed with the experiences of joy, intimacy and consolation that are the true subjects of this book.

Abbreviations

Rabbinic Sources

ARN	Avot de-Rabbi Natan
b.	Babylonian Talmud
BB	Baba Batra
BM	Baba Metzia
Deut R.	Deuteronomy Rabbah
Est R.	Esther Rabbah
Exod R.	Exodus Rabbah
Gen R.	Genesis Rabbah
j.	Jerusalem Talmud
Ket	Ketubbot
Kid	Kiddushin
Kil	Kilayim
Lam R.	Lamentations Rabbah
Lam Z.	Lamentations Zuta
Lev R.	Leviticus Rabbah
m.	Mishnah
Meg	Megillah
Mek	Mekhilta de-Rabbi Ishmael
MHG	Midrash Hagadol
Mid Pss	Midrash Psalms
MK	Moed Katan
Num R.	Numbers Rabbah
Pes	Pesahim
Pes R.	Pesikta Rabbati
PRE	Pirkei de-Rabbi Eleazar
PRK	Pesikta de-Rav Kahana
RH	Rosh Hashanah
Ruth R.	Ruth Rabbah

San	Sanhedrin
Shab	Shabbat
Sifre Deut	Sifre Deuteronomy
Sof	Soferim
Song R.	Song of Songs Rabbah
Song Z.	Song of Songs Zuta
Sot	Sotah
Suk	Sukkah
t.	Tosefta
Taan	Taanit
Tan	Midrash Tanhuma
TJ	Targum Jonathan
Yal	Yalkut Shim'oni
Yeb	Yebamot
Yom	Yoma

Secondary Sources

AB	Anchor Bible
JBL	*Journal of Biblical Literature*
JJS	*Journal of Jewish Studies*
JSOT	*Journal for the Study of the Old Testament*
MGJW	*Monatschrift für Geschichte und Wissenschaft des Judentums*
PAAJR	*Proceedings of the American Academy of Jewish Research*
ScrHier	Scripta Hierosolymitana

1

Introduction

In recent years there has been a significant shift in the scholarly understanding of the development of rabbinic Judaism and the role of the rabbis in late antique Judaism. Earlier generations of scholars relied primarily on a positivistic reading of rabbinic literature to describe the role of the rabbinic sages in late antiquity. As a result, they articulated a version of Jewish history in which the rabbis emerged as the leaders of Palestinian Judaism shortly after the destruction of the second temple. According to this narrative, rabbinic Judaism became "normative" Judaism as early as the beginning of the second century CE.[1] Through a more critical reading of the rabbinic texts, increased attention to archaeological and epigraphical evidence, and more serious consideration of the larger socio-political context of Palestine in the Roman and Byzantine periods, contemporary scholars have largely rejected this narrative of the rabbinic movement. Instead, the emerging consensus argues that the rabbis began as a marginal movement in the decades after the destruction and continued to be quite marginal for the first few centuries of the common era.[2] Into the third century, the sages were considered to be authorities only by their own circles

---

1. Gedalia Alon, *The Jews in Their Land in the Talmudic Age* (trans. Gershon Levi; Cambridge: Harvard University Press, 1989); Michael Avi-Yonah, *The Jews of Palestine: A Political History from the Bar Kokhba War to the Arab Conquest* (New York: Schocken, 1974).

2. Shaye J. D. Cohen, "The Place of the Rabbi in Jewish Society of the Second Century," in *The Galilee in Late Antiquity* (ed. L. Levine; New York: Jewish Theological Seminary, 1992), 157–73; Martin Goodman, *State and Society in Roman Galilee, A.D. 132–212* (Totowa, NJ: Rowman & Allanheld, 1983); Catherine Hezser, *The Social Structure of the Rabbinic Movement in Roman Palestine* (Tübingen: Mohr Siebeck, 1997); Lee I. Levine, *The Rabbinic Class of Roman Palestine in Late Antiquity* (New

of disciples. If they had any authority for the rest of the Jewish population, it was primarily over issues of purity, marriage and divorce, and tithes.[3] After the rise of Constantine, a combination of internal and external factors, including the urbanization of the rabbinic movement and the changing views of religion and identity prompted by the Christianization of the empire, led to the growth of rabbinic prominence and authority in the wider Jewish society. There remains debate over the speed of this process of rabbinization. Lee Levine and others argue that the rabbis' influence began to grow in the late third to fourth centuries.[4] Most recently, Seth Schwartz has argued that while a new form of Judaism was articulated in the fourth century, rabbinic Judaism did not become widely influential until, at the earliest, the sixth century.[5] While there is still ample debate over the nature and causes of this process of rabbinization, it is clear that by the late fifth to sixth centuries, the rabbis had become influential in shaping the religious culture of Palestinian Jews.[6]

The ancient synagogue has emerged as an important source of evidence for this recent re-evaluation of the role and position of the rabbis in late antique Judaism. Like the study of the rabbinic movement, the study of the ancient synagogue has undergone a significant shift in the past few decades. Until relatively recently, most scholars had assumed that synagogues were both an important part of Palestinian Jewish society and also sites for the practice of rabbinic Judaism from as early as the Yavnean period.[7] Data which countered this view, such as the paucity of archaeological evidence for Palestinian synagogues in the second and third centuries, and the discovery of lavish iconic decorations in both Palestinian and diaspora synagogues, were interpreted as anomalous or irrelevant. The scarcity of archaeological evidence for second- and third-century synagogues was dismissed as either a fault of the archaeological record or as a result of the fact that synagogues in this period might not have been dis-

---

York: Jewish Theological Seminary, 1989); Seth Schwartz, *Imperialism and Jewish Society, 200 B.C.E. to 640 C.E.* (Princeton: Princeton University Press, 2001).

3. Cohen, "Place of the Rabbi," 161; Goodman, *State and Society*, 93–118; Hezser, *Social Structure*, 191–93.

4. Lee I. Levine, *The Ancient Synagogue: The First Thousand Years* (New Haven: Yale University Press, 2000), 469–70.

5. Schwartz, *Imperialism*, 263–74.

6. I specify *religious* culture here to distinguish religious culture from other aspects of society, including the economic and jurisprudential.

7. See, for example, Ismar Elbogen, *Jewish Liturgy: A Comprehensive History* (trans. Raymond Scheindlin; Philadelphia: Jewish Publication Society, 1993); Solomon Zeitlin, "Origins of the Synagogue: A Study in the Development of Jewish Institutions," *PAAJR* 2 (1930–1931): 69–81.

tinguished from other types of buildings. The discovery of the lavish iconographic art in both diaspora and Palestinian synagogues did trigger a debate over the nature of Judaism in late antiquity. Erwin Goodenough argued that the art of the synagogue pointed to a well-developed, non-rabbinic, popular Judaism that was deeply mystical and hellenized.[8] However, since his reading of the art itself was quite problematic, his analysis of the synagogue as a locus for a non-rabbinic form of Judaism did not become regnant in scholarly circles.[9] Instead, the view of Michael Avi-Yonah, who argued that the images in the synagogue functioned as decoration, devoid of religious meaning, became dominant.[10] As a consequence of this dismissive reading, the synagogue art did not challenge the portrait of the early synagogue as a rabbinic institution.[11]

In recent years, this view of the development of the ancient synagogue has been challenged by one which is more firmly grounded in the archaeological and epigraphical evidence of the synagogues themselves, and also takes into account wider social trends in Palestine in the Roman and Byzantine periods. The prevalence of synagogues in Palestine during the first to third centuries is now a subject of debate. In his monumental work *The Ancient Synagogue: The First Thousand Years*, Lee Levine argues that, despite the scarcity of archaeological evidence, the synagogue remained a central communal institution in Roman Palestine in this era.[12] In contrast, Seth Schwartz argues that the scarcity of archaeological evidence reflects the infrequency of synagogue construction in this period. He argues that during these centuries, Jewish society had largely "disintegrated" and that most Jews in Palestine participated in the larger pagan culture of the empire, not in a particularist Jewish culture that would have supported the construction of synagogues.[13] While there is debate over the prevalence of Palestinian synagogues in the second and early third centuries, the evidence for a synagogue building boom in the late third to fourth centuries is incontrovertible. The majority of synagogues excavated in the

---

8. Erwin Goodenough, *Jewish Symbols in the Greco-Roman World* (Princeton: Princeton University Press, 1953–68).

9. Although Goodenough's particular reading of the synagogue art has been discredited, the insight that there were different "Judaisms" in late antiquity has become one of the fundamental axioms of the study of early Judaism. For a discussion of the reception of Goodenough's work, see Jacob Neusner, *Symbol and Theology in Early Judaism* (Minneapolis: Fortress Press, 1991), 172–75.

10. Michael Avi-Yonah, *Art in Ancient Palestine* (Jerusalem: Magnes Press, 1981).

11. For a discussion of this debate and its implications for the study of the ancient Judaism, see Schwartz, *Imperialism*, 133–36.

12. Levine, *Ancient Synagogue*, 171.

13. Schwartz, *Imperialism*, 175–76, 205–12.

areas of Judea, the Galilee and the Golan heights date from this period.[14] This building boom suggests that from the fourth century at the latest, the synagogue was a prominent communal institution for Palestinian Jews.

The identity of the synagogue as a consistently rabbinic institution has also come into question. Rabbinic sources from the third to fourth centuries certainly testify to substantial rabbinic interest in synagogue activities such as communal prayer and the recitation of scripture, and also report some rabbinic involvement in the synagogue. However, the combined weight of both literary and non-literary evidence demonstrates that actual rabbinic involvement in synagogues in this period was, at best, marginal. This evidence suggests that the synagogues were run and supported by non-rabbinic leaders. Of the more than 100 inscriptions found in Palestinian synagogues, not one names a sage known to us from the rabbinic corpus. In addition, discussions of the synagogue in the Theodosian Code and in the writings of the fourth- to fifth-century Church fathers identify the patriarchs, the archisynagogoi and presbyters as synagogue leaders, but never mention the sages.[15] Finally, the archaeological evidence points to norms of synagogue building which differed from rabbinic dicta. Whereas the Tosefta states that synagogue entrances should face east, only a handful of the excavated synagogues conform to this dictum.[16]

Most strikingly, the rich figural decoration on the floors and walls of many of the excavated synagogues clearly contravenes the iconoclastic dicta of the rabbis. While it is impossible to know what the images of Helios in the synagogue mosaics of Hammat Tiberias, Bet Alpha, Huseifa, Sepphoris and Na'aran meant to the synagogue community, these images clearly violated the rabbinic prohibition against images of the deity. Even where the synagogue iconography is not so blatantly non-rabbinic, it still suggests that the culture of the synagogues was distinct from that of the rabbis. As Jacob Neusner has observed, the most common set of symbols in synagogue art—the lulav, etrog, menorah and shofar—does not appear as a central set of symbols in rabbinic literature.[17]

Even the rabbinic sources themselves attest to tensions between rabbinic norms and expectations and synagogue practices. One of the most frequently cited sets of examples is found in j. Meg 4:1, 74d, which describes a series of cases in which the targum ritual of a synagogue contradicted rabbinic dicta. Thus, while the rabbinic literature testifies that the

---

14. Rachel Hachlili, *Ancient Jewish Art and Archaeology in the Land of Israel* (Leiden: Brill, 1988), 148–49.
15. Levine, *Ancient Synagogue*, 442–45.
16. T. Meg 3:22.
17. Neusner, *Symbol*, 186–90.

rabbis had developed rules to govern synagogue practice by the late third century, these rules did not yet define and determine synagogue practice.

While rabbinic involvement in the synagogue was probably marginal during the first few centuries of the common era, by the fifth to sixth centuries the rabbis and rabbinic theology had become far more influential in the culture of the Palestinian synagogues. Both archaeological and literary evidence attests to this development. In the mid sixth century, there is a shift from iconic to aniconic art on synagogue floors. In addition, in the late fifth century, synagogues are constructed with apses to hold the Torah ark. While the apse itself was borrowed from contemporary church architecture, the inclusion of a permanent and monumental Torah shrine in the synagogue reinforces the centrality of the Torah within the synagogue. While neither of these architectural trends, in isolation, necessarily points to increased rabbinic influence in the synagogue, they do correspond to rabbinic iconoclastic tendencies and to the rabbinic conviction that the synagogue derives its holiness from the presence of the Torah within it.[18] Perhaps the strongest evidence for the increasing influence of the rabbinic movement in this period comes from the liturgical poetry (hereafter, *piyyut*) of the period. The *piyyutim* (liturgical poems; sg. also *piyyut*), which were composed by professional synagogue poets, were written for performance during prayer services in the synagogue and thus are unquestionably and exclusively synagogue literature. At the same time, however, the piyyutim correspond to the statutory prayers as described and mandated in the rabbinic literature. In addition, the piyyutim are deeply informed by, and dependent on, rabbinic scriptural exegesis and rabbinic theology as it is articulated in rabbinic literature. The saturation of rabbinic motifs and traditions within the piyyutim testifies to the increased and institutionalized presence of rabbinic ideology within synagogue culture by the fifth to sixth centuries.

The emergence of piyyut in this period, supported by the evidence of the move toward iconoclasm and the increasing centrality of the Torah ark, suggests that by the fifth to sixth centuries Palestinian synagogues had increasingly become loci for the expression of rabbinic ideology and the practice of a rabbinic form of Judaism. Because the synagogue was already a popular communal Jewish institution, it became an important locus for the encounter between the rabbis and the wider Jewish community. As the rabbis sought to increase their influence within the wider community, the synagogue would have been a key place for the articulation

---

18. Schwartz, *Imperialism*, 260–61.

and propagation of a rabbinic theology which was designed for, and directed at, the Jewish populace at large.

This book contributes to the ongoing research into the emergence of rabbinic Judaism in the synagogue setting through a study of one constellation of rabbinic and synagogue literatures: the sequence of prophetic lectionary texts (hereafter, *haftarot*; sg. *haftarah*) designated for the sabbaths surrounding Tisha b'Av, and the midrashim, piyyutim and targumic texts that interpret them. The lectionary sequence for the Tisha b'Av season consists of the haftarot designated for the three sabbaths preceding Tisha b'Av; the book of Lamentations, which is read on the fast day itself; and the haftarot for the seven sabbaths that follow it. While the constituent texts of this sequence are biblical, the lectionary sequence is a distinct, post-biblical creation which was designed for liturgical use in the synagogue.

The interpretive texts that I treat in this study are:

- Chapters 13 and 22 of Pesikta de-Rav Kahana (hereafter, PRK), a collection of midrashim, probably dating from the late fifth to the early sixth century, whose chapters comment on the lectionary texts for festivals and special sabbaths. Chapters 13 and 22 correspond to the first and final sabbaths of the Tisha b'Av season sequence.

- Selections from the *kedushtot* of Eleazar Kallir (sixth to seventh century) for the first two sabbaths after Tisha b'Av. The *kedushta* is a genre of piyyut composed as part of the sabbath morning liturgy.

- Targum Jonathan's treatment of the haftarot of the Tisha b'Av cycle. Targum Jonathan (hereafter, TJ) is a highly literalist Aramaic translation of the prophetic books which probably originated in Palestine but went through several stages of revision and redaction in Babylonia.

An analysis of this literary constellation allows us to better understand two dynamics that are relevant to the discussion of the development of rabbinic Judaism in the late antique synagogue: a) the relationship between the rabbinic Judaism that was propagated in the synagogue and the non-rabbinic synagogue culture that the rabbis encountered and interacted with there; b) the relationship between rabbinic literature that was composed by sages for their rabbinic colleagues and students, and rabbinic literature that was directed toward a wider Jewish lay audience as it was imagined by the rabbis.

Interaction of Non-Rabbinic and Rabbinic Culture in the Late Antique Palestinian Synagogue

While we have little non-rabbinic Jewish literature from late antique Palestine, archaeological evidence from Palestinian synagogues from the fourth to sixth centuries bears witness to some patterns of theological concern and communal self-understanding. The appearance of central mosaics depicting Helios surrounded by the signs of the zodiac and depictions of the seasons in five synagogues in Palestine suggests that a cosmic creator theology was part of the ideology of synagogue culture in this period.[19] In addition, the ubiquity of temple-related iconography testifies to a concern with the temple and a desire to invoke the temple and temple cult in the synagogue setting. Finally, the inscriptions of several Palestinian synagogues from this period identify the synagogues as holy places and the synagogue communities as holy communities.[20] According to Seth Schwartz, by the end of the fifth century, Palestinian Jews considered their local communities to hold "the special religious status, the obligations and the promises that God granted to and imposed upon the Jews as a whole, according to the Bible."[21] While the archaeological evidence allows us to paint with broad strokes some central elements of pre-rabbinic synagogue

---

19. There is a vast literature on the iconography of ancient synagogues in general and the zodiac panels in particular. For comprehensive discussions of the Palestinian synagogue art, see Hachlili, *Ancient Jewish Art*; Levine, *Ancient Synagogue*, 194–231, 561–79. Goodenough, *Jewish Symbols* and Avi Yonah, *Art* remain valuable despite their problematic readings of the art. For discussions of the zodiac panels and their theological significance, see Joan Branham, "Vicarious Sacrality: Temple Space in Ancient Synagogues," in *Ancient Synagogues: Historical Analysis and Archaeological Discovery*, vol. 2 (ed. Dan Urman and Paul Flesher; Leiden: Brill, 1995), 319–45; Shaye Cohen,"The Temple and the Synagogue," in *The Temple in Antiquity: Ancient Records and Modern Perspectives* (ed. T. G. Madsen; Provo, UT: Religious Studies Center, Brigham Young University, 1984), 170; Gideon Foerster, "The Zodiac in Ancient Synagogues and its Place in Jewish Thought and Literature," *Eretz Israel* 18 (1987): 387–91 (Heb.); Schwartz, *Imperialism*, 252–59; Zvi Weiss and Ehud Netzer, "The Sepphoris Synagogues: A New Look at Synagogue Art and Architecture in the Byzantine Period," in *Galilee through the Centuries* (ed. Eric Meyers; Winona Lake: Eisenbrauns, 1999), 199–227.

20. Levine, *Ancient Synagogue,* 220–22. This phenomenon is part of a larger trend in late antiquity in which sanctity was ascribed to a variety of sites and figures including churches, synagogues, pilgrimage sites, charismatic figures and wonder-workers. See J. Z. Smith, *Map is not Territory: Studies in the History of Religions* (Leiden: Brill, 1978) 291–93; Peter Brown, *Society and the Holy in Late Antiquity* (Berkeley: University of California Press, 1982) 5–8, 163–65.

21. Schwartz, *Imperialism*, 275.

ideology, the details of this ideology remain obscure. For example, it is impossible to discern with certainty the precise nature of this concern for the temple. Does the iconography represent a nostalgia for the defunct temple cult, an eschatological hope for its rebuilding, or an ongoing identification of the synagogue with the temple and its functions? How did the synagogue community understand the "holiness" that they attributed to themselves and to their synagogues? How did that holiness relate to the holiness of the defunct temple and the biblical notion of the holiness of the larger community of Israel? Despite these uncertainties, the archaeological evidence is vital because, as creations of Jews who were not members of the rabbinic class, the synagogue art, architecture, and inscriptions communicate something of the self-understanding and theological outlook of this segment of Jewish society.

In contrast, the lectionary cycle, the midrashim in PRK, and the translations in TJ are products of rabbinic culture. The liturgical poems of Kallir lie somewhere in the middle of the spectrum. Kallir was a professional of the synagogue, not a professional member of the *beit midrash,* and he composed his poems for a general synagogue audience.[22] At the same time, his poems are strongly informed by rabbinic theology and rabbinic exegetical traditions. By looking at these texts in relationship to one another and to the synagogue setting, I hope to contribute a more variegated portrait of the ways in which rabbinic, non-rabbinic and "semi-rabbinic" voices contributed to late antique synagogue culture.

Synagogue and *Beit Midrash*: The Intended Audiences of Rabbinic Literature

The second distinction which is central to this study is that between two classes of rabbinic literature: literature directed toward an academic audi-

---

22. The liturgical poets known to us never appear as tradents in the canonical rabbinic literature. In addition, rabbinic literature does not identify the composition of liturgical poetry as a rabbinic activity, nor does it include anecdotal references to rabbis as synagogue poets or vice versa. Thus there is no positive evidence that would lead us to identify them as members of the rabbinic academies. The use of the term "Rabbi" with regard to these poets is not conclusive, since by this period the term was used widely as an honorific. It did not narrowly identify those who had received ordination from the rabbinic academies. In addition, the archaeological evidence suggests that synagogue leaders and professional synagogue functionaries were distinct from the professionals of the rabbinic academy. This generalization, combined with the absence of specific evidence to the contrary, leads to the conclusion that the *payyetanim* (liturgical poets) were probably not professional denizens of the rabbinic academies.

ence of rabbinic colleagues and students, and literature intended for a wider audience of Jews who were not members of the rabbinic elite.

In the past, judgments regarding the degree to which rabbinic texts were directed at a popular or academic audience often depended on scholars' intuitions and assumptions about popular discourse and ideology. For example, Joseph Heinemann identified the genre of the midrashic proem with live sermons because he thought that the proem's creation and resolution of suspense would have been pleasing to a synagogue audience.[23] A similar phenomenon occurs in targum studies where the identification of the targum's popular *Sitz im Leben* is based partially on assumptions regarding the limited exegetical abilities of the general Jewish population of late antiquity.[24]

In this study, I advocate a more sociological approach to the question of intended audience, an approach which is rooted in the demographics of the synagogue and the *beit midrash*. It is clear from both the archaeological evidence of the synagogues themselves and rabbinic comments regarding synagogues, that the synagogues were frequented by a heterogeneous Jewish population. Women and men of various social and economic positions attended, as did rabbis and non-rabbinic Jews.[25] In contrast, the study houses were the province of the sages and their students—the rabbinic intelligentsia. In this study, I consider literature which was clearly composed for the synagogue to be literature directed at a general audience. In contrast, I consider literature which was composed for and disseminated in the *beit midrash* to be academic literature. Both of these literatures can be rabbinic; however, the imagined audience of the synagogue literature was that institution's heterogeneous, lay population while the *beit midrash* literature was composed for the sages and their students.

In my view, the lectionary is the purest example of rabbinic literary production intended for a popular audience.[26] While designated lectionary

---

23. Joseph Heinemann, "The Proem in the Aggadic Midrashim: A Form-Critical Study," in *Studies in Aggadah and Folk Literature* (ed. Joseph Heinemann and Dov Noy; ScrHier 22; Jerusalem: Magnes Press), 101.

24. See for example, Leivy Smolar and Moshe Aberbach, *Studies in Targum Jonathan to the Prophets* (New York: Ktav, 1983), xiii.

25. For the presence of women in the synagogue, see Levine, *Ancient Synagogue*, 471–90; Hanna Safrai, "Women in the Ancient Synagogue," in *Daughters of the King* (ed. Susan Grossman and Rivka Haut; Philadelphia: Jewish Publication Society, 1992), 39–42. Rabbinic references to women in the synagogue include b. Sot 22a and b. Meg 18a; to children: m. Meg 4:5–6; to uneducated men: t. Pes 10:8 and t. Meg 3:12.

26. The rabbinic lectionary system, which I describe on pp. 17–19, was established before any thoroughgoing schedule of lectionary readings was established. For many centuries, individual communities determined their own haftarot and

texts may have also been read in the *beit midrash* setting, the *raison d'être* of the lectionary system and selections was the *public* recitation of scripture. The designation of Mondays and Thursdays as days for the public reading of Torah supports this assertion. If the lectionary texts were designated primarily for the *beit midrash* setting, there would have been no reason to designate market days as the days for the reading of scripture. This designation only makes sense if the intended audience of the reading was the general populace, which gathered together on these days.

Beyond the lectionary, however, the distinction between texts directed at an imagined synagogue audience and those composed for rabbis is less absolute. The intended audience of the homiletical midrashim and literalist *targumim* (pl. of "targum") has been the subject of much scholarly discussion. As I will discuss in greater detail below, many scholars have identified the homiletical midrashim closely with the synagogue setting. More recently, emphasis has been placed on the academic nature of these midrashic texts.[27] Within this study, I will argue that PRK is a text composed by rabbis for a rabbinic audience; at the same time, however, the text is dependent on, and oriented toward, scripture in its synagogue context.

The literalist targumim, Targum Onkelos and TJ, have been consistently identified as synagogue texts. While scholars have recognized in the past few decades that the targumim were also used in academic settings, the focus remains on their role as synagogue texts.[28] In this study I will argue that although Targum Jonathan came to be used in synagogues and may even have been composed partially for synagogue use, it is primarily an academic text which does not depend on or acknowledge the synagogue context of the biblical texts.

Consideration of the intended audiences of these four genres contributes to the study of the development of rabbinic Judaism in two important ways: It helps to further clarify the relationship between rabbinic "popular" theology, which was articulated for an imagined general audience, and rabbinic "academic" theology, which was articulated for members of the rabbinic elite. Attention to the intended settings of the genres high-

---

possibly the parameters of each weekly Torah portion. Beginning in the Mishnah and continuing through the amoraic and post-amoraic literature, the rabbis designated particular texts for festivals and special sabbaths. However, for regular sabbaths, great variation among haftarah traditions persisted through the middle ages and, to some degree, to modern times. For a comprehensive survey of known designated haftarot, see Natan Freid, "Haftarah," *Talmudic Encyclopedia*, X (1961), cols. 1–31, 703–23 (Heb.).

27. See pp. 91–93.
28. See p. 155.

lights the interrelationship between the *beit midrash* and synagogue settings while further clarifying the types of exegetical activity and theological production that occurred in, and for, each setting.

The Theology of the Tisha b'Av Season in the Context of Late Antique Palestine

While the lectionary, midrashic and poetic texts that I analyze were never recited together in a single synagogue setting, they provide a composite portrait of the theology of consolation that developed around the lectionary sequence of the Tisha b'Av season. This theology of consolation is particularly germane to both the liturgical season and the social and religious situation of the Jewish communities in late antique Palestine. Though the events commemorated on Tisha b'Av were long past by the fifth to sixth centuries CE, the issues raised by the season remained central to Jewish theology and Jewish identity. At the most universal level, the season raises the theological questions raised by any catastrophic event. Why did it happen? What was God's role in these events? What do these events say about our relationship with God? These issues were quite compelling for Jews in the rabbinic period. Centuries after the destruction of the second temple, Jews of both the land of Israel and the diaspora were living with the consequences of this catastrophe, namely, the absence of Jewish sovereignty and the absence of the temple cult. Thus, when the texts of the lectionary complex discuss the destructions of the temples and their aftermaths, they are also addressing the contemporary community's own situation.

The destructions of the temples and the prolonged absence of Jewish sovereignty were rendered particularly problematic by the theology of history which the Jews inherited from their biblical forebears. According to a central strand of biblical theology, God had entered into a covenant with the Israelites at Sinai. The covenant stipulated that if Israel obeyed God's commandments, the nation would prosper socially, economically and politically. If the people disobeyed, they would suffer the consequences in the spheres of both nature and politics.[29] According to this deuteronomic strand of biblical theology, political misfortune was a sign of covenantal disobedience and divine displeasure. One of the challenges faced by the theologians of the rabbinic period was the need to articulate a theology which both accommodated this biblical legacy and also asserted an ongoing, positive relationship between God and Israel despite continu-

---

29. E.g., Deut 11:13–25; 28.

ing political misfortune. Because Tisha b'Av commemorates catastrophes in Israel's past and draws attention to their enduring consequences, the Tisha b'Av season becomes a locus for the articulation of this theology. When the texts of the liturgical anthology articulate consolatory responses to the catastrophes commemorated on Tisha b'Av, they are also articulating strategies for dealing with the theological challenges posed by the continuing lack of Jewish political power and the absence of the temple in the land of Israel.

As I will demonstrate below, these are subjects which were confronted and negotiated both within the rabbinic literature and within the contemporaneous synagogue culture. To cite just one example, the prevalence of temple cult iconography in third- to fourth-century synagogues testifies to both a concern with the temple and an attempt to forge some sort of connection between the synagogue and the defunct temple cult.

Exegesis and Theology in the Literature of the Tisha b'Av Season

While this project is cultural and theological, it is also exegetical. The literary features and exegetical strategies of each of the constituent genres of the Tisha b'Av season literature shape the theological meanings of the individual texts. The lectionary cycle itself is a carefully constructed sequence of biblical texts. The targum, midrash and piyyut employ different strategies to interpret, comment on, and develop the messages of the lectionary texts. For example, Targum Jonathan uses the strategies of translation and emendation to subtly transform the theology of the lectionary texts while Eleazar Kallir uses the poetic techniques of rhyme and allusion to explore the emotional and relational dynamics suggested by them. The divergent messages of these texts are not only a result of the authors' individual understandings or proclivities—they are also the result of the different exegetical projects represented by targum and piyyut. In order to understand the theological messages of each of these texts, it is first necessary to understand how they function as works of literature and exegesis. Thus, the core of my study consists of literary analyses of selected texts of the literature of the Tisha b'Av season. Through close readings of the haftarot, as well as of selected texts from the midrashic, targumic, and poetic strata of reception and interpretation, I show how the literary and exegetical features of each genre shape the theology articulated by the individual texts. In my analysis of the haftarot, I show how literary structures, tropes and patterns function in the lectionary context to articulate a theology of consolation which is different from that articulated by the haftarot in their biblical contexts. In my analyses of the interpretive genres, I show how the literary strategies and structures central to midrash, poetry and translation are used once again to expand and transform the meanings of the received texts.[30]

The nexus of exegesis and theology in any one of these genres merits a book-length study; consequently, it would be impossible to treat any of them comprehensively in a single chapter. I have dealt with this issue by focusing each chapter on particular exegetical strategies and theological issues. Each chapter conforms to a single structure. I begin by briefly addressing the question of the *Sitz im Leben* of the genre and the extant texts. I then discuss in theoretical terms the particular literary and exegeti-

---

30. Though literary analysis has become an important tool for biblical and midrashic scholarship, it remains underutilized in the study of targum and piyyut. Most targum scholarship has focused on historical and philological issues or on theological topics. (For philological studies, see, for example, Paul Kahle, *Masoreten des Westens* [Stuttgart: Kohlhammer, 1927]; Edward Yehezkel Kutscher, *A History of Aramaic* [Jerusalem: Academon, 1971] [Heb.]. For theological studies, see Bruce Chilton, *The Glory of Israel: The Theology and Provenience of the Isaiah Targum* [Sheffield: JSOT Press, 1983]; Martin McNamara, *Targum and Testament; Aramaic Paraphrases of the Hebrew Bible: A Light on the New Testament* [Shannon: Irish University Press, 1972]; Etan Levine, *The Aramaic Version of the Bible: Contents and Context* [Berlin: Walter de Gruyter, 1988]). However, the work of Avigdor Shinan, Esther Menn and Michael Klein represent important exceptions to these trends. Shinan and Menn have both analyzed the narrative expansions in the Palestinian targumim (Esther Menn, *Judah and Tamar (Genesis 38) in Ancient Jewish Exegesis: Studies in Literary Form and Hermeneutics* [Leiden: Brill, 1997], 267–346; Avigdor Shinan, *The Biblical Story as Reflected in its Aramaic Translations* [Tel Aviv: Hakibbutz Hameuchad, 1993] [Heb.] and *The Embroidered Targum: The Aggadah in Targum Pseudo-Jonathan of the Pentateuch* [Jerusalem: Magnes Press, 1992] [Heb.]). Klein carefully identifies and analyzes signature features of the targumic texts (for example, *Anthropomorphisms and Anthropopathisms in the Targumim of the Pentateuch* [Jerusalem: Makor, 1982]).

Surprisingly, there have also been few attempts to apply the tools of literary criticism to the analysis of the piyyutim. Thus far, scholars of piyyut have identified and described piyyut structures, rhyme patterns and meter. See, for example, Ezra Fleischer, *Hebrew Liturgical Poetry in the Middle Ages* (Jerusalem: Keter, 1975) (Heb.); and Leon Weinberger, *Jewish Hymnography: A Literary History* (London: Littman Library of Jewish Civilization, 1998); Joseph Yahalom, *Poetic Language in the Early Piyyut* (Jerusalem: Magnes Press, 1985) (Heb.). Other scholars have analyzed the ideological and theological content of the piyyutim. See, for example, Schwartz, *Imperialism*, 268–73; Michael Swartz, "Sage, Priest, and Poet: Typologies of Religious Leadership in the Ancient Synagogue," in *Jews, Christians, and Polytheists in the Ancient Synagogue* (ed. Steven Fine; New York: Routledge, 1999), 101–17. However, scholars have not attempted to integrate thematic analysis with analysis of the poetic features of the piyyutim.

cal strategies which will be the foci of the chapter. The third part of each chapter consists of close readings of selected texts. In these analyses I focus on the dual role of the texts as receptors and creators of meaning. The goal of the readings is to demonstrate that at each level of the literary constellation, particular exegetical strategies are employed to interpret and re-present the lectionary texts. The new interpretations and renderings of the lectionary texts in turn represent new responses to the issues raised by the Tisha b'Av season and the lectionary texts themselves. Because the lectionary sequence is the primary articulation of the themes and theology of the Tisha b'Av lectionary complex, it receives the most comprehensive treatment.

In chapter 2, I discuss the narrative and dialogic structures of the lectionary cycle as well as the more localized exegetical strategies of conjunction, echo and allusion. Through these strategies, the redactors of the lectionary cycle articulate a narrative of sin-punishment-redemption which extends from Israel's past through the present into the future. At the same time, the lectionary cycle articulates a theology of divine attention and intimacy which might serve as immediate consolation for the worshiping community. In addition to these major themes, I discuss the ways in which the lectionary cycle suggests particular standpoints regarding issues such as the power of prayer and the reliability of prophecy.

In chapter 3, I analyze chapters 13 and 22 of PRK, which correspond to the first sabbath of rebuke and the final sabbath of consolation. In these analyses I focus on the exegetical features of the proem and the *davar aḥer* (additional comment), and on the overall structure of the chapters. I demonstrate how the midrashic authors and redactors use these literary structures to reinforce the lectionary's narrative theology and elaborate on the lectionary's assertion regarding the redemptive nature of divine love. In addition, I show how they use these literary strategies to explore and express the peculiar theological ambiguity which the exile comes to represent in rabbinic culture.

Chapter 4 focuses on the opening poems of the *kedushtot* by Eleazar Kallir for the first two sabbaths of consolation following Tisha b'Av. Here, I focus on the poetic strategies of rhyme and allusion and demonstrate how Kallir employs these strategies to explore the dynamics of the relationship between God and Israel that is described by the lectionary texts.

The structure of the case studies in chapter 5 differs slightly from that of the preceding chapters. Unlike the lectionary cycle, the midrashic pericopes and the piyyutim, Targum Jonathan's interpretation of the haftarah texts does not underscore the romantic, erotic aspects of the God-Israel relationship. Rather, the targum downplays these aspects of the biblical text. In order to demonstrate the comprehensive nature of this revision, I first demonstrate how TJ's characteristic exegetical strategies revise and reshape the portrait of God in the text by preserving certain anthropomorphic features and revising and replacing others. I then analyze TJ's treatment of romantic and erotic language within the haftarot of consolation in order to show how TJ subverts the sexual aspects of the biblical text.

In the conclusion I integrate the results of the individual analyses into a discussion of the function of the Tisha b'Av season as a whole and the relevance of this season to the study of the spread of rabbinic culture in late antiquity.

2

The Tisha b'Av Lectionary Cycle

The Synagogue Bible and Popular Jewish Theology

An investigation of the Bible in its liturgical setting is particularly important to the study of late antique Judaism because, unlike the scribal workshop or the *beit midrash,* the synagogue was the locus of the popular encounter with the Bible. While the rabbinic sages and their students might have had access to complete texts of the Hebrew Bible, the lay people who frequented the synagogue probably did not. Rather, they encountered only the biblical texts that were recited in the synagogue service. Thus, the selection of lectionary texts, and the rituals which developed around them, determined the nature and content of the Bible as it was experienced by most Jews in the early centuries of the common era. The lectionary texts that were recited in the synagogue were the "required reading" for Jewish lay people. The literature and rituals that developed around the public recitation of the Torah were the means through which the Bible was defined, shaped and continually resignified for the popular audience.

The rabbinic lectionary system defines a synagogue Bible that is different in both content and form from the 24 books of the canonical Hebrew Bible. The central text of the synagogue canon is the Pentateuch. According to m. Meg 4:1–2, portions from the Pentateuch are read on sabbaths, festivals, new moons, Mondays, Thursdays, and public fast days. Within the synagogue context, the recitation of the Torah is governed by a conservative hermeneutic which functions to assure the audience that the Torah text that is being recited is identical to the Torah which was revealed at Sinai. Through the rules governing scribal practice, the synagogue audience is assured that the text from which the lector is reading has been meticulously copied and therefore is identical with its Sinaitic prototype.[1] The rules governing the recitation of the Torah text assure that the recitation of the text corresponds in all details to the written text. The Mishnah notes that the reader is not permitted to skip text within a given pericope (m. Meg 4:4). T. Megillah 3:10 dictates that the Pentateuch should be read sequentially from week to week.[2] In addition, if a reader makes a mistake in the reading, he is obligated to return and correct his mistake.[3] Thus, the rules governing the recitation of scripture insure that the recitation is an accurate representation of the written scroll which is, in turn, an accurate copy of its original Sinaitic prototype.[4] To underscore this point, the ritual surrounding the Torah reading is modeled on the Sinai event. In j. Meg 4:1, R. Samuel bar R. Isaac scolds a man for leaning on a post while translating the Torah portion; he then scolds another for both reading and translating the portion. He rebukes them by saying that since Torah was given in fear and trembling, through the hand of an intermediary, we must treat it with fear and trembling and recite it through an intermediary.

While the synagogue Torah is identical to the canonical Torah, there is a wide discrepancy between the prophetic canon of the Hebrew Bible and the prophetic canon of the synagogue in terms of function, size and order. First, within the synagogue context the prophetic texts are identified as important, but subordinate to Torah. Unlike the Torah portion (Heb. *parashah*; pl. *parashot*), the haftarah was read only on sabbaths, festivals and public fast days (m. Meg 4:1–2). In addition, b. Meg 23a states that the person who reads the haftarah must first read the final verses of the parashah "out of respect for the Torah." This custom articulates an intrinsic connection between the parashah and the haftarah; it suggests that the haftarah is connected to, and dependent on, the Torah portion. The rules governing the stacking of scripture texts reinforce the higher status of the Pentateuch. According to b. Meg 27a, one is permitted to place single books of the Torah on top of single books of the prophets or writings but the re-

---

1. Soferim 1–10.
2. According to a baraita cited on b. Meg 31b, there were differing opinions regarding the consecutive reading of the Torah. R. Meir stated that consecutive texts should be read on sabbath morning, sabbath afternoon, Monday, and Thursday. R. Judah stated that consecutive texts should be read on consecutive sabbath mornings. On the intermediate days, the beginning of the weekly portion should be recited again. The Gemara rules in accordance with the latter opinion.
3. J. Meg 4:5.
4. The division of the texts into lectionary units and the mode of cantillation are the only means through which the pentateuchal text itself is shaped in the public recitation ritual.

verse is prohibited. This dictum translates the differing statuses of the Torah and the prophetic books into concrete terms.

This status differential is reflected in the synagogue reading practices as well. Unlike the Pentateuch, which was recited sequentially, in its entirety, over the course of the lectionary cycle, only a small percentage of the biblical prophetic texts were recited as haftarot. In addition, the prophetic texts were always read in conjunction with, and as a coda to, the pentateuchal texts. Thus, Jews who encountered the Bible only in the synagogue would have no concept of a prophetic *book*. For these audience members, the basic prophetic unit would have been a single pericope which was conjoined to a "corresponding" pentateuchal text. By creating these parashah/haftarah pairs, the rabbinic redactors of the lectionary cycle create new, second-order biblical texts which might underscore, subvert or transform the meanings of the lectionary texts in their biblical contexts. The first parashah/haftarah pair of the lectionary year provides an illustrative example. Isaiah 42:5–43:11 is designated as the haftarah which accompanies Gen 1:1–6:8. This prophetic text adds a particularist valence to the relatively universalist primeval history of Gen 1–6. The Torah portion describes the creation of the earth and God's interaction with the earliest humans. The text makes no mention of particular nationalities or of the special status of the Israelites. The haftarah, however, makes a connection between God's creative acts and God's selection of Israel:

> Thus says God, YHWH,
> Who creates the heavens and stretches them out, who spreads
>   out the earth and its offspring;
> Who gives breath to the people upon it and spirit to those who
>   walk on it.
> I, YHWH, have called you in righteousness and I have taken you
>   by the hand; I have created you and made you a covenant
>   people, a light to the nations. (Isa 42:5–6)

By selecting Isa 42:5–6 as the haftarah for the beginning of Genesis, the redactors of the lectionary cycle retroject the special status of Israel to the beginning of time and assert that it is an intrinsic part of the created order of the world.[5]

The parashah/haftarah pair for any week of the lectionary would demonstrate certain redactional strategies and would potentially articulate interesting theological assertions. However, no single pair would demonstrate the range of strategies operative within the lectionary genre.

---

5. For analyses of the relationships between parashot and haftarot throughout the lectionary year, see Michael Fishbane, *JPS Bible Commentary: Haftarot* (Philadelphia: Jewish Publication Society, 2002).

In contrast, the Tisha b'Av cycle is the most extensive, coherent lectionary example within the "synagogue Bible." Because the sequence is so extensive, it provides an excellent case study for an analysis of the lectionary as a vehicle for the rabbinic construction of a public Bible.

In this chapter I will show how the redactors of the lectionary cycle use the strategies of identification, selection and arrangement to create the new second-order biblical compilation which is the lectionary cycle. Through a close reading of the lectionary cycle, I will show how the literary structures, patterns and features of the cycle transform the meanings of the constituent biblical texts. Despite their disparate origins and contexts within the Bible, within the context of the lectionary sequence the biblical texts all respond both theologically and emotionally to the events commemorated on Tisha b'Av.

History of the Tisha b'Av Lectionary Cycle

The complete lectionary cycle for the Tisha b'Av season is first attested to in the Pesikta de-Rav Kahana, a fifth- to sixth-century collection of midrashim which comment on the lectionary texts for festivals and special sabbaths. According to PRK, the lectionary cycle consists of texts beginning with the following verses.[6]

Three of Rebuke:[7]

- Jeremiah 1:1

- Jeremiah 2:4

- Isaiah 1:21/Lamentations 1[8]

---

6. Since PRK only identifies the first verses of each pericope, it is impossible to deduce the extent of the haftarot from this source.

7. The rubrics are first attested to in the twelfth century in *Mahzor Vitry* and in the tosafists' comment to b. Meg 31b.

8. There is a discrepancy between early and later traditions regarding the third haftarah of rebuke. Chapter 15 of PRK, which is the third chapter in the treatment of the Tisha b'Av season, is a composite chapter which treats both Isa 1:21 and Lam 1:1 as the opening verses of the lectionary text. This conflation is motivated by the parallelism between the two verses and the inclusion of both texts in the lectionary cycle. However, it makes it impossible to determine decisively the exact nature of the third haftarah. There are three possibilities: 1) PRK preserves a tradition of two special haftarot before the ninth of Av, in which case chapter 15 corresponds to the lectionary texts of the holiday itself. 2) Isaiah 1:21ff. was recited on the sabbath immediately preceding the ninth of Av. If this is the case, then chapter 15 represents a

Seven of Consolation:

- Isaiah 40:1
- Isaiah 49:14
- Isaiah 54:11
- Isaiah 51:12
- Isaiah 54:10
- Isaiah 60:1
- Isaiah 61:10

This haftarah cycle eventually became a canonical part of the major liturgical rites throughout the Jewish diaspora. However, as a consequence of the particular development of liturgical traditions in the gaonic and medieval periods, its fifth- to sixth-century Palestinian origin was identified only in the past century. By the end of the amoraic period, two major systems of lectionary practice had developed. In the system that became dominant in Babylonia, the entire Torah was read over the course of a year. In the system that was prevalent in Palestine, the entire Torah was recited over a period of three to four years.[9] By the fourteenth century, the Babylonian system became canonical throughout most of the Jewish world. As a result, it became impossible to reconstruct the triennial lectionary traditions or to identify which elements of the extant reading customs originated in the now defunct triennial tradition. It was not until the pioneering work of Leopold Zunz and the discovery of the Cairo genizah material that scholars were able to reconstruct the Palestinian lectionary cycles and, as a result, identify the origins of the Tisha b'Av cycle.

Gaonic and medieval sources refer frequently to a midrashic collection known alternately as *Pesikta, Piskot,* and *Pesikta Zuta.* However, by the sixteenth century, references to the work cease to appear—suggesting that

---

composite treatment of the texts for the sabbath preceding the ninth of Av and for the holiday itself. 3) Lamentations 1:1ff. was recited on the sabbath preceding the holiday.

The extant poems of the sixth- to seventh-century liturgical poets Yannai and Kallir identify Lam 1:1 as the opening verse of the third lectionary text of the cycle. The poems of Yannai include liturgical poems for the three weeks preceding Tisha b'Av and the three weeks after. The poems for the three weeks preceding the holiday are based on Jer 1, Jer 2:4, and Lam 1, respectively. The situation is further complicated by a statement by the tosafists which asserts that the *Pesikta* designates Isa 1:1 as the opening verse of the third haftarah.

9. See n. 1.

all manuscripts were lost. In 1832, Leopold Zunz reconstructed the text from references in the later midrashic compilations.[10] Zunz's reconstruction ignited scholarly interest in the lost text, and in 1868 Solomon Buber published a composite edition of the work based on manuscripts which had been discovered since Zunz's reconstruction.[11] The publication of Buber's edition of PRK made possible the scholarly study of the early Palestinian midrashic traditions relating to the lectionary texts for festivals and special sabbaths, including those for the weeks surrounding Tisha b'Av.

Like PRK, the poems of the sixth- to seventh-century liturgical poets Yannai and Kallir attest to the antiquity and Palestinian origins of the cycle. The surviving poems of Yannai include liturgical poems for the three weeks preceding Tisha b'Av and the first, second, and fourth weeks following it. The poems preceding the holiday are based on Jer 1, Jer 2:4 and Lam 1:1, respectively. Thus, with the exception of the third week, Yannai's haftarot of rebuke correspond to those of PRK. Yannai's poems for the weeks following the holiday are based on Isa 40:1, Isa 49:14 and Isa 51:2. The surviving poems of Eleazar Kallir include poems for the three weeks preceding Tisha b'Av and the first six weeks following it. Kallir, like Yannai, seems to know Lam 1:1 as the opening verse of the lectionary text for the third Sabbath preceding Tisha b'Av. Kallir's haftarot for the six weeks following the holiday correspond to those invoked in PRK.

The Talmud and post-talmudic commentaries, as well as extant lectionary traditions, provide more data for determining the original form and development of the Tisha b'Av cycle. While the Talmud does not attest to the full lectionary cycle, it does designate Isa 1:14 as the haftarah for Rosh Hodesh Av when it falls on a sabbath. This tradition is not attested in the midrash, the piyyut, or later lectionary lists. The tosafists of the twelfth century recognize the discrepancies between the Talmud on the one hand, and PRK and contemporary practice on the other. In their comment on the statement, "On Rosh Hodesh Av that falls on shabbat, recite as haftarah: *My soul despises your new moons and festivals* (Isa 1:14)," they state:

> We do not do this. Rather, we recite the haftarah from Jeremiah, *Hear the words of the Lord* (Jer 2:4). On the sabbath before Tisha b'Av we recite, *The vision of Isaiah* (Isa 1:1), and the reason is that we behave according to the *Pesikta*, which is to say, three of rebuke before the ninth of Av. They are: *The words of Jeremiah* (Jer 1:1), *Hear the words of the Lord* (Jer 2:4), *The vision*

---

10. Leopold Zunz, *Die gottesdienstlichen Vorträge der Juden historisch entwickelt* (Berlin: A. Asher, 1832).

11. Solomon Buber, *Pesikta: ve-hi agadat Erets Yisra'el meyuḥeset le-Rav Kahana* (Lyck: Ḥevrat mekitse nirdamim, 1868).

of Isaiah (Isa 1:1). After the ninth of Av come the seven of consolation and the two of repentance. (b. Meg 31b)

With the exception of the sabbath immediately preceding the holiday, the cycle cited by the tosafists is identical to that found in PRK. With a few exceptions, the major liturgical sources, which reflect Ashkenazic, Sephardic, North African, Italian and Romanian practices, follow the lectionary cycle designated by the tosafists.[12] In addition, these sources attest to the extent of each haftarah pericope. While the extent of the texts is attested only in medieval sources, the high degree of consistency among the different rites suggests that the traditions regarding the extent of the pericopes, like the traditions regarding their opening verses, are ancient.

Though there is no explicit attestation regarding the authorship of the Tisha b'Av lectionary cycle, it is clear that it is of rabbinic provenance. First, the presence of lectionary lists in b. Meg 31a–b shows that the rabbis of the academy whose comments are preserved in the Talmud were also responsible for determining certain lectionary traditions. In addition, the appearance of the cycle in PRK and the early piyyutim, as well as the later ubiquity of the cycle throughout a wide range of lectionary rites, demonstrates that it was authorized and utilized by the rabbis from an early date. Finally, as I will argue in the following chapters, the affinities between the rabbinic theology which is articulated in the midrashic collections and the theology articulated in the Tisha b'Av cycle testifies that the lectionary cycle was born in the same rabbinic, academic milieu as the midrashic collections. Just as there is no explicit evidence regarding authorship of the lectionary, there is also no explicit evidence regarding the process of redaction. One might argue that the lectionary texts were chosen as paradigmatic texts of rebuke and consolation and bear no intrinsic relationship to one another; or one might argue that the cycle was constructed haphazardly and reflects no principles of selection at all. While I can make no definitive statements regarding authorial intent, the coherent structure of the cycle seems to reflect a high degree of intentional redaction.

The coherence of the structure was noted by medieval Jewish commentators. First, the rubrics "three of rebuke" and "seven of consolation," which are used by the twelfth-century *Maḥzor Vitry*, the tosafists, and later commentators, attest to a thematic coherence which unites the sections of the cycle. In addition, both *Maḥzor Vitry* and the fourteenth-century Spanish commentator Abudarham understand the structure of the entire cycle to be meaningful. *Vitry* notes that the haftarot of consolation proceed "little by little"—in a manner which is appropriate to the consolation of

---

12. See Nathan Freid, "Haftarah," *Talmudic Encyclopedia*, X (1961), cols. 701–23 (Heb.) for a complete list of the lections designated by the various rites.

grief.[13] Abudarham notes the dialogic structure of the haftarot of consolation. He understands the order of the haftarot to reflect a dialogue between God, the prophets, and Israel.[14] Thus both *Maḥzor Vitry* and Abudarham saw the cycle as a coherent and ordered sequence, not a random collection.

This impression of coherence is supported by the cycle itself. First, the haftarot of consolation are selected from the sections of Isaiah that allude most frequently to Lamentations.[15] This fact suggests that the redactors chose texts which would create an impression of coherence within the cycle. Second, the order of the haftarot of consolation does not reflect the order of the canonical text. Isaiah 54:11–55:5 is the haftarah for the third sabbath of consolation. It is followed by Isa 51:12–52:12 and Isa 54:1–10. While rabbinic culture did subscribe to the dictum "there is no before or after in Torah," the fact that the redactors of the lectionary cycle separated and reversed the order of two consecutive texts suggests that they were operating according to some intentional principles of arrangement. Ultimately though, the degree of intentionality underlying the lectionary cycle is irrelevant to my project. My analyses will demonstrate that the literary structures which undergird the cycle as a whole and the literary relationships which connect individual texts to one another generate meaning within the cycle and serve as vehicles for the articulation of theological and ideological assertions.

Lectionary Poetics

There are no precise Jewish literary parallels to the Tisha b'Av cycle. While the cycle shares some features with individual parashah/haftarah pairs from other parts of the lectionary, its scope is far greater than the scope of any of these pairs. In addition, while the conjunctions of the parashah/haftarah texts are motivated by verbal and/or thematic correspondences, they are not marked by the same degree of structural coherence as the larger cycle. The Tisha b'Av cycle also bears some resemblance to other sequences of biblical pericopes which occur within the liturgy, most notably, the *shema* and the *pesukei dezimra*.[16] Like the Tisha b'Av lectionary

---

13. *Maḥzor Vitry* (ed. S. Hurwitz; Nurnberg: J. Bulka, 1923), 224.
14. *The Complete Abudarham* (Jerusalem: Usha, 1958), 203. See pp. 68–69.
15. See pp. 61–66 for a discussion of Second Isaiah's allusions to Lamentations.
16. Other liturgical compositions, such as the *malkhuyot, zikhronot,* and *shofarot* sections of the Rosh Hashanah liturgy and the medieval additions to the *pesukei dezimra* consist of concatenations of single biblical verses. While these compositions share some important features with the lectionary sequence, they are distin-

cycle, these units are sequences of biblical texts which have been arranged in a new order in their liturgical settings. In both of these cases, the re-ordering of the material shapes the meaning of the new, liturgical composition. For example, m. Ber 2:2 understands the order of the first two paragraphs of the *shema* to reflect the order of the worshiper's submission to God. First one accepts the authority of God's kingship and then that of the commandments.[17] However, neither of these texts provide precise parallels to the Tisha b'Av cycle: While the order of the *shema* certainly affects its meaning, its arrangement is not nearly as elaborate or exegetically powerful, and while the *pesukei dezimra* is a more elaborate composition, it was formed through the gradual aggregation of thematically related texts; it was not constructed as a coherent unit.[18]

Although it is not a precise parallel, the genre of anthology bears a resemblance to the lectionary cycle, and the study of anthologies provides a starting point for my analysis of the cycle's poetics. Like the lectionary sequence, anthologies "present themselves consciously and openly as collections of preexisting sources and traditions."[19] In addition, while anthologies reproduce their constituent texts verbatim, the inclusion and arrangement of the texts within the anthology can affect and transform their meaning. As David Stern notes,

> Even anthologies that simply present texts "as they really are" (to paraphrase Ranke) can radically alter and shape their readers' reception and understanding of their contents by placing them within the anthological context in one place and not another.[20]

Despite these similarities, lectionary sequences are not identical to other anthologies. Whereas anthologies' primary identification is that of a collection, the Tisha b'Av lectionary sequence is a new, discrete text with its own narrative coherence and dialogic structure. Whereas the creation

---

guished from it by being thematic collections of isolated verses rather than structured compositions consisting of larger pericopes.

17. For other interpretations of the structure of the *shema*, see Reuven Kimelman, "The Shema' Liturgy: From Covenant Ceremony to Coronation," in *Kenishta: Studies of the Synagogue World* (ed. Joseph Tabory; Ramat Gan: Bar Ilan University Press, 2001), 12–25.

18. For the history of the formation of the *pesukei dezimra* see Elbogen, *Jewish Liturgy*, 72–76.

19. David Stern, "The Anthological Imagination in Jewish Literature," *Prooftexts* 17 (1997): 4. For detailed discussions of the hermeneutics of anthology, see David Roskies, "The Holocaust According to its Anthologists," *Prooftexts* 17 (1997): 95–113, and Hannan Hever, "'Our Poetry is Like an Orange Grove': Anthologies of Hebrew Poetry in Eretz Yisrael," *Prooftexts* 17 (1997): 199–225.

20. Stern, "Anthological Imagination," 3.

of an anthology is primarily an act of accretion, the creation of the lectionary first involves a process of extraction, whereby the lectionary texts are removed from their context in the biblical anthology and recombined in the lectionary sequence. Finally, the goal of the lectionary sequence differs from that of other anthologies. While the process of anthologization often subtly transforms the meaning of the anthologized texts, anthologizers do not attempt to appropriate the pre-existent texts and transform them into expressions of their own ideas and values. This is precisely the project of the authors of the lectionary sequence. Through the creation of the lectionary, they transform the biblical texts into "bi-lingual" texts: texts which continue to articulate the messages of the biblical authors but also become the constituent parts of the lectionary—a post-biblical text which preaches a post-biblical theology of consolation, which is foreign to the biblical canon. While the lectionary sequence is more than an anthology, anthological strategies provide a useful heuristic device for understanding the lectionary process. Like anthologies, the lectionary is created through a process of identification, selection, correspondence, and arrangement.

Identification

The conventions which govern the selection of lectionary texts determine the parameters of the Tisha b'Av lectionary. On the ninth of Av itself a hagiographical text may be read. On the surrounding sabbaths, the haftarot must be prophetic texts. In addition, the lectionary texts must address the events commemorated on the ninth of Av and the religious themes of the season.[21] This final criterion is both the most elusive and the most interesting. By the mishnaic period, the seventeenth of Tammuz, the ninth of Av, and the period between them had been identified as occasions of both historical and supernatural doom and danger.[22] However, the period which extends from the ninth of Av through the fifteenth of Av to Rosh Hashanah is not signified liturgically in the tannaitic literature. Consequently, there is no evidence that the seven weeks following Tisha b'Av had a "theme" to which the lectionary texts should correspond. Rather, the lectionary itself defines the significance of the seven week period. In addition, the lectionary defines the significance of the "three weeks" in a way which echoes, but is not identical to, the significance attached to this period in the mishnaic and midrashic sources.

---

21. B. Meg 29b.
22. See p. 29.

Selection

In the case of anthologies, two general motives govern the processes of selection: preservation and selection. David Stern identifies anthologies whose primary purpose is preservation as "archives." At the other end of the spectrum lies the "anthology proper" in which "a very strong principle of selection regardless of desire for preservation is the operative criterion of inclusion."[23]

The lectionary cycle corresponds to this second type of anthology, which bears witness to a distinctive process of selection. When compared to the biblical books from which they are derived, it is clear that the haftarot of rebuke and consolation are not a representative selection or microcosm of the collections from which they come. Instead, the redactors of the lectionary cycle isolated pericopes from the biblical anthology which articulated certain themes. When compared to Second Isaiah as a whole, for example, the haftarot of consolation emphasize themes of consolation and downplay themes of rebuke. However, the process of selection differs from that of even an anthology proper. The haftarot of consolation do not represent the best examples of consolatory discourse in Second Isaiah. Rather, they are selected strategically to articulate the variety of positions and moments necessary to the cycle's argument.

Correspondence

The principle of correspondence underlies the process of selection. Each anthology proclaims that there are correspondences among its constituent texts which were obscured by the texts' prior transmission and dissemination. By bringing these texts together, the anthologist is able to reveal the relationships among previously scattered texts. The texts of the lectionary cycle are connected by a dense web of thematic and poetic correspondences. These correspondences were present in the biblical context as well, but they were obscured by the canonical arrangement of the biblical text. By bringing together these corresponding texts, the creators of the lectionary cycle assert that the texts have something to do with one another. The correspondences alone, however, are raw data. It is the particular arrangement of the corresponding texts which gives significance to the pre-existing correspondences.

---

23. Stern, "Anthological Imagination," 4.

Arrangement

"There is no anthological organization devoid of an ideological orientation. In the anthology, literary form, organization, even sequence, are all ideological subjects."[24] Even seemingly neutral anthological ordering principles such as geography, alphabet, and chronology bear ideological messages. An anthology that is arranged alphabetically by author identifies the individuality of the author as the most significant identifying feature of a text. An anthology which is organized chronologically necessarily suggests some form of teleology, be it of development, decay or transformation. The power of (re)arrangement is deployed even more strongly in the lectionary cycle. The arrangement of the lectionary texts provides the high degree of coherence that differentiates the cycle from anthologies. By arranging the biblical texts into a narrative and dialogic sequence, the redactors of the lectionary cycle highlight certain themes and assert that the correspondences among the texts are signs that the texts are part of a single story and part of a single consolatory conversation. Through the structures of narrative and dialogue, the redactors of the lectionary cycle transform the meaning of the texts and make them applicable to the contemporary situation of the post-70 CE Jewish audience.

Analysis of the Lectionary Cycle

Lamentations

The book of Lamentations is the anchor of the Tisha b'Av lectionary cycle. It defines the historical and theological significance of the ninth of Av within the liturgical complex and defines and articulates a communal, liturgical response to the events commemorated on the holiday. By designating Lamentations as the central lectionary text for the ninth of Av, the redactors of the cycle assert that the events of 587 BCE and by extension, those of 70 CE, are the events which give meaning to the day of mourning and commemoration.[25] This primary act of selection shapes the meaning of the Tisha b'Av season significantly.

---

24. Stern, *Anthological Imagination*, 3, paraphrasing Lucia Re, "(De)Constructing the Canon: The Agon of the Anthologies on the Scene of Modern Italian Poetry," *Modern Language Review* 87 (1992): 585–602.

25. The rabbinic literature often conflates the two destructions. Shaye J. D. Cohen ("The Destruction: From Scripture to Midrash," *Prooftexts* 2 [1982]: 20) observes that in Lam R., the midrashists often do not identify which temple, destruction or enemy they are discussing.

Several rabbinic texts attest to the range of significances attached to Tisha b'Av and the weeks preceding it in ancient Jewish culture. From at least mishnaic times, the seventeenth of Tammuz and the ninth of Av were days of mourning and commemoration for tragic events in Israel's past.

> Five things happened to our ancestors on the seventeenth of Tammuz and five occurred on the ninth of Av. On the seventeenth of Tammuz the tablets were broken, the *tamid* sacrifice was eliminated, the city was breached; Apostomos burned the Torah and he erected an idol in the palace. On the ninth of Av it was decreed that our ancestors would not enter the land; the first and second temples were burned; Betar was captured and the city was destroyed. Whoever enters the month of Av should lessen his joy. (m. Taan 4:6)[26]

This mishnah reveals the mythic character of Tisha b'Av as a day of doom. The identification of the seventeenth of Tammuz and the ninth of Av as the dates of multiple tragic events is symbolic and paradigmatic rather than historical. The Bible does not indicate a precise date for the breaking of the tablets or for God's decree that the exodus generation would not enter the land of Israel. In addition, the assignation of the destruction of the first temple to the ninth of Av contradicts two biblical accounts:

> In the fifth month on the tenth day of the month, which is the nineteenth year of the reign of king Nebuchadrezzar, the king of Babylon, Nebuzaradan, the chief of the guards who represented the king of Babylon in Jerusalem, came. He burned the house of YHWH and the house of the king and all the houses of Jerusalem; every house of importance he burned with fire. (Jer 52:12–13)

This passage also appears in 2 Kgs 25:8–9, but there Nebuzaradan's arrival occurs on the seventh day of the fifth month. While b. Taan 29a attempts valiantly to justify the Mishnah's dating of both the pentateuchal events and the events of 587 BCE, the text also acknowledges the mythic, paradigmatic logic that underlies the Mishnah's view of history. In commenting on the Mishnah's assertion that the second temple was also destroyed on the ninth of Av, b. Taan 29a states, "How do we know this? It has been taught: Meritorious events occur on meritorious days and doom occurs on days of doom." This suggests that the seventeenth of Tammuz and the ninth of Av were days of doom on which a series of catastrophes occurred over time. The dates themselves are catastrophic, so catastrophic events accrue on them. Lamentations Rabbah 1:3 further describes the

---

26. The reference to Apostomos remains obscure; the name does not appear in any other sources. Neither the Mishnah nor the talmudic passages which comment upon it elaborate on this "lessening of joy."

mythic malevolence of the period between the seventeenth of Tammuz and the ninth of Av.

> *All her pursuers overtook her amid the narrow places.*[27] In the days of distress from the seventeenth of Tammuz to the ninth of Av in which *ketev meriri* (קטב מרירי) is found. As it is said, "From the plague that walks in darkness and from the pestilence (מִקֶּטֶב) that destroys at noon" (Ps 91:6). R. Abba b. Kahana and R. Levi comment. R. Abba b. Kahana says: It stalks through the midday period from the beginning of the sixth hour until the end of the ninth. R. Levi said: It stalks through the day from the end of the fourth hour until the beginning of the ninth. It does not walk in the sun or in the shade but in the shadow near the sun. R. Yohanan and R. Simon b. Lakish also commented. R. Yohanan said: It is covered all over with eyes, scaly scales and hairy hair. R. Simon b. Lakish said: One eye is located on its heart and anyone who looks at it falls down and dies. It happened that a pious man who saw it fell on his face and died. Some say it was R. Judah b. Rabbi. Samuel saw it and did not fall. He said: It is the snake of the house. R. Abahu was sitting and teaching in a synagogue in a place in Caesarea. He saw a man carrying a stick who was about to hit his neighbor. He saw a demon standing behind him who was holding an iron rod. He [R. Abahu] got up and restrained him [the man]. He said to him, "Do you want to kill your neighbor?" The man said to him, "Can a man kill his neighbor with this [stick]?" He [R. Abahu] said to him, "There is a demon standing behind you with an iron rod. You hit him with this stick and he hits him with that one and he dies." R. Yohanan warned elementary and Mishnah teachers not to use a strap on children in these days. R. Samuel b. Nahmani would warn elementary teachers and Mishnah teachers that they should dismiss the young children during those four hours.[28]

In this text, three forms of malevolence are conflated. The demon, *ketev meriri,* is a figure of both natural and supernatural malevolence. It is a supernatural creature, but it is associated with the blistering heat of midsummer and stalks only during the hottest hours of midsummer days. The demon is also associated with human aggression which normally remains relatively restrained. Usually, when a man hits his neighbor or a teacher hits a student, the assailant can limit the damage through choice of weapon and restraint of his own force. However, *ketev meriri* serves as a disinhibiting force: he overrides the assailant's restraint and caution and causes the death of the victim. According to this pericope, there is a con-

---

27. "Amid the narrow places" (בֵּין הַמְּצָרִים) is used as an epithet for the three weeks between the seventeenth of Tammuz and the ninth of Av.

28. A version of this pericope also appears in Num R. 12:3. Here the demon has "a head like that of a calf and a horn grows out from the center of his forehead and he rolls like a pitcher."

fluence of natural and supernatural malevolent forces during the period between the seventeenth of Tammuz and the ninth of Av. Humans must take precautions not to fall victim to them. Thus, in the rabbinic sources, the seventeenth of Tammuz, the ninth of Av, and the three weeks between them are days of both historical and supernatural danger and misfortune. In the lectionary cycle, however, the cosmic and natural valences of the period are subordinated to a historical-theological paradigm. By designating Lamentations as the lectionary text for Tisha b'Av, the redactors of the cycle assert that of all the historical calamities and supernatural dangers associated with Tisha b'Av, the events of 587 BCE and, by extension, 70 CE, are central. According to the lectionary cycle, the catastrophes described in Lamentations, not the cosmic malevolence of midsummer, are the primary events commemorated on Tisha b'Av.

The designation of Lamentations as lectionary text not only defines the subject of the holiday, it also articulates a particular portrait and interpretation of that subject. To a large extent, the destruction of the temple and the conquest of Jerusalem as they are recounted in Lamentations determine the contours of the rest of the lectionary anthology. The redactors of the lectionary cycle surround Lamentations with a sequence of prophetic texts which serve to both anticipate and respond to Lamentations' portrayal of the catastrophes of Tisha b'Av. Within the biblical anthology, these prophetic texts correspond to varying degrees to the text of Lamentations. Within the lectionary anthology, however, these biblical correspondences are brought to a new, explicit level. The resonances between Lamentations and the haftarot of rebuke and consolation form the infrastructure for the lectionary's treatment of, and response to, Lamentations. A literary reading of the texts of the cycle both underscores these correspondences and reveals their significance within the lectionary cycle.

Lamentations presents a vivid and harrowing portrait of the events of 587 BCE. According to the text, the tragedies caused by the Babylonian conquest include the starvation and death of the populace (1:11, 19; 2:11–12, 20–21; 4:3–10; 5:4–5, 9–10) and the exile of the survivors (1:3–5, 18; 2:9; 4:15). The text laments the destruction of the Temple (2:1, 4, 6–7; 5:18) and describes the mourning and despair of the city's inhabitants. Zion's empty roads are a sign of her devastation (1:1, 4; 4:18) and the walls of the city itself mourn the destruction (2:8, 18). While Zion suffers, her enemies benefit from, and rejoice over, her misery (1:2, 5, 8–10, 21; 2:15–16, 22). Throughout the text, the effects of siege, war and exile are described with powerful pathos. Lamentations 2:10–13 provides an eloquent example:

> They sit on the ground and are silent, the elders of the daughter
>   of Zion,
> They raise dust on their heads and gird sackcloth;

32 *From Rebuke to Consolation*

> They lower their heads to the ground, the maidens of Jerusalem.
>
> My eyes overflow with tears, my insides are in tumult;
> My heart is poured out on the ground over the shattering of the
>   daughter of my people,
> As the infants and the sucklings faint away in the streets of the
>   city.[29]
>
> They say to their mothers, "Where are grain and wine?"
> As they faint like the wounded in the streets of the city;
> As their lives run out on their mother's breasts.
>
> What can I compare to you? To what can I liken you, O daughter
>   Jerusalem?
> What can I compare to you that I might comfort you, maiden
>   daughter Zion?
> For as vast as the sea is your ruin; who can heal you?

The choice of Lamentations as the lectionary text for Tisha b'Av identifies these images, and others like them, as the grounds for mourning and commemoration on the day of lament. According to Lamentations, Jerusalem's inhabitants are not the only victims of the Babylonian invasion. The city itself, personified as a woman, is victimized by the invasion and both suffers and laments its consequences:

> Alas! She sits solitary, the city, once great with people.
> She has become like a widow, who was once great among the
>   nations;
> The queen of the nations has become a slave.
>
> Bitterly, she weeps in the night and her tears are on her cheeks.
> She has no comforter from among all her lovers;
> All her companions have betrayed her; they have become her
>   enemies. (Lam 1:1–2)

Throughout the lectionary cycle, the female personification of Zion, which is drawn so forcefully in Lamentations, will be a protagonist in the drama of the Tisha b'Av season.

Lamentations not only paints a particular portrait of the events commemorated on Tisha b'Av, it also articulates a theological interpretation of these events. The Babylonian conquest of Judea and the subsequent exile and temple destruction generated two distinct theological anxieties which left their mark on the Hebrew Bible. The exile suggested that the God of Israel was an impotent God who was unable to protect his temple and his

---

29. The word כְּבֵדִי, which I translate as "my heart," literally means "my liver." I translate it as "heart" because here the organ is used to represent the seat of the emotions.

people from the Babylonians. While this anxiety is rarely articulated explicitly, its refutation occupies much biblical theology and historiography. Deuteronomy states in no uncertain terms that Israel's historical situation is the consequence of her obedience or disobedience to God:

> And if you diligently obey the voice of YHWH, your God, by carefully performing all his commandments which I command you this day, YHWH, your God, will grant you ascendancy over all the nations of the earth. And all these blessings shall come upon you and overtake you when you obey the voice of YHWH, your God. (Deut 28:1)

> But if you will not obey the voice of YHWH, your God, by carefully performing all his commandments and his statutes which I command you this day, then all these curses shall come upon you and overtake you. (Deut 28:15)

The deuteronomic historian applies this theological principle to the history of the kingdoms of Judea and Israel. By insisting that the fortunes of the Israelite and Judean monarchies correlated neatly to the degrees of obedience and disobedience of individual kings, these authors articulated a clear theology of divine control over history. God, not politics, determined the fate of kings and kingdoms. Similarly, the exilic and post-exilic prophets repeatedly assert that God controls the workings of international politics. Foreign enemies who triumph over Israel are merely God's vehicles for punishing Israel.[30] While this ideology seems deeply counterfactual to modern ears, its theological benefits are clear. The deuteronomic theology asserts that the God of Israel is in control of history even when Israel's enemies are ascendant. In addition, this ideology asserts that the universe is a moral system. Fortune and misfortune are not results of divine caprice, but rather are the consequences of moral and immoral behavior.

The book of Lamentations supports this deuteronomic principle. Throughout the poems, the speakers avow that the suffering of the people is a consequence of their sin.[31] For example, Lam 1:5 states: "Her foes have become the head, her enemies prosper / Because YHWH has caused her to suffer for the multitude of her transgressions." In addition, the poems consistently identify God as the agent of Israel's suffering. "Look and see if there is any sorrow like my sorrow which he dealt to me / which YHWH caused me to suffer on the day of his fierce anger" (Lam 1:12).[32]

While these assertions of divine control of history counter anxieties about divine impotence, they spawn a second theological problem. The

---

30. Examples in Isa 40–66 include Isa 41:2–4; 44:28; 45:1; 47:6.
31. Lam 1:5, 8–9, 14, 18; 3:42; 4:13; 5:7, 16.
32. See also Lam 1:13–15, 17–18; 2:1–8, 17, 20, 22; 3:1–18, 38, 43–45; 4:11, 16.

events of 587 BCE, as they are described in Lamentations, are catastrophic. According to the text, the Babylonians murdered, raped, deported and looted. In addition, the Judeans suffered from famine and shame and witnessed the destruction of their city, its social fabric, and their way of life. If these atrocities are the consequences of God's anger, then God's anger must be extreme—so extreme that reconciliation seems impossible.

Lamentations expresses two distinct positions regarding the possibility of a permanent rupture between God and Israel. Chapter 3 of the book assuages the concern on theological grounds and expresses hope for reconciliation. After lamenting the sufferings that God has inflicted, the speaker has a change of heart and invokes a series of conventional arguments against the possibility of divine abandonment. God is essentially compassionate and just; misfortunes are finite divine punishments, not arbitrary or permanent divine acts:

> But this I call to mind, and therefore I have hope;
> The steadfast love of YHWH never ceases;
> His compassion never comes to an end. (Lam 3:21–22)[33]
>
> For YHWH will not cast off for ever;
> Rather, he inflicts suffering and has compassion according to the abundance of his steadfast love.
> For he does not afflict of his own accord or grieve the sons of men. (Lam 3:31–33)[34]

These verses employ two distinct strategies to allay the anxiety. First, even though God is causing the speaker to suffer now, God's past compassionate acts are signs of God's true, compassionate nature. Since God has treated the speaker well in the past and responded to his pleas, the speaker can assume, or at least hope, that God will respond to him again. "I called on your name, O Lord, from the pit of the lowest places / You heard my plea; do not deafen your ears to my relief, to my cry " (Lam 3:55–56).[35] This strategy of consolation is common in the Psalms. In both

---

33. Reading תָמְנוּ from the root תמם. According to Ibn Ezra, the *nun* is in place of the doubled *mem*.

34. The translation of מִלִּבּוֹ as "of his own accord" rather than the more common "willingly" is influenced by the covenantal nuances of the word חֶסֶד (steadfast love). In his comment on this verse, Rashi notes that God does not inflict suffering "from his heart." Rather, the people's sins cause their suffering.

35. The phrase לְרַוְחָתִי לְשַׁוְעָתִי is difficult. The Septuagint translates the phrase, "to my supplication." See Bertil Albrektson, *Studies in the Text and Theology of the Book of Lamentations* (Lund: CWK Gleerup, 1963), 164 for a discussion of the Septuagint version. The targum translates צלותי לארווחותני בגין בעותי, "[And now you will not shut your ear from hearing] my prayer in order to release me on account of

communal and individual laments, a confession of trust reassures the speaker that God is on his side. As Claus Westermann states, "confidence in the previously experienced activity of God for his people is expressed in the present in faith and praise."[36] Even though the speaker's current situation is grim, he invokes past beneficent acts of God to console himself and give himself hope.

Second, the invocation of God's steadfast love (חֶסֶד) has strong covenantal overtones. The tropes of covenantal theology which are invoked through the word חֶסֶד head off the fear of a permanent rupture between God and Israel. According to much of the Bible, the rules of the covenant are predictable, binding and fair. Just as the Israelites can be sure that transgression will lead to misfortune, so too can they be sure that repentance and obedience will lead to reconciliation and restoration. Leviticus 26:40–42 articulates this principle explicitly:

> They will confess their guilt and the guilt of their fathers—for the treachery which they performed against me and because they walked in opposition to me. Yea, I will walk in opposition to them and I will bring them to the land of their enemies. Then their uncircumcised hearts will be humbled and their guilt will be forgiven. Then I will remember my covenant with Jacob and also my covenant with Isaac and my covenant with Abraham I will remember, and I will remember the land.

God, like Israel, is bound by the terms of the contract. If Israel repents, God will restore its fortunes. If God punishes and has compassion according to his covenantal love, then both the punishment and the compassion are influenced and shaped by the covenant. Neither one is arbitrary or capricious.

Thus, Lam 3 echoes consolations which are common elsewhere in the Bible. God's past acts of compassion are evidence of God's essential goodness. Consequently, God can be depended upon to act compassionately again. At the same time, the chapter asserts that God's love is a covenantal love. Therefore, the catastrophes bemoaned throughout Lamentations must be punishments that are limited by the terms of the covenant rather

---

my plea." רְוָחָה appears elsewhere only in Exod 8:11, where it means "relief." Many commentators, including Abraham Cohen (*The Five Megilloth* [London: Soncino, 1946]) and Claus Westermann (*Lamentations* [trans. C. Muenchow; Minneapolis: Fortress Press, 1994]), translate לְרְוָחָתִי as a synonym for לְשַׁוְעָתִי. Delbert Hillers (*Lamentations* [AB 7a; Garden City: Doubleday, 1972]) emends לְשַׁוְעָתִי to לְיִשְׁעָתִי and translates the phrase "Do not close your ears—to relieve me—to save me." I have chosen to translate the verse as literally as possible, although I think that "cry for relief" would also capture the meaning of the phrase.

36. Claus Westermann, *The Praise of God in the Psalms* (trans. K. Crim; Richmond: John Knox Press, 1965), 59.

than unbounded acts of fury. Within Lamentations, these theological arguments are accompanied by a surge of optimism on the part of the speaker. In Lam 3:21 attention to these theological assertions causes the speaker to have hope. In 3:58–64 he is optimistic enough to ask God to avenge his enemies, and in 3:58–59 he states: "You, Lord, have argued my case; you have redeemed my life / You, YHWH, have seen my suffering, vindicate my right!" By the end of the chapter, the speaker is confident enough in future reconciliation that he is able to ask God for help.

The covenantal optimism of chapter 3 is not the dominant theme of Lamentations. Chapters 1, 2, 4 and 5 are unrelenting expressions of grief and despair, devoid of consolations and expressions of hope. In his commentary on Lamentations, Westermann notes how these chapters deviate from the other communal laments in the Bible. Communal laments usually include units of complaint, supplication and praise.[37] In the complaint sections, the speaker bemoans his current situation and then uses strategies of praise and supplication to try to invoke a response from God. According to Westermann, the lament form allows the speaker to express anger and a sense of alienation from God while affirming an ongoing relationship and expressing hope for reconciliation and restoration. The accusatory units express the negative feelings while the sections of praise and supplication affirm God's compassionate nature and testify to the fact that the speaker still feels in relationship with God.[38] In his analysis of Lamentations, Westermann identifies chapters 1, 2 and 4 as communal laments which have been influenced by the genre of the dirge. As a result of this influence, the laments in Lamentations devote an uncharacteristic amount of space to descriptions of misery and accusations against God. The poems also reduce or omit entirely expressions of praise and supplication.[39] In other words, the majority of laments in Lamentations deviate from the communal lament genre in that they are primarily expressions of alienation and abandonment which are not tempered by the expressions of connection and reliance which are intrinsic to the communal lament genre.[40] Westermann's analysis of the final verses of the text provides a characteristic example. Westermann identifies 5:21, "Return us to you,

---

37. Westermann, *Praise*, 52.
38. Westermann, *Lamentations*, 93.
39. Westermann notes that the two conventional elements of petition—a plea for divine attention and a plea for restoration—occur together only in chapter 5. Elsewhere, the speakers plead only for divine attention or for the punishment of Zion's enemies. He also notes that 5:19 is the only statement of praise outside of chapter 3.
40. Lamentations' thoroughgoing fatalism makes it anomolous among Ancient Near Eastern city laments as well. See F. W. Dobbs-Allsopp, *Weep, O Daughter of*

YHWH, so that we may return. Renew our days as of old," as the only petition for restoration in chapters 1, 2, 4 and 5:

> Where God can be addressed in this fashion, it is no longer necessary for the speaker to remain trapped and unconsoled in a desperate situation. Still, in v. 22 there follows an anxious question, *one that runs contrary to the whole tradition of the concluding verses of the communal laments.* Tersely put, "have you totally rejected us?" Nothing could more forcefully depict the situation in which this particular song of lamentation arose. Nothing could more poignantly express the solemnity with which the survivors voiced the lament.[41]

In addition, Lamentations 1, 2, 4 and 5 also ignore the potential consolations which are implicit in the Bible's covenant theology. While chapter 3 underscores the temporally limited nature of covenantal punishment, chapters 1, 2, 4 and 5 emphasize the brutality of God's wrath:

> YHWH has destroyed without mercy all the dwellings of Jacob.
> He has torn down in his wrath the strongholds of the daughter
>   of Judah . . .
>
> He has cut down in fierce anger the horn of Israel;
> He has drawn back his right hand from before the enemy;
> He has burned in Jacob like a flaming fire, consuming all
>   around. (Lam 2:2–3)

If God's actions are manifestations of divine fury, then there is no assurance that the suffering will ever end. Once, in 4:22, the text considers the possibility that there is a finite amount of punishment which corresponds to Israel's sins. "The punishment of your guilt, O daughter of Zion, is accomplished, he will not continue to exile you." However, the entire book ends with the fear that the God who reigns eternally might be angry for all time: "Rather, you have utterly rejected us, you have raged against us exceedingly" (Lam 5:22).[42]

Zion: A Study of the City-Lament Genre in the Hebrew Bible (Rome: Editrice Pontificio Istituto Biblico, 1993), 93–94.

41. Westermann, *Lamentations,* 217; my emphasis.

42. The particle כִּי אִם makes this verse notoriously difficult to translate. It often functions to contradict what precedes it (Deut 7:5; 1 Sam 8:19). In other cases, it restricts what precedes it (Gen 32:27). These usages suggest translations such as "Unless you have rejected us . . ." or "Rather, you have rejected us." The RSV translation, "Or have you utterly rejected us?" attempts to capture the the meaning of "unless you have rejected us . . ." in more poetic form. Robert Gordis argues in his article "The Conclusion of the Book of Lamentations [5:22]" (*JBL* 93 [1974]: 289–93) that the phrase should be read "even if, although" on the basis of its usage in Isa 10:22, Jer 51:14 and Amos 5:22. Other interpreters read כִּי אִם as an emphatic:

The presence of these two conflicting attitudes in Lamentations has led to debate over the meaning of the book as a whole. For many scholars, chapter 3 is the crux of Lamentations and articulates its deepest theological truths.[43] For these critics, the speaker in Chapter 3 is finally able to move beyond lament and see the larger deuteronomic picture. Israel has been punished for its sins but God's mercy is everlasting and gives grounds for hope and motivation for repentance. Delbert Hillers serves as a representative example. After describing the theocentric explanation of catastrophe proffered throughout Lamentations, Hillers states:

> Central to the book, however, is an expression of hope . . . the book offers, in its central chapter, the example of an unnamed man who has suffered under the hand of God . . . From near despair, this man wins through to confidence that God's mercy is not at an end, and that his final, inmost will for man is not suffering. From this beginning of hope the individual turns to call the nation to penitent waiting for God's mercy.[44]

Claus Westermann resists this optimistic reading of Lamentations. Although he is unwilling to acknowledge the full theological implications of Lamentations' deviation from the genre of communal lament, Westermann does reject the identification of chapter 3 as the essence of the book. Westermann insists that Lamentations should be read as a lament—an emotional reaction to suffering, rather than as a didactic text or a program for coping with misfortune.[45]

The scholars who view chapter 3 as the essence of Lamentations point to its placement in the center of the book as a sign of its importance. However, as Tod Linafelt notes, these scholars do not take into account the fact that the last two chapters of Lamentations revert to the hopelessness of the earlier chapters.[46] Despite the tentative optimism of the middle chapter, the book ends on a note of plaintive despair in which the speaker doubts the possibility of divine-human reconciliation:

"Indeed!" The Septuagint emends the verse by omitting the particle altogether. The resulting phrase is "For you have certainly rejected us . . ." I have chosen the reading "rather" because it best preserves both the emphatic and reversing functions of כִּי אִם.

43. Brevard Childs, *Introduction to the Old Testament as Scripture* (Philadelphia: Fortress Press, 1979); Norman Gottwald, *Studies in the Book of Lamentations* (London: SCM Press, 1962); Hillers, *Lamentations*; Alan Mintz, "The Rhetoric of Lamentations and the Representation of Catastrophe," *Prooftexts* 2 (1982): 1–17.

44. Hillers, *Lamentations*, xvi.

45. Westermann, *Lamentations*, 78–79.

46. Tod Linafelt, *Surviving Lamentations: Catastrophe, Lament and Protest in the Afterlife of a Biblical Book* (Chicago: University of Chicago Press, 2000), 2–3.

> But you, YHWH are enthroned forever; your throne endures for
> eternity.
> Why have you forgotten us forever? Abandoned us for all time?
> Return us to you, YHWH, so that we may return. Renew our
> days as of old.
> Rather, you have utterly rejected us, you have raged against us
> exceedingly. (Lam 5:19–22)

In the final two chapters of Lamentations, the consolation and optimism of chapter 3 are suspended. The speaker feels so abandoned by God that he fears that the abandonment may last forever. His grief and despair over the destruction of Jerusalem are so overwhelming that the brief moment of optimism and consolation expressed in chapter 3 cannot be sustained.

Summary

As the lectionary text for Tisha b'Av, Lamentations identifies the destruction(s) of the temple and Jerusalem as the catastrophe commemorated on the holiday. The historical grounds for lament include the suffering of the city's population, the destruction of the temple and the exile of the Judeans from the city. In addition, the sufferings of personified Zion herself are grounds for lament and commemoration. Lamentations also articulates potent theological anxieties which were raised by the events of 587 BCE and 70 CE. If Zion's misfortunes are a result of divine fury, then the intensity and duration of those misfortunes suggest that God's anger is fierce and potentially unbounded. From the standpoint of the speaker in Lamentations, it appears as though God and Israel might never be reconciled again. Finally, Lamentations gives voice to overwhelming grief and despair over the catastrophic destruction of Jerusalem and devastation of her inhabitants. According to the lectionary cycle, the emotional tenor of the holiday is one of utter despair.

Haftarot of Rebuke and Consolation

The designation of Lamentations as the lectionary text for Tisha b'Av identifies the significance of the holiday, its theological implications and its emotional tenor in a particular way. According to the lectionary cycle, it is not a day marked by timeless, supernatural, malevolent forces. Instead it is a day which marks Israel's historical catastrophes and laments the divine anger and alienation which seem to be manifested by those events. This particular delineation of Tisha b'Av determines the significance of the surrounding season. The lectionary cycle defines the periods preceding and following the holiday according to the same historical-theological paradigm. The three weeks preceding the holiday are identified with the periods preceding the catastrophes of 587 BCE and 70 CE. The haftarot of rebuke not only chastise Israel for wrongdoing, they also warn the people of the disasters which are to come. The seven weeks following the holiday are identified with the redemptive future which will follow the disasters' aftermath. The haftarot surrounding Tisha b'Av not only elaborate on, and participate in, the theological-historical paradigm; they also respond to the emotions and theological anxieties raised by Lamentations. Through the strategic selection and arrangement of haftarot, the redactors of the lectionary cycle assert the validity of the covenantal paradigm, counter the accusation of ongoing divine abandonment, and enact a process of consolation in which the community, as represented by Zion herself, moves from grief and alienation to consolation and reconciliation.

The tripartite structure of the lectionary cycle forms a narrative which defuses Lamentations' anxiety that God and Israel are permanently estranged. The three sections of the lectionary cycle articulate a narrative of sin-punishment-restoration. The three haftarot of rebuke decry Israel's numerous transgressions. Jeremiah 1:16 and 2:4–28 accuse Israel of straying from the God of Israel and worshiping other gods. Isaiah 1 accuses the people of forsaking God (v. 4) and of performing rituals while behaving immorally (vv. 11–17). The text also targets the immorality of Israel's leaders (v. 23). The haftarot of rebuke not only describe Israel's sins, they also warn the people of the disastrous consequences of continued transgression:

> Then YHWH said to me:
> Out of the north misfortune will break out on all the inhabitants of the land.
> For here I am calling all the tribes of the kingdoms of the north, says YHWH;
> And they shall come and each of them shall set his throne at the entrance of the gates of Jerusalem;
> Against all its surrounding walls and against all the cities of Judah.
> And I will utter my judgments against them, for all their wickedness—because they forsook me;
> And offered incense to other gods and prostrated themselves before the work of their hands. (Jer 1:14–16)[47]

Within the lectionary cycle, the haftarot of rebuke are followed by Lamentations. Within the cycle's narrative, Lamentations describes the catastrophes which occurred as punishment for the sins decried in the hafta-

---

47. See also Isa 1:5–9, 19–20, 24–25.

rot of rebuke. Thus far, the lectionary cycle as a whole concurs with Lamentations' conviction that Israel's misfortune is the consequence of its sins. However, whereas Lamentations ends on a note of fatalistic despair, the lectionary sequence does not end with Lamentations. Instead, the recitation of Lamentations is followed by seven weeks of consolation and promises of redemption and restoration. In its biblical context, Lamentations suggests that Israel's narrative ends with catastrophe and alienation from God. The lectionary cycle assures its audience that catastrophe is the fulcrum of the nation's story, not its conclusion.

Haftarot of Rebuke

Within the lectionary anthology, the haftarot of rebuke are linked to Lamentations through both thematic and verbal correspondences. Through strategies of selection and arrangement, the redactors of the lectionary cycle use these correspondences to articulate particular theological messages. Within the cycle, the haftarot of rebuke articulate the sin segment of the sin-punishment-restoration narrative. In addition, the conjunction between the haftarot of rebuke and Lamentations itself serves to justify God's punishment of Israel. The conjunction also serves to assert the reliability of the prophetic word.

Jeremiah 1:1–2:4

The first haftarah describes Jeremiah's prophetic commission and recounts the content of his first prophetic vision: an omen of the invasion of the Babylonians. It also establishes the prophet's credentials and introduces the theme of the reliability of the divine word. This text is linked to Lamentations through both the traditional identification of Jeremiah as the author of Lamentations and through literary correspondences between the two texts.[48] Like Lamentations, this passage includes images of destruction and siege (1:10, 15) and portrays Jerusalem in sexualized female terms (2:2–3).

Jeremiah 2:4–28, (4:1–2)[49]

The second haftarah is the most vituperative of the three haftarot of rebuke. The text is a scathing condemnation of the sins of Israel's ancestors

---

48. B. BB 15a identifies Jeremiah as the author of Jeremiah, Lamentations and Kings.

49. The addition of 4:1–2 reflects the custom of ending haftarot on a positive note. J. Meg 3:7 (also Sof 12:1) records an opinon of R. Yose b. R. Bun, who states that "the one who stands to read from the Torah must open with a good thing and

as well as those of the current generation. Throughout the text, the prophet condemns Israel's worship of other gods and its reliance on foreign nations. In the context of a holistic reading of the lectionary cycle, the enumeration of the people's sins in this pericope resonates with the unspecified sinfulness of Zion in Lamentations (Lam 1:5, 8–9, 14, 18; 2:14; 3:42; 4:13; 5:7, 16). The description of Israel's polytheism as a form of nymphomania in Jer 2:20–26 resonates with Lamentations' sexualized representations of the invasion of Jerusalem, and of Zion's relationship with other nations.

Isaiah 1:1–27

The parameters of the earliest form of this haftarah are difficult to determine. The chapter in PRK which corresponds to the third sabbath of rebuke is a composite chapter which deals with both Lam 1:1 and Isa 1:21. The poems of Yannai and Kallir also identify Lam 1:1 as the lectionary verse. However, the tosafists state that the *Pesikta* designates Isa 1:1 as the haftarah. This tradition becomes canonical in the major liturgical rites. The short and long forms of the haftarah which are attested in PRK and the later rites, respectively, manifest different types of correspondences to Lamentations.

The long form of the haftarah (1:1–27) condemns the Judeans for their sins and decries their obstinate refusal to understand that their misfortune is a result of their sinfulness (1:1–20). The last section of the chapter (1:21–31) decries the moral corruption of Zion and announces that God will punish the city for its immorality. This punishment will serve as a purification, which will in turn lead to the restoration and redemption of the city. This version of the haftarah manifests the sort of thematic correspondence which links the first two haftarot of rebuke to the rest of the lectionary cycle. Like Lamentations, Isa 1 speaks of the sins of the people (1:2–5, 21–24) and declares that the people's misfortunes are, and will be, punishment for those sins (1:5–9, 25–26). It also deals with the subjects of the temple cult (1:13–15) and Jerusalem (1:21, 26–28). The short form of the haftarah (1:21ff) contains a more precise verbal correspondence to Lamentations. It begins, "Alas (אֵיכָה), she has become like a harlot, the faithful city." This verse resonates strongly with Lam 1:1. "Alas (אֵיכָה), she sits alone, the city once great with people." Both verses begin "Alas"; both de-

---

close with a good thing." Although this statement is made with regard to the Torah portion and not the haftarah, the appending of positive verses at the end of otherwise pessimistic haftarot in certain rites suggests that the custom was extended to the haftarot as well.

scribe the city in feminine terms, and both are succinct, poetic descriptions of the city's reversal of fortune.

Within the biblical context, many of the correspondences between Lamentations and the haftarot of rebuke are quite unremarkable. Countless biblical texts enumerate Israel's sins, predict doom, and make exhortations regarding the temple cult. In the context of the biblical anthology, these correspondences are merely signs that texts which are scattered throughout the biblical canon share common concerns which were central to the world view of the biblical authors. Within the lectionary cycle, however, these correspondences become the raw material from which a set of theological responses to Lamentations is constructed.

Sin-Punishment-Restoration

The conjunction of the haftarot of rebuke and Lamentations articulates the sin-punishment portion of the sin-punishment-restoration narrative discussed above. Within their biblical contexts, the warnings and rebukes of Jer 1:1–2:28 and Isa 1:1–26 are followed by more prophetic exhortations. In its biblical context within the Masoretic text, Lamentations is an isolated self-contained lament which is not linked meaningfully to the books on either side of it.[50] In the lectionary cycle, however, the prophecies of rebuke are followed by Lamentations' description of the devastation of Jerusalem. This lectionary arrangement presents the catastrophes lamented on the ninth of Av as the consequences of the sins, and the fulfillment of the prophecies, recited during the three weeks preceding the holiday.

While the haftarot of rebuke narrate the sin portion of the lectionary drama, they also foreshadow the entire sin-punishment-restoration narrative. In Jer 1:10, God appoints Jeremiah to "pluck up and pull down, to destroy and to overthrow, to build and to plant." In its biblical context, this verse serves to soften the harshness of Jeremiah's prophecy. By appointing Jeremiah to build and to plant, God informs the prophet's audience that their future is not entirely bleak. The verse serves a similar function for the lectionary audience. It informs the worshiping community that the future contains building and planting as well as destruction. When read from the vantage point of the cycle as a whole, this verse not only injects a note of optimism into the prophecies of doom; it also foreshadows the end of the lectionary narrative. From the outset, the redactors of the lectionary cycle assure the audience that the destruction described on Tisha b'Av will give way to acts of restoration and renewed fertility. The verse's foreshadowing is particularly potent because images of planting and building figure

---

50. In Christian bibles, Lamentations is placed after Jeremiah. This arrangement reflects the traditional attribution of the book to Jeremiah.

prominently in the visions of restoration in the haftarot of consolation (Isa 54:2, 12; 55:10, 13; 60:10–13, 21; 61:11; 62:9–10).

Similarly, the third haftarah summarizes the entire cycle in terms that resonate both with Lamentations and with the final haftarah of consolation:

> Alas, she has become like a harlot, the faithful city!
> She was filled with justice, righteousness dwelled in her; but now, murderers. (Isa 1:21)

> Then I will restore your judges as they were at the start and your counselors as in the beginning.
> After this they will call you "City of righteousness, faithful city." (Isa 1:26)

These verses not only articulate the sin-punishment-redemption narrative. They also echo the corresponding parts of the lectionary cycle. The "alas" (אֵיכָה) of Isa 1:21 foreshadows the "alas" (אֵיכָה) which begins Lamentations. The renaming of the city in Isa 1:26 foreshadows the triumphant renaming of Zion in Isa 62:4: "You will no longer be called 'Forsaken'and your land will no longer be called 'Desolate' / For you will be called 'My delight is in her' and your land will be called 'Espoused.'"[51] Thus, the haftarot of rebuke form an essential part of the lectionary's response to accusations of eternal divine estrangement and fury. By articulating the first segment of the overarching narrative and foreshadowing the narrative as a whole, they counter Lamentations' anxiety that God's fury will last forever.

Measure-for-Measure Punishment

The redactors of the lectionary cycle also use the haftarot of rebuke to assert that the catastrophes described in Lamentations are just and fitting consequences of Israel's sins. Within the lectionary cycle, the correspondences between the texts of rebuke and Lamentations become signs of a precise measure-for-measure relationship between Israel's sins and her punishment.

---

51. Here, the redactors of the lectionary cycle are capitalizing on one of the correspondences which links the pre-exilic and post-exilic sections of Isaiah to one another (Rolf Rendtorff, *Canon and Theology: Overtures to an Old Testament Theology* [ed. and trans. Margaret Kohl; Minneapolis: Fortress, 1993], 158 n. 45). The redactors of the cycle use this correspondence, which serves a unifying purpose in the Book of Isaiah, to assert the coherence of the lectionary narrative.

Destruction of the Temple

Lamentations describes the destruction of the temple as an act of divine fury: "Alas, the Lord in his anger has beclouded daughter Zion / He threw down from heaven to earth the splendor of Israel / He did not remember his footstool in the day of his anger" (Lam 2:1–2). A few verses later it comments: "He has broken down his booth like a garden; He has destroyed his tabernacle / YHWH has rejected his altar, spurned his sanctuary" (Lam 2:6–7). This destruction of God's own footstool/booth and tabernacle is the manifestation of God's unbridled anger and a sign of the ruptured relationship between God and Israel. In destroying the temple, God destroys the prime symbol of his special relationship with Israel. In the context of the lectionary cycle, however, the destruction of the temple becomes the fitting punishment for the abuse of the temple cult. Isaiah 1:10–17 accuses Israel of empty ritual observance which is unaccompanied by moral obedience:

> What are your many sacrifices to me? says YHWH.
> I have had enough of your burnt offerings of rams and the fat of
>   fatted calves;
> The blood of cows and of sheep and of he-goats I do not desire.
> When you come to see my face,
> Who asks this of your hand, this trampling of my courts?" (Isa
>   1:11–12)

In light of this charge, the destruction of the temple is devastatingly "appropriate" to the people's crime. Desecration of the festivals results in their violent abolition. The punishment embodied in the destruction of the temple is both punitive and preventive. The destruction of the temple and the mechanisms of the cult prevents Israel from transgressing in the particular fashion decried in Isa 1.

Rape of Zion

The conjunction of the haftarot of rebuke and Lamentations transforms the sexualized vision of the devastation of Jerusalem into another example of measure-for-measure punishment. Lamentations employs the trope of the female personification of Zion. This trope, which may arise from the genre of Ancient Near Eastern city laments, serves a multitude of rhetorical purposes. The personification of the city as a woman both humanizes and feminizes its destruction. The city becomes all the more pathetic and helpless. The personification of the city as a woman generates or facilitates the description of the invasion and destruction in sexual terms: "Jerusalem has sinned a sin; therefore she has become like a menstruant (לְנִידָה) /

All of her admirers despised her, for they have seen her nakedness / She can only sigh and turn (her) back. Her uncleanness is on her skirts . . ." (Lam 1:8–9). A few verses later, the invasion of the temple is described. "The foe has laid his hand on all of her treasures / Surely, she has seen nations enter her sanctum; about whom you commanded, they will not enter your congregation" (Lam 1:10). The language of the biblical text is steeped in sexual allusion.[52] The term נִידָה in 1:8 means "impure one" in its broadest sense but refers particularly to a menstruant.[53] The subsequent reference to the uncleanness on Zion's skirts supports this reading. The city is described as an impure menstruant who has exposed herself to a multitude of lovers. Now they have turned against her and all she can do is sigh and turn her back in an attempt to hide herself. The subsequent invasion of the temple is equally suggestive. The verb לבוא (to enter) is also used in the Bible to mean "have sex with."[54] At the plain sense level, the phrase "surely, she has seen nations enter her sanctum" refers to the invasion of the temple. However, in the context of the sexual imagery of Lam 1:8–9, the phrase has a strong allusive character which continues the sexual motifs. It not only describes a military invasion, it also suggests images of sexual penetration.[55] As Alan Mintz notes, this sexualized language is enormously powerful rhetorically:

> The serviceableness of the image of Jerusalem as an abandoned fallen woman lies in the precise register of pain it articulates. An image of death would have purveyed a false comfort of finality; the dead have finished with suffering and their agony can be evoked only in retrospect. The raped and defiled woman who survives, on the other hand, is a living witness to a pain that knows no release.[56]

Within the biblical context, this sexual language is generated by the persistent personification of Jerusalem as a woman in Lamentations. If the city is personified as a woman, then the stripping of its defenses and the subsequent invasion become imagined as the stripping and rape of the woman. In the context of the lectionary cycle, the sexual language of Lamentations resonates with the sexual language of Jer 2:23–25. The conjunction of the sexualized text of rebuke and the sexualized account of the de-

---

52. Mintz, "Rhetoric," 3–4.
53. E.g., Lev 12:2; 15:19, 20, 24, 25, 26, 33; 18:19.
54. E.g., Gen 6:4, 30:3.
55. This sexual meaning is reinforced when the text is read by speakers of rabbinic Hebrew. By the rabbinic period, יָד (hand) becomes a euphemism for penis. Thus the beginning of v. 10 reads as a reference both to the grasping hand and the thrusting phallus of the enemy who invades the city's most precious parts.
56. Mintz, "Rhetoric," 3. See also Linafelt, *Surviving*, 43–49.

struction suggests that Zion's sexual disgrace and violation is the "fitting" result of sexual transgression. The second haftarah of rebuke describes Israel's ritual and political transgressions in terms of sexual infidelity and chronic nymphomania:[57]

> How can you say, 'I am not defiled, I have not gone after the
>   Baalim?'
> Look at your way in the valley; know what you have done;
> A running she-camel twisting her path.
> A wild ass, desert-trained, snuffing the wind in her eagerness,
>   whose hot passion none can restrain;
> None that seek her grow weary; in her season, they'll find her.
>   (Jer 2:23–25)

By asserting that ritual "promiscuity" was one of Israel's central transgressions, the lectionary provides a narrative, causal motivation for the ensuing sexual violation. The lectionary suggests that Israel was, once again, punished measure-for-measure. The consequences of her promiscuity were rape and humiliation.

Zion's Isolation

The literary correspondences between Jer 2:4–28 and Lamentations also provide moral causation for the dual tropes of isolation and vulnerability that pervade Lamentations. Lamentations 1:3 states: "All her pursuers overtook her in the narrow places." The violence of this "overtaking" becomes the dark consequence of Zion's availability to all comers in Jer 2:24. Similarly, Lam 1:2 states: "She has no comforter from among all her lovers; all her companions have betrayed her; they have become her enemies." In the context of Lamentations, the designation of *"all* her lovers" and *"all* her companions" is one of many tropes of totality, of devastation and isolation without exception. When conjoined to the accusation that

---

57. For further discussion of the trope of Israel as harlot, see Phyllis Bird, "'To Play the Harlot': An Inquiry into an Old Testament Metaphor," in *Gender and Difference in Ancient Israel* [ed. Peggy Day; Minneapolis: Fortress Press, 1989], 75–94; Tikva Frymer-Kensky, *In the Wake of the Goddesses: Women, Culture, and the Biblical Transformation of Pagan Myth* (New York: Free Press, 1992), 144–52; Moshe Greenberg, *Ezekiel* (2 vols.; AB 22, 22a; New York: Doubleday, 1983, 1997), 22:297–306, 22a:491–94 and Renita J. Weems, *Battered Love: Marriage, Sex, and Violence in the Hebrew Prophets* (Minneapolis: Fortress Press, 1995). Weems' reading of the erotic trope in the Bible is particularly relevant here. She notes that in most cases where the Bible uses sexual tropes to portray the relationship between God and Israel, these tropes serve to describe dynamics of power and violence, not love and romance. This pattern is certainly evident in the conjunction of the haftarot of rebuke and Lamentations.

"*none* that seek her grow weary" (Jer 2:24), the assertion in Lam 1:2 is no longer merely a statement of the extreme nature of Zion's isolation but also another example of fitting punishment: If you have so many lovers, they are bound to desert and betray. Lastly, the accusation that Israel has abandoned God, articulated in Jer 2:5 ("What wrong did your fathers find in me that they abandoned me"), becomes the justification for the abandonment of Israel by God in Lamentations.

This literary reading of the Tisha b'Av cycle demonstrates how the redactors of the cycle use the correspondences among scattered biblical texts to assert a causal relationship among the texts. Literary motifs shared in common by the prophetic texts and Lamentations serve as evidence for a cause-and-effect relationship between the sins condemned by the prophets and the catastrophes suffered by Zion. Through the establishment of measure-for-measure correspondences between the texts of rebuke and Lamentations, the lectionary cycle asserts that the catastrophes bemoaned in Lamentations are fair and appropriate punishments for Israel's sins. Through this assertion, the creators of the lectionary cycle counter Lamentations' accusation that the events of 587 BCE are "cruel and unusual." Thus, the conjunction of the haftarot of rebuke with the text of Lamentations not only places the catastrophes commemorated on Tisha b'Av within a sequence of events, it also asserts that a deep moral causality underlies that sequence.

Reliability of the Prophetic Word

Within the lectionary cycle, the conjunction of the haftarot of rebuke and Lamentations not only articulates a structure of cause and effect; it also establishes a paradigm of prophecy and fulfillment. The prophecies of rebuke themselves warned the people of the upcoming disasters and, in effect, determined their occurrence. The paradigm established by the conjunction of the two lectionary units asserts that what is prophesied will occur. In the early weeks of the Tisha b'Av cycle, this assertion is far from comforting. For audience members who are schooled in the ideology of the reliability of prophecy, the prophecies of doom can only lead to disaster. However, from the perspective of the cycle as a whole, the reliability of the prophetic word provides grounds for optimism and hope.

At a fundamental level, the efficacy of the lectionary's strategies of consolation depends on the reliability of the prophetic word. The lectionary cycle articulates a chronological scheme which extends from past sin and catastrophe to future redemption. Within this chronology, the redactors of the lectionary cycle, along with the rest of the worshiping community, were situated somewhere between acute past catastrophe and future redemption. While the situation of the fifth- to sixth-century CE Jewish community was nowhere near as dire as the situation described in Lamentations, it certainly was not as glorious as the redemption described in the haftarot of consolation. In addition, with the exception of a few periods of messianic fervor, the historical reality of the community did not suggest that redemption was imminent. Throughout much of Jewish history, the only grounds for hope for future redemption lay in the messianic promises of the prophets, and in beliefs in God's ultimate forgiveness and compassion. If the words of the prophets were not reliable, then the community had little grounds for hope.

There is also a political rationale for the insistence on the reliability of the biblical prophetic word. Throughout the rabbinic literature, the rabbis repeatedly insist that prophecy came to an end during the biblical period. After the close of that era, divine revelation occurs through the study of Torah, not through direct divine revelation to individuals.[58] This ideology identifies the rabbis as the primary conduits of the divine word. It is the Torah scholars, not the independent prophets or messianic aspirants, who communicate the word of God. The assertion of the reliability of the divine word is fundamental to this ideology of revelation. If the veracity of the prophetic word is questionable, then the rabbinic study and interpretation of that word is also unreliable.

The reliability of the divine word is asserted explicitly in the third haftarah of consolation:

> For my thoughts are not your thoughts and your ways are not my ways, says YHWH.
> For as high as the heavens are from the earth, so are my ways higher than your ways and my thoughts than your thoughts.
> Just as the rain and the snow fall from heaven,
> And there they do not return but instead they water the earth,
> And cause it to give birth and blossom, and they produce seed for the sower and bread for the eater;
> So will be the word which goes forth from my mouth; it will not return to me empty,
> But will do what I please and succeed in the purpose for which I sent it. (Isa 55:8–11)[59]

The haftarot of rebuke contribute to the assertion of this ideology. The first haftarah recounts Jeremiah's prophetic commission and states definitively that God is the true power behind his prophecies:

---

58. E.g., b. Sot 48b, b. Yom 9b, and b. San 11a.
59. The insistence on the reliability of the divine word recurs repeatedly throughout Isa 40–66. E.g., Isa 42:9; 43:12; 44:7–8, 26; 45:19, 21, 23; 46:10–11; 48:3–5, 15.

> Before I created you in the belly, I knew you; and before you came out from the womb, I consecrated you; I made you a prophet to the nations.
> And I said, "Oh Lord, YHWH, behold I do not know how to speak for I am a lad."
> And YHWH said to me, "Do not say 'I am a lad';
> Because wherever I send you, you will go, and whatever I command, you will say." (Jer 1:5–6)

Thus, the opening pericope of the cycle averts any accusations regarding the human source or human fallibility of the ensuing prophecies. Jeremiah's commission shows that the prophet is merely an agent of God's word and God's will.[60]

By joining the haftarot of rebuke to Lamentations, the redactors of the lectionary cycle assert further "proof" for the reliability of the prophetic word. Within the lectionary cycle, the prophecies of doom in Jer 1–2 and Isa 1 are fulfilled in the catastrophes described in Lamentations. Jeremiah 1 foretells the invasion and siege of Jerusalem (1:13–15). Jeremiah 2 predicts the desolation of the land (2:15). Isaiah 1 also foretells the desolation of the land and the destruction of the people at the hand of God (1:7–8, 25). Each of these predictions is fulfilled in Lamentations. The fulfillment of the prophecies of doom in the early parts of the cycle set up the, as yet unproven, reliability of the prophecies of restoration in the latter part of the cycle. If Jeremiah's and Isaiah's prophecies of destruction and devastation were fulfilled, there is reason to believe that Isaiah's prophecies of restoration and redemption will also come to pass.

Summary

Through the strategic selection and arrangement of the haftarot of rebuke, the redactors of the lectionary transform biblical prophecies of doom and destruction into essential parts of a consolatory structure. Although the prophecies of rebuke themselves do not offer much consolation, their function within the lectionary cycle is deeply comforting. When the haftarot of rebuke are placed before Lamentations and the haftarot of consolation, they form part of the narrative which assures the worshiping community that the catastrophes commemorated on Tisha b'Av and the state of divine displeasure and estrangement that they represent are only a tem-

---

60. For a discussion of this trope in the biblical prophetic literature, see Michael Fishbane, "Biblical Prophecy as a Religious Phenomenon," in *Jewish Spirituality* (vol. 1 of *From the Bible through the Middle Ages*, ed. Arthur Green; New York: Crossroad, 1986), 62–81.

porary stage in Israel's history. In addition, the selection of the haftarot of rebuke underscores the verbal and thematic correspondences between the prophetic discourse of warning and rebuke and Lamentations' discourse of catastrophe. The redactors of the lectionary cycle use these correspondences to contextualize God's acts of fury in Lamentations within a judicial framework. Although God's punishments are brutal, they are calibrated in mode, if not in degree, to Israel's sins. Finally, the recitation of the haftarot of rebuke in the weeks preceding Tisha b'Av asserts the reliability of the prophetic word. The fulfillment of the prophecies of doom becomes the grounds to assert the reliability of the prophecies of restoration.

Haftarot of Consolation

Like the haftarot of rebuke, the haftarot of consolation articulate a response to the theological challenges posed by Lamentations and by the ongoing political situation of the Jewish community in the fifth to sixth centuries CE. The haftarot respond to Lamentations' despair over the destruction and exile by promising a future restoration and return. At the same time, the haftarot of consolation counter Lamentations' accusations of divine abandonment by asserting that God and Israel are engaged in an ongoing intimate relationship. As is the case in the haftarot of rebuke, the articulation of these responses is effected through redactional techniques. Through the strategies of selection and arrangement, the redactors of the lectionary cycle create a consolatory dialogue between God and Israel which both enacts, and serves as evidence for, the reconciliation between God and Israel. The haftarot of consolation not only articulate and demonstrate grounds for comfort, they model an emotional journey from grief to consolation for the worshiping community.

Lamentations and the Haftarot of Consolation

In isolation, the haftarot of consolation are forward-looking texts. They describe vivid portraits of the future restoration of Zion and the return of the exiles. In the context of the lectionary cycle, these texts not only point toward a messianic future, they also respond retrospectively to the texts of Lamentations and speak to the contemporary needs of the worshiping community.

While most of the correspondences between the haftarot of rebuke and Lamentations seem to be the result of shared cultural concerns and a common cultural and literary milieu, the correspondences between Lamentations and the haftarot of consolation seem to be intentional allusions by the authors of Isa 40–66.⁶¹ In *Studies in the Book of Lamentations*, Norman Gottwald states:

> As Lohr indicated, the affinities between Lamentations and Isa 40–66 are numerous, and a close study reveals many more than he mentioned. Some of these are shared by other early writings and cannot be of much help in determining influence between the two books. But others are unique or nearly so, thus demonstrating to the satisfaction of the present writer that both Deutero- and Trito-Isaiah knew the Book of Lamentations.⁶²

Gottwald supports this assertion with a list of 28 words or phrases which are shared in common by the two texts.⁶³ The most extensive treatment of the correspondences between Second Isaiah and Lamentations occurs in Patricia Tull Willey's *Remember the Former Things*. Here, Willey employs a more sophisticated method for identifying and analyzing allusions within Second Isaiah.⁶⁴ Like Gottwald, Willey cites cases of verbatim citation to prove that Second Isaiah repeatedly alluded and responded to earlier texts, including Lamentations. Once she has made a compelling case for allusion based on verbatim citation, Willey extends her analysis to explore the larger relationship between the alluding and alluded texts that contain the verbal parallels. Her analysis of the relationship between Lam

---

61. The following scholars have documented correspondences between Lamentations and Second Isaiah: Gottwald, *Studies*, 44–5; Yehezkel Kaufmann, *History of the Religion of Israel* (Jerusalem and Tel Aviv: Bialik and Devir, 1937–56), 592 n. 7 (Heb.); Carol Newsom, "A Response to Norman Gottwald, 'Social Class and Ideology in Isaiah 40–55,'" *Semeia* 59 (1992): 73–78; Alan Mintz, *Hurban: Responses to Catastrophe in Hebrew Literature* (New York: Columbia University Press, 1984), 42–46. Linafelt, *Surviving*, 62–79; Benjamin Sommer, *A Prophet Reads Scripture: Allusion in Isaiah 40–66* (Stanford: Stanford University Press, 1998), 152–67.

62. Gottwald, *Studies*, 44–45.

63. Ibid.

64. She utilizes the methodology outlined by Richard Hays in *Echoes of Scripture in the Letters of Paul* (New Haven: Yale University Press, 1989). Hays outlines a seven-part "test" for identifying allusions. Availability: Would the author of the later text have had access to the earlier text? Volume and Recurrence: Does the author cite significantly large sections of the earlier text and does he refer repeatedly to the earlier text? Thematic coherence: Is there a relationship between the meaning of the echoed words or phrases? Here Hays does not insist on an identity of meaning. The later text might be revising or refuting the meaning of the cited text. Historical Plausibility: Is it reasonable to assume that the author of the later text could have intended the allusion as it is being interpreted? History of Interpretation: Have other readers seen the allusion? Satisfaction: Does the identification and interpretation of the proposed allusion make sense? Does it illuminate the meaning of the later text?

4:15 and Isa 52:11 provides a representative case.⁶⁵ Lamentations 4:15 states, "Depart! Unclean! they call to them. Depart! Depart! Do not touch! / So they wandered and roamed for they said among the nations, 'they will not continue to live.'" Isa 52:11 states, "Depart! Depart! Go out from there! Uncleanness do not touch / Go out from its midst! Purify yourselves! bearers of the vessels of YHWH." First, Willey uses a philological method to determine conclusively that Isa 52:11 is an allusion to Lam 4:13. She notes that the imperatives סוּרוּ (depart!) and אַל־תִּגָּעוּ (do not touch!) are relatively rare in the Hebrew Bible and notes that the word טָמֵא (unclean) appears infrequently outside of the book of Leviticus. Isaiah 52:11 and Lam 4:13 are the only verses in which all three terms appear together.⁶⁶ Consequently, it is unlikely that the correspondences between the two verses are coincidental.

On the grounds of these linguistic correspondences, Willey asserts that Isa 52:11 is an allusion to Lam 4:15. She then interprets the nature and effect of the allusion. Second Isaiah's verse represents a sophisticated reversal of the Lamentations verse. In Lamentations, the exiles are figured as ritually unclean creatures who are forced to leave Jerusalem because of their impurity. In Second Isaiah, the exiles are now the ritually pure addressees who are commanded to leave the unclean city of their exile. The allusion asserts that the exile from Judea would be reversed by the exodus from Babylon. The exodus from Babylon also marks a return to normal conditions of purity and uncleanness. Once again, the Israelites are clean and they are exhorted to stay away from the unclean space and property of the gentiles.

Through her analysis of specific cases of allusion, Willey establishes that Second Isaiah knew Lamentations and regarded it as a text to be reckoned with. Once a literary relationship has been established between the two texts, it becomes plausible to read various forms of correspondence as allusions and responses.⁶⁷ Willey observes that Second Isaiah alludes to Lamentations in a variety of ways—through verbatim citations, re-use of vocabulary clusters and through the treatment of similar themes. In some cases, the Second Isaiah text will allude in a concentrated fashion to a particular Lamentations text.⁶⁸ In other cases, Willey argues that Second Isa-

---

65. Patricia Tull Willey, *Remember the Former Things: The Recollection of Previous Texts in Second Isaiah* (SBL Dissertation Series 161; Atlanta: Scholars Press, 1997), 125–28.

66. Benjamin Sommer (*Prophet*, 68) further notes that the splitting in half of the alluded verse is a common strategy of allusion in Second Isaiah.

67. Willey, *Remember*, 129.

68. Willey notes that Isa 51:11–12 alludes heavily to Lam 1:2–4 (ibid., 130–77). Isa 51:17–23 alludes heavily to Lam 4 (ibid., 125–30); Isa 50:4–11 and 52:12–53:12

54 From Rebuke to Consolation

iah echoes scattered texts within Lamentations. Without the more concentrated allusions to particular texts, it would be difficult to identify these cases conclusively as allusions. However, since the more concentrated cases of allusion establish a relationship between Second Isaiah and Lamentations, it becomes plausible to hear the more scattered echoes as intertextual allusions as well.[69]

The work of Gottwald, Kaufmann, Sommer, and Willey establishes conclusively that Second Isaiah alluded and responded to the text of Lamentations. These scholars have compiled extensive lists of verbatim correspondences between the two texts and have analyzed many of the correspondences in order to determine whether or not they can be considered intertextual allusions. The following list of thematic correspondences assumes the intertextual relationship established by these scholars. In some cases, the correspondences cited below are cases of verbatim echo; in other cases, they are thematic correspondences in which the same image is invoked in different ways by the authors of Lamentations and Isa 40–66 .

I. Second Isaiah's visions of restoration and redemption reverse the catastrophes bemoaned in Lamentations. In many cases, Second Isaiah's vision surpasses the pre-exilic situation whose demise is lamented in the earlier texts.[70]

1. Lamentations repeatedly bemoans the exile of the people from Jerusalem (1:3–5, 18; 2:9; 4:15). Second Isaiah proclaims the imminent, triumphant return of the exiles (Isa 40:10–11, 49:17–22; 52:11–12; 54:1–3; 55:12; 60:4, 9).[71]

2. Lamentations laments the destruction of the temple (Lam 2:1–2, 6–7; 5:18) and bewails the effects of the invasion and siege on the population. Food is scarce; the people are starving and dying in the streets from both hunger and battle wounds (Lam 1:11, 19; 2:11–12, 20–21; 4:3–10; 5:4–5, 9–13). In Second Isaiah, the temple will be rebuilt gloriously (Isa 54:11–12; 60:7), food is plentiful (Isa 55:1) and the scenes of mourning and despair are replaced with sounds of joy and rejoicing (Isa 51:3; 52:7; 54:1; 55:12; 60:18; 61:10; 62:5). The punishment that Jerusalem suffered will be turned on her enemies (Isa 51:23; 60:14–16).

---

invoke Lam 3 (ibid., 214–21); Isa 54:6–8 invokes Lam 5:19–22 (ibid., 233–39); Isa 54:11–13 alludes to Lam 4:1–2 (ibid., 239–41).
   69. Ibid., 188–91.
   70. Ibid., 239–41, for a more detailed discussion of this trope.
   71. I cite examples only from the texts which are used as haftarot of consolation because these are the only cases which are relevant to the main part of this study.

3. The ascendancy of Jerusalem's enemies and their mockery of the defeated city in Lamentations (Lam 1:2, 5, 8–10, 21; 2:15–16, 22; 4:19) are transformed into obeisance to both God and Jerusalem in Second Isaiah (Isa 49:22–23; 52:10; 55:5; 60:5–16; 62:2).

4. Lamentations declares that Zion has no comforter (Lam 1:2, 9, 16–17, 21). In the haftarot of consolation, God declares his intention to comfort Zion (Isa 40:1; 51:3, 12).[72]

5. In Lamentations, the foreign nations witness Zion's misery (Lam 1:7–8, 12, 18, 21; 2:15–16). In Second Isaiah, all people witness God's redemptive power (Isa 40:5; 49:7, 23; 52:8; 62:2).

6. In Lamentations, Zion's empty roads are a sign of her devastation (Lam 1:1, 4; 4:18). In Second Isaiah, the roads will be filled with returning exiles and pilgrims (Isa 49:19–20; 60:4–9; 62:10).

7. In Lamentations, the Judeans barter their treasures for food (Lam 1:11) and pay for water and wood (Lam 5:4). In Isa 55:1, water and milk will be free.

8. In Lamentations, prohibited gentiles enter the sanctuary (Lam 1:10). In Isa 52:1 God promises that Zion will never be invaded by the unclean and uncircumcised again.

II. In addition to these thematic correspondences, many of the dominant literary tropes and images of devastation in Lamentations are reversed in the haftarot of consolation.

1. In Lamentations, the elders of Zion sit on the ground and the maidens of Jerusalem bow their heads to the ground (2:10). The speaker in Lam 3 advises a similar strategy of repentance (3:28–29). In addition, God casts down to earth the majesty of Israel (Lam 2:1). In Second Isaiah, Zion is repeatedly exhorted to rise (Isa 51:17; 52:2; 60:1).

2. In Lamentations, fire is a dominant divine trope (Lam 1:13; 2:3–4; 4:11). In Second Isaiah, God is identified with water instead (Isa 54:9; 55:10).

3. In Lamentations, the walls of the city mourn (Lam 2:8, 18). In Second Isaiah, they shout with joy (Isa 52:9).

---

72. This thematic correspondence is the one noticed most frequently by scholars. See Claus Westermann, *Isaiah 40–66, A Commentary* (trans. D. M. G. Stalker; Philadelphia: Westminster Press, 1969), 33 and Mintz, *Hurban,* 44–45.

4. In Lamentations, Zion wears soiled clothing (Lam 1:9) and God wears clothing of anger (Lam 3:43). In Second Isaiah, Zion puts on her children like jewelry (Isa 49:18) and will don garments of majesty (Isa 52:1; 61:10). God will wear Zion like a crown (Isa 62:3) and will wear splendid garments to vanquish her enemies (Isa 63:1–2).

5. In Lamentations, the reversal of the city's fortunes is described as the dulling of gold and the murder of her inhabitants is described as the spilling of sacred gems (4:1–2). In Second Isaiah, God will rebuild Jerusalem with precious stones and metals (54:11; 60:17).

6. In Lamentations, the people are described as orphans and as widows (5:3). In Second Isaiah, Zion is a fertile woman, re-espoused to God (Isa 54:1, 5–6; 62:4).

By selecting the haftarot of consolation from those sections of Second Isaiah which allude most consistently to Lamentations, the redactors of the lectionary cycle capitalize on potent, pre-existent correspondences between the two texts in order to articulate a theology of consolation which addresses the needs of the fifth- to sixth-century-CE community.

While Second Isaiah provides excellent material for the lectionary response to Lamentations, its theology does not provide full consolation for the Jewish community in the fifth to sixth centuries CE. In many ways, the theological situation of this community resembled that of the exilic community in the sixth century BCE. Like the authors of Lamentations and Isa 40–55, the Jews of the later period lived in the absence of both a temple and Israelite/Jewish sovereignty. While the situation which prompted the composition of Lamentations resembled, in some ways, the post-70 CE situation, the sort of historical circumstance which motivated Second Isaiah did not recur during the period of redaction of the lectionary cycle. Isaiah 40–55 was written after Cyrus' ascent to power and on the eve of the return of the Judean exiles from Babylon. Unlike Second Isaiah's contemporaries, who could reasonably expect a return to Judea, the Jews of Palestine and the diaspora in the fifth to sixth centuries CE had no reason to expect a return to Jewish sovereignty. The community did not live in a state of imminent messianic expectation.[73] It did not expect that great his-

---

73. At least the rabbinic leadership which authored the surviving literature did not. It is difficult to know whether other classes within the Jewish community expected the messiah imminently.

torical change was going to provide a solution to theological dilemmas any time soon.[74]

This difference radically mitigates the consolatory potential of Second Isaiah's message. In the biblical context, Second Isaiah responds to Lamentations by identifying and interpreting recent historical events as the "antidote" to Lamentations' woes. In Lamentations, Zion complains that her city is destroyed, her God has forsaken her and she has no comforter. Second Isaiah interprets the advent of Cyrus and the imminent end of the exile as signs that God and Israel are reconciled and that Jerusalem will be restored. Through these historical events, Zion will be consoled; as the agent of these historical events, God acts as Zion's comforter. Within Second Isaiah, Israel's political situation serves as the barometer of her relationship with God. Exile is a sign of divine displeasure; return from exile is a sign of divine reconciliation. Thus, for Second Isaiah, reconciliation and redemption, and, consequently, consolation, are simultaneous events.[75] According to this ideology, the situation of the Jews after 70 CE might have been interpreted in deeply pessimistic terms. The ongoing lack of sovereignty could have been read as a sign of continuing divine

---

74. Until the failure of the Jewish revolt in 135 CE, there was a high degree of messianic expectation among certain segments of the Jewish community as witnessed by the Dead Sea Scrolls, the New Testament, and references in the rabbinic literature to R. Akiba's identification of Bar Kokhba as the messiah (Lam R. 2:2). The failure of the Bar Kokhba revolt seems to have led the rabbinic sages to discourage imminent messianic expectation. For a discussion of the rabbinic tendency to downplay messianic fervor, see Judah Goldin, "Of Midrash and the Messianic Theme," in *Studies in Midrash and Related Literature* (ed. B. Eichler and J. Tigay; Philadelphia: Jewish Publication Society, 1988), 359–78. For a compendium of rabbinic messianic beliefs, see b. San 97a–99a.

75. Isa 55–66 also confronts the failure of earlier messianic expectations. The return to Judea had not been as glorious as had been expected and the post-exilic Judean society was far from perfect. In Isa 56–66, the author deals with this disappointment through two central strategies. First, he rebukes Israel for ongoing sins and misbehavior (i.e. 56:9–57:13). Second, he describes the restoration and redemption in even more miraculous and cosmic terms than the author of Isa 40–55. At the same time, he pushes the redemption into the future. The sixth haftarah provides a characterstic example. In Isa 60:1–22, God proclaims that the redemption will bring both political and cosmic change. The exiles will return and Jerusalem will gain ascendancy over the nations (60:4–12) . She will no longer need the sun and the moon because God will be her light (60:19–20). In addition, the nature of the city and its inhabitants will be spiritualized (Isa 60:17–18, 21). However, these miracles are no longer imminent. Rather, they will occur when God decides that their time has come. The pericope ends, "I am YHWH. In its time, I will hasten it."

disfavor and alienation.[76] Through the strategies of selection and arrangement, the redactors of the lectionary cycle transform texts of Second Isaiah into a consolatory collection which articulates an alternate reading of the ongoing political limbo. In the lectionary cycle, reconciliation is unhitched from redemption. Lamentations' complaints about the destruction of the city and the exile of the people will be redressed gloriously sometime in the future. However, her accusation of divine abandonment and her complaint that "she has no comforter" (Lam 1:17) are addressed in the present in the midst of the worshiping community. Thus, through the strategies of selection and arrangement, the redactors of the lectionary cycle adapt the consolatory tropes of Second Isaiah to respond to the situation of the community in the sixth century CE.

The lectionary cycle includes copious promises of restoration and redemption that meticulously reverse Lamentations' complaints. By the sixth century CE, however, these prophecies of restoration no longer represented immediate expectations. Rather, they were part of a complex of messianic expectation which, for the most part, was postponed to some indefinite time in the future. While this postponement of messianic expectation is not articulated explicitly by the lectionary cycle, it was part of the cultural milieu in which the lectionary cycle was developed.

The Dialogic Structure

Thus far, I have discussed the ways in which the redactors of the lectionary cycle shaped the biblical material into a narrative structure. Attention to this narrative structure highlights issues of plot within the cycle—the narrative tells a story of cause and effect, of prophecy and fulfillment. This narrative coexists alongside a second structure within the cycle. The conjunction of Lamentations and the haftarot of consolation and, in particular, the arrangement of the haftarot of consolation themselves, form a dialogue which unfolds in the period beginning with Tisha b'Av and ending at Rosh Hashanah. The dialogic arrangement of the haftarot of consolation is noted by the fourteenth-century Spanish commentator, Abudarham:

> It says in the midrash, in high language, that they decided to begin the haftarot of consolation with *Comfort, comfort my people* (Isa 40:1), which is to say that the Holy One Blessed be He says to the prophets, *Comfort, comfort my people*. The congregation of Israel responds to this, *And Zion says YHWH has abandoned me* (Isa 49:14). Which is to say, "I am not appeased by

---

76. The claim that the ongoing exile was a sign of God's continuing displeasure with Israel was made by Christian polemicists as well. See Robert L. Wilken, *The Land Called Holy* (New Haven: Yale University Press, 1992), 143.

the consolations of the prophets." And he says, *Arise, arise, don strength, arm of YHWH. Arise as in days of old* (Isa 51:9). And in the places where they recite *Unhappy, storm-tossed one, uncomforted* (Isa 54:11) instead of this haftarah, this is to say that the prophets respond and say before the Holy One Blessed be He, "Behold, the congregation of Israel is not pacified by our consolations." To this the Holy One Blessed be He replies, *I, I am he who comforts you* (Isa 51:12). And he says further, *Rejoice, barren one who has not given birth* (54:1) and he says, *Arise, shine, for your light comes* (60:1). To this, the congregation of Israel responds, *I will greatly rejoice in YHWH* (61:10), which is to say, "Now I have reason to rejoice and be happy." *My soul rejoices in God because he clothed me in garments of salvation* (Isa 62:10).[77]

This lectionary dialogue is simultaneously consolatory and radical. Through the strategies of selection and arrangement, the authors of the lectionary re-characterize the voice of Zion and invest it with the authority that it lacks in Isa 40–55. In the biblical context, the voice of Zion/Israel is usually cited in a polemical context. The prophet, or God speaking through the prophet, cites Israel's words in order to rebut them. In many cases, the rebuttal is a harsh one.[78] In the lectionary cycle, the people's voice is far more prominent both in terms of reliability and influence. The lectionary cycle gives the impression that God takes Israel's protests and challenges quite seriously. The correspondences between Lamentations and the haftarot of consolation provide the most obvious evidence. The audience of the lectionary cycle would hear Lamentations recited on the ninth of Av and, in the weeks following, would hear God promise the meticulous reversal of Lamentations' complaints. This sequence of lectionary texts would suggest that God was listening very carefully to Israel and that the precise nature of her complaints shaped the nature of the future redemption and restoration. In addition, the lectionary presents a theology of consolation that, while common to rabbinic literature, is absent from the biblical canon. Through the constructed dialogue between God

---

77. In PRK 16:8 Israel rejects the prophets' consolations because they foretold doom as well as consolation and she does not know which to believe. At the end of the pericope God says to the prophets, "You and I will go together to comfort her." Thus, "comfort, comfort my people (עַמִּי)" means "comfort, comfort, with me (עִמִּי)." In PRK, as well as in the parallel versions in PR 29/30 (139) and Yal 443, the pericope serves as a comment on Isa 40:1, not 51:12. The association of the tradition with Isa 51:12, however, seems to be more natural. In Abudarham's version, the plain sense of the biblical verse serves as the punchline to the pericope, whereas in the extant midrashic versions 40:1 needs to be revocalized in order to serve as a punchline.

78. E.g., Isa 40:27–28.

and Israel, the redactors of the lectionary assert that reconciliation is a present event which occurs independently of redemption.[79]

The Dialogic Paradigm and the Theology of Intimacy

According to the lectionary cycle, Israel's voice not only shapes God's presentation of the redemption and restoration, it also shapes the nature of divine consolation. The conjunction of the first two haftarot of consolation serves as a critique of the consolation proffered by Second Isaiah in its canonical form. The juxtaposition of the two texts suggests that during a situation of ongoing Jewish powerlessness, assertions of divine power and future redemption are not adequate consolation. The lectionary cycle, like Second Isaiah in its canonical form, begins with Isa 40:1:

> Comfort, comfort my people, says your God.
> Speak tenderly to Jerusalem and declare to her
> That her time of service is over, her guilt has been expiated;
> She has received from YHWH's hand double for all her sins. (Isa 40:1–2)

The pericope continues with God's announcement of his triumphant return to Zion with the exiles in tow (Isa 40:3–5, 9–11). These announcements are followed by assertions of divine power which support these proclamations (40:12–26). The pericope ends with a masterful description of divine power:

> Lift up your eyes and see, who created these?
> The one who brings out the hosts by number and calls each one
>   by name;
> On account of his great strength and mighty power, not one fails
>   to appear. (Isa 40:26)

In the Bible, Isa 40:1–26 is followed by a quoted challenge to divine power and justice. "Why do you say, O Jacob, and speak, O Israel / My way is hid from YHWH and my just cause passes by my God?" (Isa 40:27). While v. 27 seems to be an accusation regarding both divine attention and divine justice, the prophet interprets it only as a challenge regarding divine power and responds with further proofs of divine potency and omniscience. "Have you not known? Have you not heard? / YHWH is the everlasting God, the creator of the ends of the earth; he does not faint or grow weary, his wisdom is unfathomable" (Isa 40:28).

---

79. This notion is not revolutionary within rabbinic Judaism. To the contrary, rabbinic Judaism is grounded in the assumption that the relationship between God and Israel continues despite the ongoing exile. The innovative move is the transformation of the Second Isaianic texts into a vehicle for this message.

In the lectionary cycle, Isa 40:1–26 is followed in the second week by Isa 49:14–51:3. The resulting sequence reads as follows. End of the first haftarah:

> Lift up your eyes and see, who created these?
> The one who brings out the hosts by number and calls each one by name;
> On account of his great strength and mighty power, not one fails to appear. (Isa 40:26)

Beginning of the second haftarah:

> But Zion says: YHWH has abandoned me, my Lord has forgotten me.
> Can a woman forget her suckling child, not have compassion on the child of her womb?
> These may forget, but I will not forget you.
> Behold I have engraved you on my palms, your walls are always before me.
> Your children hurry; your destroyers and your ruiners depart from you. (Isa 49:14–17)

In the lectionary cycle, the substance of the argument of Isa 40:1–26 is not challenged. Zion does not dispute the assertion of divine omnipotence. Instead, she rejects the consolatory power of the claim. Zion responds to Isa 40:1–26 by accusing God of abandonment. It is as though Zion says that divine omnipotence is not comforting without evidence of reconciliation between God and Israel.

The juxtaposition of the two texts transforms the status of Isa 40:1–26. It is no longer identified as an inadequate theological argument; it is identified as an ineffective consolatory strategy. Zion does not contest the validity of the claims of divine power, she refuses to be consoled by them. Within the context of the lectionary cycle, God's response in Isa 49:15–16 becomes a divine revision of the first attempt at consolation. God replaces the portrait of himself as powerful captain of the heavenly hosts with a portrait of himself as the devoted lover of Israel. The cosmic portrait of God directing the stars at their stations is replaced by the shockingly intimate image of God engraving Israel into the flesh of the divine body. The shift in consolatory strategy is underscored by the parallels between Isa 40:26 and Isa 49:18. In the verse from the first haftarah, God commands Israel to "lift up your eyes and see" the stars, which are evidence of divine omnipotence. In the second haftarah, which opens with Zion's disconsolate accusation of divine abandonment, God commands:

> *Lift up your eyes and see,* all are gathered; they have come to you.

> As I live, says YHWH, you shall put them all on as an ornament,
> you shall bind them on as a bride does. (Isa 49:18)

Within the lectionary, God replaces the failed discourse of divine power with the discourse of intimate restoration. The tropes of military might and creation are replaced with tropes of marriage and family. The tropes of sending out in martial order are replaced by tropes of ingathering and arrival.

By underscoring the differences between God's first and second attempts at consolation, the redactors of the lectionary cycle set up a dynamic relationship between two distinct discourses of consolation: the discourse of historical redemption and restoration and the discourse of reconciliation and relationship. The assertions of divine power in the first haftarah and the attendant descriptions of God as creator, sovereign, judge, and military hero are part of the discourse of redemption. In these texts, Second Isaiah assures his audience that God is powerful enough to intervene in history and effect Israel's redemption. The assertion that God is eternally devoted to Israel and the attendant rhetoric of parental, romantic, and otherwise intimate relationships are part of the discourse of reconciliation. God's proclamations of devotion and attachment assure the audience that God still loves Israel and is devoted to her. The innovation of the lectionary cycle is the isolation of these two discourses from one another. It is their isolation, which is highlighted by their juxtaposition within the cycle, that allows for their temporal separation. God can testify to reconciliation and devotion even in the absence of historical redemption. The author of *Maḥzor Vitry* (twelfth century) noted this lectionary assertion. In commenting on the choice of 49:14ff as a haftarah, he states, "Even though she is destroyed, do not say that she is abandoned."[80]

The tension between consolation based on divine power and consolation based on divine intimacy and attention is articulated most clearly through the juxtaposition of Isa 40:1–26 and Isa 49:14ff. However, negotiation over consolation continues in more subtle ways throughout the cycle. Some of the features that I will discuss in this analysis are constructed through the processes of selection and arrangement. As in the case of the final lines of the first haftarah and the opening lines of the second, the juxtaposition of distant texts changes the meaning and functions of the texts. Other features are present in the texts in their biblical contexts, though the canonical arrangement of Isa 40–66 does not necessarily draw attention to them. The tension between the consolatory power of God as redeemer and God as intimate consoler, which is articulated in the first and second haftarot, heightens the audience's awareness of these features throughout the

---

80. *Maḥzor Vitry*, 224.

text. In the following analysis, I will read the haftarot of consolation through the lens established by the juxtaposition of the first two texts.

Third Haftarah (Isa 54:11–55:12)

Despite God's protestations of devotion and promises of redemption and restoration in the second haftarah, Zion remains disconsolate at the beginning of the third. The juxtaposition of Isa 49:14–51:3 and Isa 54:11–55:12 suggests that the consolations of the second haftarah are also inadequate. In Isa 54:11 God addresses Zion as "Afflicted, storm-tossed one, uncomforted." In the subsequent verses, God attempts to console Zion through promises to rebuild the city (vv. 11–13) and keep Zion safe and secure (vv. 14–18). After an exhortation to hearken to God (Isa 55:6–8) and an assertion regarding the efficacy of the divine word (vv. 9–11), the text ends with a divine promise to end the exile. The redemption of Israel will cause nature to rejoice and grow more bountiful. These supernatural changes in turn will serve as an everlasting sign to God:

> For you will go out in joy and you will be led in peace.
> The mountains and the hills will burst forth in joyous song before you and all the trees of the field will clap their hands.
> Instead of thorns, cypress will rise; instead of nettle, myrtle will rise;
> And it will be a testimony to YHWH, an everlasting sign which will never be cut off. (Isa 55:12–13)[81]

Within its biblical context, this verse articulates two of Second Isaiah's common themes. The return to Judea will be a second exodus—similar to, but surpassing the first. In addition, nature will join in celebration at the moment of redemption. Within the lectionary cycle, these verses also resonate with the end of the first haftarah. There, nature in all its order was a sign of divine power. Here, nature will become a player in the relationship between God and Israel. In other words, in Isa 40:26 God's power is the factor that determines nature's behavior and is manifest in it. The relationship between God and Israel generates miraculous events in the natural world.[82]

---

81. Another possible translation of the verse is, "It will be for God's name, an everlasting sign," meaning that the growth of myrtle and cedar in the desert will serve to praise or bear witness to God's name. See Westermann, *Isaiah,* 291.

82. Westermann (*Isaiah,* 292) notes that these verses articulate the unity of God the creator and God the redeemer. However, he does not emphasize the particularist nature of that conjunction here. Nature responds not just to God's actions in history but to the vicissitudes of the God-Israel relationship. This notion is also

Fourth Haftarah (Isa 51:12–52:6)

The transition between the third and fourth haftarot mirrors the transition between the first and second. The declaration of God's control over nature in 55:12 is followed by a shift toward a more intimate theology in the opening of the fourth haftarah. In Isa 51:12, God states: "I, I am he who comforts you." Within the canonical arrangement of Isa 40–66, this text resonates with Isa 40:1: "Comfort, comfort my people." Both texts use a trope of doubling and both announce the comforting of Israel. Commentators have observed the resonances between the two verses and have understood them as signs of a continuity of theme in Isa 40–55.[83] Within the context of the lectionary's concern for divine attention to Israel, not only the parallels but also the differences between the two texts become significant. In the first text, God assigns the job of comfort to a group of unnamed addressees. In Isa 51:12 God assumes the task of comfort personally.[84] The ensuing pericope marshals the now familiar arsenal of consolation. It invokes God's creative power (51:12–16) and promises that the time of punishment has ended and that the time of vindication has begun (51:17–23).[85] In addition, it urges Jerusalem to rise from her mourning and prepare for the triumphant advent of God (51:17; 52:1–3, 7–9). The pericope ends with a vision of the return from exile as a new exodus:

> Depart! Depart! Go out from there! Uncleanness do not touch;
> Go out from its midst! Purify yourselves! bearers of the vessels
>   of YHWH;
> For you will not go out in haste, nor will you go in flight;
> For YHWH goes before you and the God of Israel is your rear
>   guard. (52:11–12)

Here, Second Isaiah makes an obvious reference to the exodus, but once again, the new exodus will surpass the old. Here, the refugees will not leave in haste. Rather, they will go in security and calm. Instead of being accompanied by the divine manifestations of the pillars of smoke and fire, they will be enveloped by God himself. Within the biblical context, this

---

reflected in PRK 13:10. See pp. 94–96 for an analysis of this pericope and parallel sources.

83. Westermann, *Isaiah*, 243; James Muilenburg, "Isaiah, chapters 40–66," in *The Interpreter's Bible* (ed. G. Buttrick; New York: Abingdon Press, 1956), 5:599; Rendtorff, *Canon and Theology*, 151. Rendtorff notes that divine proclamations of comfort in Isa 40:1, 51:12 and 66:13 punctuate the three sections of Isa 40–66.

84. This shift is noted by Abudarham as well as by the author of *Maḥzor Vitry*.

85. This section contains a dense web of allusions to Lamentations. For detailed analysis, see Willey, *Remember*, 159–65.

new exodus is clearly better than the old.[86] However, in the context of the lectionary cycle the second "improvement"—the enveloping presence of God himself—serves as another assertion of greater intimacy by God.

Within the lectionary cycle, the assumption of divine responsibility for consolation in 51:12 marks a pivotal moment in the negotiation over consolation. The verse is placed strategically at the beginning of the middle haftarah of the cycle and there is a marked difference between the two haftarot which precede it and the two that follow. The second and third haftarot opened with the recognition of Zion's ongoing despair. Both the fifth and sixth haftarot open with exhortations to rejoice.

Fifth Haftarah (Isa 54:1–9)

The fifth haftarah marks a shift in the process of consolation. In this pericope, central theological tropes are recast in the language of intimate relation. The pericope opens: "Rejoice, barren one who has not given birth / Burst forth in joy, shout gladly, you who did not writhe [in birth-pangs]." This exhortation suggests that God has become bolder in his attempts to console. He now dares to ask for rejoicing and shouts of joy. This boldness is followed by a pericope which depends nearly exclusively on the discourse of relationship, espousal and love. God assures Zion that the children of her destruction will outnumber the children of her espousal (Isa 54:1). God then declares that he, himself, is Zion's husband (54:5). God even revises his theory of catastrophe and puts it in relational terms. Rather than stating that Israel's time of servitude is over (Isa 40:1), this pericope states:

> For like an abandoned woman and a woman of downcast spirit
>   YHWH called you;
> And [like] a wife of a man's youth who is cast off, says your
>   God.
> For a brief moment, I forsook you, but with great compassion, I
>   will gather you.
> In a flood of anger, I hid my face from you for a moment;
> But in everlasting, steadfast love I will have compassion on you,
>   says your redeemer, YHWH. (Isa 54:6–8)

Within the context of the lectionary cycle, this verse, like Isa 40:1, serves to answer the query at the end of Lamentations. Once again God assures Israel that the estrangement was temporary but the reconciliation will be

---

86. For further discussion of the new exodus trope, see Westermann, *Isaiah,* 253; Muilenberg, "Isaiah," 613; Bernhard Anderson,"Exodus Typology in Second Isaiah," in *Israel's Prophetic Heritage: Essays in Honor of James Muilenberg* (ed. B. W. Anderson and W. Harrelson; New York: Harper and Row, 1962), 177–95.

permanent. In contrast to Isa 40:1, however, God does not define the relationship between God and Israel in judicial terms; rather, he defines it as one of everlasting, intimate love. This pericope also ends with the assimilation of a universalist creation trope to the particularist relationship between God and Israel. God avows,

> This is like the waters of Noah to me;
> Just as I swore never to make pass again the waters of Noah over the earth,
> So do I swear never to be furious with you and never to rebuke you.
> For the mountains may move and the hills may totter,
> But my steadfast love will never move from you and the covenant of my peace will not totter,
> Says the one who has compassion on you, YHWH. (Isa 54:9–10)

This haftarah, like the third, ends with the assertion that nature is not neutral, but is instead a trope in the service of the relationship between God and Israel.

Sixth Haftarah (Isa 60:1–22)

The sixth haftarah comes from the portion of Isa 56–66 which resonates most strongly with Isa 49–55. Consequently, it shares many features with the preceding haftarot. It begins with an exhortation to the personified city (Isa 60:1). It continues to address Zion in the second person feminine singular and continues to refer to the exiles as children (Isa 60:4, 9).

However, this pericope backs off from both the radical personification of Israel and the portrayal of the intimate relationship between God and Israel. The text presents a vision of a spiritualized, utopian Jerusalem (Isa 60:17–18) whose claim to fame is the temple (Isa 60:7, 13, 14). Consequently, the relationship between God and Israel is no longer described in romantic terms. In contrast to Isa 54:5, which states "For your husband is your maker," Isa 60:16 states "Know that I am YHWH your savior and your redeemer, the mighty one of Jacob." The lover/creator dyad has been replaced with the savior/redeemer pair. In addition, the male personification "Jacob" is invoked instead of the female personification "Zion."[87] Elsewhere in the pericope, God is imagined as a light which both illuminates and radiates from Zion (Isa 60:1–3, 19–20). The introduction of these new divine images and the attendant retreat from the radical personification of the city and erotic representation of the divine-human relationship mutes the dialogic paradigm. The sixth haftarah serves as an abstract re-

---

87. This represents only a partial shift in gender because the rest of the verse uses the second person feminine singular form of address.

sponse to the earlier complaints, not a response which is imbedded in a conversation and relationship between two characters.

This muting of Israel's voice and consequent suppression of the dialogic paradigm is quite disjunctive. One might read the apparent dissolution of the personified Israel and the silence of her voice as a sign that the resistance has been conquered. Zion's position has been assimilated into the dominant, divine voice. However, the lectionary itself resists this reading. Throughout the haftarot, Israel is repeatedly exhorted to rejoice (Isa 40:9; 52:9; 54:1). According to these texts, the expression of joy is the litmus test for the success of the consolation. In light of that exhortation, acquiescent silence is insufficient.

Seventh Haftarah (Isa 61:10–63:9)

Only in the final haftarah does the speaker vow to rejoice. The pericope begins, "I will greatly rejoice in YHWH; my soul will rejoice in my God" (Isa 61:10). Finally, after seven weeks of dialogue, the human voice has accepted divine consolation. Israel has accepted the command to rejoice. However, the cycle does not end with the vow of praise. In 62:1 the speaker acknowledges that Zion has not yet been redeemed and vows to pester God until he fulfills his promises of redemption. The subsequent verses serve as a catalogue of those promises and, within the lectionary cycle, as a reminder of the range of consolatory discourses. Zion will adorn God's hand (Isa 62:3; cf. Isa 49:14); Zion and her inhabitants will be triumphantly renamed (Isa 62:2, 4, 12; cf. Isa 1:26); God has sworn by his mighty arm (Isa 62:8; cf. Isa 50:2); Zion's inhabitants will reap their grain and wine (Isa 62:9; cf. Isa 55:1–2). The chapter ends with two allusions to the first haftarah:

1. Isaiah 62:10 states: "Pass through, pass through the gates! Prepare a road for the people. Build up, build up the path! Clear it of stones." This verse resonates strongly with Isa 40:3: "In the wilderness, prepare a road for YHWH. Make straight in the desert a path for our God."

2. Isaiah 62:11 contains a direct allusion to the herald's cry in Isa 40:10: "[Behold your redeemer comes], behold, his reward is with him and his recompense is before him."

Within its biblical context, this densely allusive chapter serves to link the third, post-exilic section of Isa 40–66 with the earlier sections. Within the lectionary context, it forms an *inclusio* to both the haftarot of consolation and to the cycle as a whole. This framing device serves to reinforce the coherence of the cycle and to underscore its teleology. In the final haftarah, the renaming of the city prophesied in the third haftarah of rebuke finally occurs. Isaiah 1:26 promises, "After this they will call you 'City of righteousness, faithful city,'" and Isa 62:4 states:

> You will no longer be called "Forsaken" and your land will no longer be called "Desolate."
> For you will be called "My delight is in her" and your land will be called "Espoused."

In addition, the advent of God announced in the first haftarah of consolation is reiterated. Chapter 62, however, does not end the cycle. The final pericope continues with a gruesome vision of God, returning bloodspattered from the vanquishing of Israel's enemies (Isa 63:6). This vision is followed by the speaker's avowal to remember God's steadfast love and all that he has done for Israel on account of it (Isa 63:7).[88] The final verse of the cycle asserts that "In his love and in his mercy He redeemed them / And lifted them and carried them all the days of old" (Isa 63:9). Thus the pericope opens with a vow of praise and continues with the protest that Zion is not yet redeemed. The protest then becomes an occasion to rehearse God's redemptive promises. This unit is followed by a ghastly vision of vindication which in turn gives way to a nostalgic rehearsal of God's past saving deeds.[89] Thus, the final haftarah, like the juxtaposition of the first and second haftarot, highlights the contrasts between the rhetoric of reconciliation and the rhetoric of redemption.

The haftarot of consolation foreground the tropes of intimate divine relation and consolation. During the seven weeks following the ninth of Av, God repeatedly assures Israel that he has not abandoned her; he is her intimate partner and consoler. These assertions of divine attention are supported by the invocation of correspondences among the lectionary texts. The strategic redaction of the haftarot of consolation creates a text in which God responds quickly and meticulously to Israel's complaints. In response to Israel's accusation of abandonment, God revises his self-presentation and his presentation of the relationship between God and Israel. The resulting portrait emphasizes the intimate nature of the God-Israel relationship and even revises the tropes of creation and exodus to make them evidence of God's intimate attention to Israel.

Finally, the fact of the lectionary dialogue itself supports the assertion that God and Israel are reconciled and engaged in an intimate, ongoing relationship. The haftarot of consolation take up nearly one-seventh of the liturgical year. For this seventh of the year, God and Israel are engaged in dialogue in the midst of the worshiping community. Whereas in the bibli-

---

88. This verse resonates with Lam 3:21–22, in which the speaker also calls to mind God's steadfast love.

89. For a detailed analysis of this pericope, see p. 71.

cal context, God often responds to Israel's complaints and demurrals with rebuke or polemic, within the lectionary context, God responds patiently to her stubborn disconsolation, returning week after week with new attempts at consolation. The enactment of this dialogue in the synagogue setting proves the cycle's point. It provides experiential proof of the presence of God and the continuity of the covenantal relationship despite the ongoing reality of the exile.

The construction of this consolatory dialogue is one of the most powerful transformative moves of the lectionary cycle. By separating avowals of redemption from evidence of reconciliation, the redactors of the lectionary cycle unhitch these events temporally from one another. At some time in the future, God will use his sovereign power to redeem Israel from exile, vanquish her enemies, and restore Jerusalem. In the meantime, however, Israel can take consolation in the knowledge that God is intimately engaged in conversation with the community and is deeply attentive to the community's emotional needs.

Redemptive Nature of Divine Love

While the redactors of the lectionary cycle refute the simultaneity of redemption and reconciliation that is so strongly articulated by the Isaiah texts in their biblical context, they reinforce a causal relationship between reconciliation and redemption which is only hinted at in the biblical context. In Second Isaiah, assertions of omnipotence provide the most prominent causal arguments for the inevitability of redemption. God has declared his intention to redeem Israel, and since God controls the universe, nothing can impede his will. The redactors of the lectionary cycle preserve this argument for the inevitability of redemption, although it is proportionally less prominent in the cycle than in Second Isaiah.[90] While the redactors of the lectionary cycle downplay this argument, they underscore a second causal argument which is present, though less prominent, in Second Isaiah. Because the omnipotent God is the God who loves Israel, it is inevitable that he will use his power to redeem her.[91] The creators of the lectionary cycle once again use the strategies of selection and redaction to make the point. In the fifth haftarah, the prophet states:

> Fear not, for you will not be ashamed; do not be confounded, for
> you will not be put to shame;

---

90. The argument appears at least nine times in Second Isaiah, but appears only three times in the haftarot of consolation.

91. The redactors include every articulation of this argument in the lectionary cycle.

> You will forget the shame of your youth, and the reproach of your widowhood you will not remember any longer.
> For your husband (בְּעֲלַיִךְ) is your maker; the Lord of hosts is his name;
> And the Holy One of Israel is your redeemer, the God of the whole earth he is called. (Isa 54:4–5)

This text asserts that the powerful creator God and the God who loves Israel are one and the same. If this is the case, then Israel can be confident that the omnipotent God will use his power to redeem her.[92]

The repetition of the word בעל as a *leitwort* within the cycle communicates a similar message. The root בעל appears seven times in Isa 40–66. Six of these occurrences are included in the haftarot.[93] The root בעל has two central meanings: "master" and "husband."[94] This congruence of meaning is particularly powerful within the lectionary sequence. Just as Isa 54:4–5 asserts that Zion's husband is her maker, so too do the other uses of the word בעל remind the audience that in the case of God, husband and master are true synonyms:

> You will no longer be called "Forsaken" and your land will no longer be called "Desolate."
> For you will be called "My delight is in her" and your land will be called "Espoused" (בְּעוּלָה).
> For the Lord delights in you, and your land shall be married (תִּבָּעֵל).
> For as a young man marries (יִבְעַל) a virgin, so shall your sons marry you (יִבְעָלוּךְ);
> The joy of the bridegroom over the bride will your God rejoice over you. (Isa 62:4–6)

Not only is God Israel's husband; he is also the master of nature and history. These two forms of mastery are inextricable. Consequently, God's espousal of Zion is manifest in her restoration and redemption.[95] The word

---

92. Isa 51:16 and 55:12–13 also assert a connection between God's power over creation and his intention to redeem Israel.

93. Isa 50:8; 54:1; 62:4 (twice); 62:5 (twice). The root also appears in Isa 41:15, but does not mean "master"/"husband" there.

94. The nominal form can also mean "citizen"/"inhabitant" and can serve as a noun of relation. בעל is also the proper name of a Canaanite god and appears in the names of various cities.

95. This trope appears in Hos 2–3 as well. There God describes himself as the husband of Israel, a wayward wife. God punishes Israel's infidelity by making her suffer political and natural devastation. Their re-espousal in Hos 2:14–23 is manifest in renewed fertility, peace, and prosperity.

itself contains the conjunction of relationship to Israel and universal power that is underscored in the lectionary cycle.[96]

The strange redaction of the final haftarah makes the same point. At the beginning of the pericope, the prophet describes the relationship between God and Israel in highly eroticized terms (Isa 62:4–6). This unit is followed by an exhortation to set out watchmen to wait for God and the promised redemption. The vision of the redeemed city gives way abruptly to a gory vision of God, spattered in the blood of Israel's enemies.

> Who is this that comes from Edom, in crimsoned garments from Bozrah?
> He that is glorious in his apparel, crouching in the magnitude of his strength.
> I, speaking in righteousness, mighty to save. (Isa 63:1)
>
> I trod them (the nations) in my anger and trampled them in my wrath;
> Their lifeblood is sprinkled upon my garments and I have defiled all my raiment. (Isa 63:3)[97]

The haftarah ends with a testimony to God's steadfast love and God's past acts of redemption. The various units of the pericope are quite distinct and their conjunction within the single lectionary unit is jarring.[98] However, the redaction of the unit unites a powerful assertion of God's love for Israel with a vivid description of God's exercise of power in history. The textual conjunction of the two suggests a logical connection as well. This logical connection is articulated in the last verse of the pericope, which is also the last verse of the entire haftarah sequence. "In his *love* and in his mercy He *redeemed* them / And lifted them and carried them all the

---

96. The repetition of the root בעל is particularly significant within the lectionary cycle as a whole. According to the narrative logic of the cycle, the catastrophes of the ninth of Av occurred because Israel rebelled against God and ignored the rebuke of the prophets. In other words, the people denied God's mastery over them. When, in the final pericope, the prophet proclaims that the land will be called בְּעוּלָה, he not only proclaims the erotic reconciliation of God and Israel but also Israel's renewed submission to divine authority. Cf. Hos 2:16–20, where the trope functions in a similar fashion.

97. In a conversation in August 1998, Tikva Frymer-Kensky suggested that this conjunction of romantic language and military power language resonates with the trope of the bride-price. She drew a comparison between God's act of vengeance here and David's bloody acquisition of Philistine foreskins as the bride-price for Michal in 1 Sam 18.

98. Most commentators identify discrete thematic units within Isa 61–63. For example, in his Anchor Bible commentary, John McKenzie divides the pericope into four units: Isa 61, Isa 62, Isa 63:1–6, and Isa 63:7–64:11.

days of old" (Isa 63:9). The sequence ends by asserting that redemption is a function of divine love and divine pity. The love for Israel that God manifests in the present provides the framework for the redemption which he will effect in the future. While this idea is hinted at in Second Isaiah, it is not a dominant theme in the biblical text. The redactors of the cycle raise the trope to a new level of prominence through the strategic selection and arrangement of the lectionary texts. The high concentration of occurrences of the root בעל and the jarring redaction of the final haftarah underscore the redemptive and consolatory potential of the trope of divine love.

Thus far, I have demonstrated how a literary reading reveals the lectionary cycle's theology of catastrophe and consolation. However, the lectionary cycle is not only a literary and theological text. It is also a liturgical text. As such, it performs certain functions within the worshiping community.[99]

Enactment of Divine Reconciliation

As I mentioned above, the lectionary cycle not only argues that God and Israel are reconciled, it also enacts that reconciliation through the consolatory dialogue. While this enactment supports the lectionary's theological argument, it also serves a liturgical function. Through the recitation of the haftarot, the worshiping community both witnesses and participates in the reconciliation between God and Israel. The community itself, through the proxy voices of the lectionary, is addressed and comforted by God. The reconciliation occurs in their midst. Thus, the lectionary dialogue serves not only as theological argument but also as sacred drama in which the communal feelings of alienation and despair which are articulated on Tisha b'Av are countered and comforted by the consoling God.

From Grief to Consolation

Through the enactment of Zion's journey from despair to consolation, the lectionary cycle provides an opportunity for the worshiping community to express grief, anger and despair over Israel's historical situation without becoming mired in a state of grief and alienation. In the liturgical context, the composite voice of Zion and the individuals who advocate for her within the liturgical cycle represent the voice and experience of the worshiping community. In Lamentations, the speaker who witnesses Zion's

---

99. It is more precise to say that it can *potentially* perform certain functions. If no one is listening to the haftarot or if people are listening to the melody but not the words, then any potential effect worked by the literary features of the texts will not be realized. Nevertheless, those potential effects are inscribed within the texts themselves.

devastation stands in the same position as the worshipers who commemorate and mourn the destruction of the city. In the haftarot of consolation, it is Zion herself who grieves over the exile and destruction. As the survivor of the devastation, she speaks for the worshiping community. Finally, in the last haftarah of consolation, it is once again an individual human who speaks. He accepts consolation and agrees to rejoice in God. In the biblical contexts, these voices represent different speakers and different viewpoints; in the lectionary cycle, however, they all cohere in the communal voice—the voice of those who mourn and must cope with the catastrophic events of Israel's past and present. Over the course of the lectionary cycle, this composite communal voice experiences the grieving process in realistic psychological terms. On Tisha b'Av, when the catastrophes themselves are invoked in graphic and horrific detail, the lectionary text expresses overwhelming grief and despair. Zion is devastated and both she and the speaker who advocates for her can hardly even imagine the possibility of a reconciliation with God. At this moment, the optimism which is briefly expressed in Lam 3 cannot be sustained. It gets drowned out by the overwhelming grief and despair of the rest of the book. In the ensuing weeks, God, through a process of trial and error, articulates a consolation which assuages the anxieties and counters the accusations of Lamentations. From a theological perspective, the articulation of an adequate consolation seems to catalyze the expression of joy in the final haftarah. However, from the perspective of the grief process, it is important to remember that the journey from grief to consolation occupies one-seventh of the liturgical year. The community, like an individual mourner, takes significant time to move from grief and despair to consolation and renewal.[100] The lectionary cycle provides a liturgical experience in which the community mourns intensely, experiences the slow but ultimately successful journey from grief to consolation, and arrives at Rosh Hashanah ready to accept the divine sovereignty which is the central theological trope of the holiday.

Exhortation and Efficacy

As liturgy, the lectionary cycle not only provides a model for expressing and coping with national grief; it also demonstrates a mechanism for persuading God to act on Israel's behalf. Individual haftarah texts suggest that if Israel bombards God with lamentation, supplication and reminders

---

100. *Maḥzor Vitry* states, "It is the way of comforters to offer consolation little by little. The one who delivers too much consolation to the despairing is like one who says to a beggar, 'tomorrow you will be king'—he will not be believed."

of God's promises, God may be moved to respond. In Isa 62:6–7, the speaker states:

> On the walls of Jerusalem, I have stationed guards;
> All day and all night they will never be still.
> You who remind God—do not rest.[101]
> And do not give rest to him until he establishes
> And makes Jerusalem praiseworthy in the land.

Here the speaker suggests that the perpetual pestering of God to fulfill his promises can have an effect on divine behavior. Lamentations 2:18–20 implies a similar argument regarding lament. In 2:18–19, the speaker urges the walls of Zion to cry out and cry ceaselessly. He urges Zion to get up in the night and weep and raise her hands before God in supplication. Finally, in 2:20 the speaker turns his address to God and exhorts: "Look, YHWH, and observe, whom you have caused to suffer so." The concatenation of verses suggests that the weeping and lamenting of the personified Zion can draw God's attention to her plight and spur God to act on her behalf.

This belief in the power of exhortation, articulated in the individual haftarot, is relevant to the lectionary cycle as a whole. Through the recitation of the promises of restoration and redemption in the haftarot of consolation, the worshiping community, like the guards of Isa 62:6–7, constantly remind God of his promises. Although it does not state so explicitly, the cycle suggests that the recitation of divine prophecies of restoration might move God to act on those prophecies.

The Theology of Consolation in the Context of the Synagogue

Attention to the context of the late antique synagogue further illuminates the relationship between the rabbinic theology of consolation articulated in the lectionary cycle and the non-rabbinic theology that may have been espoused by synagogue communities before the advent of widespread rabbinic influence. In my discussion of the culture of the non-rabbinic synagogues, I noted that the archaeological evidence suggests that the synagogue communities saw their local communities as analogues to the nation of Israel as it is described in the Bible. While this notion seems to be part of the self-understanding of many Jews in late antique Palestine, Seth Schwartz notes that it runs counter to the rabbinic focus on the nation as a

---

101. הַמַּזְכִּרִים (You who remind) is the hiphil participle form of זכר. The form can mean "to remind" or "to mention." Here, I think both meanings are operative. The watchers invoke both God's name and God's deeds, and remind God of his promises and obligations to Israel.

whole.¹⁰² The performance of the Tisha b'Av sequence in the synagogue testifies to the negotiation of these two ideologies. On the one hand, the language of the lectionary texts is resolutely national. The players in the drama are God and Israel/Zion. However, when this drama is enacted in the synagogue, the local community becomes conflated with the Israel/Zion of the texts. The voice of Zion serves as the spokesperson for the worshiping community and the worshiping community becomes the concrete, ongoing manifestation of Israel/Zion. Thus, the performance of the rabbinic Tisha b'Av lectionary sequence in the synagogue facilitates the coexistence of these two conflicting ideologies of community.

The lectionary cycle also echoes the identification of the synagogue with the temple. This identification, which seems to have been a central part of synagogue culture, was the subject of some ambivalence in the tannaitic literature, and was not fully espoused until the amoraic period, at which time the rabbinic anxiety over this identification seems to dissipate. Amoraic and post-amoraic sources develop more fully the ideas of synagogue sanctity, kinship between the synagogue and the temple, and kinship between synagogue practices and the defunct temple cult.¹⁰³

The performance of the Tisha b'Av lectionary sequence in the synagogue attests to rabbinic willingness to accept this identification in the fifth to sixth centuries. Tisha b'Av is the day of the most intense and concentrated mourning for the temple in the Jewish calendar. Since the temple was the historic locus for the encounter between God and Israel, this prolonged and intense meditation on its destruction raises the spectre, articulated at the end of Lamentations, of a permanent rupture in the God-Israel relationship. However, in the weeks following Tisha b'Av, the haftarot of consolation assert that the relationship between God and Israel continues despite the absence of the temple. The enactment of the dialogue of reconciliation in the synagogue draws an analogy between the synagogue and the absent, lamented, temple. Whereas in biblical times, necessary reconciliations between God and Israel occurred in the temple, now they occur in the synagogue through the enactment of the lectionary dialogue.

Lastly, while it is difficult to articulate the precise significance of the synagogue iconography, the frequency of zodiac and sun-god imagery suggest that God's role in the cosmic order was a major point of interest or concern for the synagogue-building communities of late antiquity. While

---

102. Schwartz, *Imperialism*, 287.

103. For discussions of the growth of the idea of the sacrality of the synagogue in rabbinic literature and growing rabbinic comfort with assertions of relationship between the synagogue and the temple, see Steven Fine, *This Holy Place: On the Sanctity of the Synagogue During the Greco-Roman Period* (Notre Dame: University of Notre Dame Press, 1997), 35–94; Schwartz, *Imperialism*, 230–38.

the rabbinic literature—both the professional literature and the liturgy—retains a belief and interest in God's role in the cosmic order, this interest is subordinate to a concern with Israel's covenantal history and covenantal relationship with God. In his analysis of several piyyutim, Schwartz has argued that one of the features of the rabbinization of the synagogue was a historicization of the cosmic theology articulated by the synagogue iconography. The Tisha b'Av lectionary sequence reinforces Schwartz's hypothesis. The rabbinic literature testifies to a wide range of understandings of segments of the season stretching from the seventeenth of Tammuz through Tisha b'Av to Rosh Hashanah. The fast day itself is identified as an unlucky day on which unlucky events occur; the "three weeks" are identified as times of cosmic malevolence. The fifteenth of Av was once a fertility festival, and Rosh Hashanah itself is associated with the judgment of humanity and the birthday of the world. While traces of each of these layers of meaning exist, to greater and lesser extents, throughout the rabbinic literature and liturgy, the lectionary sequence ascribes a covenantal significance to the period. Through the articulation of the sin-punishment-restoration narrative and through the description of the repaired relationship between God and Israel, the lectionary posits a covenantal significance while excluding other possible meanings. Thus, like the piyyut that Schwartz analyzes, the Tisha b'Av lectionary bears witness to rabbinic attempts to assert a covenantal-historical theology as the central framework for the community's self-understanding.

Conclusion

The preceding analyses reveal the ways in which the literary features of the lectionary cycle communicate a theology of catastrophe and consolation which is different from that expressed by the lectionary texts in their biblical contexts. The patterns of repetition and echo, as well as the larger structures of narrative and dialogue, bring the texts of the lectionary into meaningful relationship with one another. In many cases, these relationships are grounded in pre-existent correspondences among the biblical texts. It is the strategies of selection and arrangement, however, which highlight and signify these correspondences.

The lectionary cycle as a whole asserts that the events of 587 BCE and 70 CE are the catastrophes commemorated on Tisha b'Av. Through the designation of Lamentations as the lectionary text for the fast day, the redactors of the cycle identify the destructions of Jerusalem as heart-rending and devastating events which victimized not only the inhabitants but also the personified city itself. By selecting Lamentations, the redactors also give voice to theological anxieties and concerns which are raised by the events of Tisha b'Av. Lamentations worries that the historical devastation is a sign of unbounded divine anger. It expresses the concern that the alienation between God and Israel, which was represented by the destructions, will last forever. While the lectionary cycle gives full voice to the despair and anxiety of Lamentations, it also situates the text within a larger sequence which responds to its theological concerns and challenges. The lectionary cycle as a whole asserts that Lamentations and the historical misfortune and divine alienation that it describes are only a single episode in a larger national and theological narrative. According to the lectionary cycle, Israel's history does not end with devastation but instead it moves from sin through devastating punishment to reconciliation and redemption.

One of the most significant innovations of the lectionary cycle is the separation of redemption from reconciliation. Through the creation of the dialogue of consolation, the redactors of the lectionary assert that while redemption lies in the future, reconciliation and the establishment of an ongoing intimate relationship between God and Israel occur in the present. In addition to these theological assertions, the lectionary accomplishes certain liturgical functions. It provides a structured vehicle for the expression of communal grief and despair and for the movement from grief to consolation and renewal. In addition, it articulates and enacts a strategy for influencing divine action. Persistent lament, supplication, and recitation of divine promises of restoration might move God to act on the community's behalf. The lectionary cycle also contributes to the ongoing exploration of the rabbinization of the synagogue in late antiquity. The lectionary cycle echoes the concern for the temple which is expressed in the archaeological remains of the late antique Palestinian synagogues and resonates with the understanding, articulated in the synagogue inscriptions, that the worshiping community is a microcosm of Israel itself. At the same time, the lectionary bears witness to the amoraic acceptance of notions of synagogue sanctity and identification of the synagogue with the defunct temple.

The lectionary constellation not only represents a striking appropriation and re-presentation of biblical material; it also serves as a base text for interpretation at successive levels of cultural and literary transmission. The themes which are revealed through a close reading of the lectionary anthology recur throughout the midrashim and piyyutim which interpret the lectionary texts. In the next two chapters, I will show how these two interpretive genres employ particular literary and exegetical strategies to expand, elaborate on, and nuance these themes.*

---

*An earlier version of this chapter appeared as "Transforming Comfort: Hermeneutics and Theology in the Haftarot of Consolation," *Prooftexts* 23 (2003): XXX–XXX.

3

Pesikta de-Rav Kahana 13 and 22

The thematics outlined in chapter 2 emerge from a close reading of the lectionary anthology as a whole. It is quite possible that a person who encountered the texts aurally, week-by-week, in their synagogue context would miss many of the nuances and intricacies which are visible only to the close reader. The interpretive texts which comment on the lectionary cycle therefore explicitly identify and further elaborate on the themes of the lectionary texts and the season as a whole.

The chapters regarding the Tisha b'Av cycle in the Pesikta de-Rav Kahana serve as a case in point. These chapters are ostensibly collections of individual exegeses of the opening verses of each haftarah. Through serial exegeses of the opening verses, the chapters of PRK define for the reader/audience the themes which, according to the midrash, are implicit in the biblical verses themselves. As I will demonstrate, the chapters in this midrashic collection identify and underscore the central lectionary themes that I identified in chapter 2.

*   *   *

The Pesikta de-Rav Kahana is a collection of midrashic materials organized around the lectionary cycle. It is Palestinian in origin and probably dates from the late fifth or early sixth century CE.[1] The collection consists

---

1. In his pioneering work on PRK (*Die gottendienstlichen Vorträge der Juden historisch entwickelt* [Berlin: Asher, 1832]), Leopold Zunz posited the existence of a collection of midrashim organized around the lectionary calendar called Pesikta de-Rav Kahana, which he dated to circa 700 CE. Zunz's judgment was based on his assumption that PRK used the Palestinian Talmud, Gen R., Lev R., and Lam R. However, because of the striking stylistic and literary similarities between Lev. R and

of 28 chapters, each of which is an anthology of midrashic material pertaining to the lectionary text for a festival or special sabbath. While there is debate over the original order of the chapters, the oldest available manuscript, the Oxford manuscript (thirteenth century), begins with the chapter relating to Hanukah.[2] The subsequent chapters follow the order of the festal calendar.

- Chapter 1: Hanukah
- Chapters 2–5: four special sabbaths preceding Passover
- Chapters 6–12: Passover, the Omer, Shavuot
- Chapters 13–22: Tisha b'Av season
- Chapters 23–26: Rosh Hashanah through Yom Kippur
- Chapters 27–28: Sukkot and Shemini Atzeret

The Mandelbaum edition also includes several chapters in the appendices which were found only in certain manuscripts. With the exception of chapters 13–22 (Tisha b'Av season), 24 (the sabbath after Rosh Hashanah) and 25 (*Seliḥot*), the chapters all deal with the pentateuchal readings for the designated holy days. Only the chapters regarding the Tisha b'Av season and the sabbath immediately following Rosh Hashanah treat the des-

---

PRK, contemporary scholars such as Bernard Mandelbaum (*Pesikta de Rav Kahana: According to an Oxford Manuscript with Variants*, ed. Bernard Mandelbaum [New York: Jewish Theological Seminary, 1987], 2:x), and Lewis Barth ("'The Three of Rebuke and the Seven of Consolation': Sermons in the *Pesikta de Rav Kahana*," *JJS* 33 [1982]: 503–15) assign the work to the fifth century. This early date is supported by the suggestion, first made by Zunz, that the liturgical poet Eleazar Kallir (sixth to seventh century) knew of the work.

2. According to Zunz's reconstruction, PRK began with the chapter on Rosh Hashanah and followed the order of the festal calendar. Thirty-six years later Solomon Buber discovered and collected four manuscripts of PRK and published the first critical edition (*Pesikta: ve-hi agadat Erets Yisra'el meyuḥeset le-Rav Kahana* [Lyck: Ḥevrat Mekitse Nirdamim, 1868]). Buber's edition follows the order of the Safed manuscript, which begins with the chapter for Hanukah. Since Buber's publication, three additional manuscripts and a number of fragments have been discovered. One of these, Oxford$_1$, conforms to Zunz's hypothesis that PRK begins with Rosh Hashanah. While Mandelbaum agrees that this ordering probably reflects the original order, he bases his edition on the Oxford manuscript and consequently begins with the chapter regarding Hanukah.

ignated haftarot. The chapter for *Seliḥot* is also anomalous; it revolves around a series of texts dealing with repentance and forgiveness.[3]

Each of the chapters of PRK consists of a series of *petiḥtot* (proems) which end in the opening verse of the designated lectionary texts. The *petiḥtot* are followed by a series of exegetical comments on the first verse or verses of the lectionary text. Each chapter ends with a messianic or eschatological interpretation of the lectionary verse.

Sitz im Leben

For many years, an extensive scholarly conversation took place regarding the *Sitz im Leben* of the homiletical midrashim in general, and the *petiḥta* genre in particular. Scholarly consensus in the middle of the twentieth century identified the *petiḥtot* as literary versions of oral sermons that were, if not verbatim transcripts, at least close approximations of the sermons themselves. In recent years, this opinion has given way to the judgment that the *petiḥtot* are literary compositions. While individual exegeses within them may have originated as oral exegeses, the *petiḥtot* themselves are rabbinic literary creations which were authored in the academic setting of the *beit midrash*. and were probably written for other members of the rabbinic elite.[4]

---

3. Abraham Goldberg (review of Bernard Mandelbaum, ed., *Pesikta de Rav Kahana, Kiryat Sefer* 43 [1967]: 77) suggests that this chapter was designated for the fast of Gedaliah and perhaps other fast days as well. He notes that in several of the manuscripts, it is appended to the previous chapter, but he agrees with Mandelbaum's decision to treat it as a separate unit because it deals with pentateuchal texts, whereas chapter 24 deals with prophetic texts.

4. The earlier view is articulated by Julius Theodor, "Zur Composition der agadischen Homilien," in *MGWJ* 28 (1879): 97–112; Philipp Bloch, "Studien zur Aggadah" in *MGWJ* 4 (1885): 166–84; Sigmund Maybaum, *Die ältesten Phasen in der Entwicklung der jüdischen Predigt* (Berlin: H. Itkowitz, 1901); Wilhelm Bacher, *Die Proömien der alten judischen Homilie* (Leipzig: Hinrichs, 1913); Leo Baeck, "Zwei Beispiele midraschischer Predigt," *MGWJ* 69 (1925): 258–70; Jacob Mann, *The Bible as Read and Preached in the Old Synagogue* (Cincinnati: Hebrew Union College, 1940–66); Joseph Heinemann, "Ha-petiḥtot be-midrashe ha-agadah: mekorotan ve-tafkidan" in *Papers of the Fourth World Congress of Jewish Studies* (Jerusalem: World Congress of Jewish Studies, 1965), II, 43–47, and "Proem," 100–102; Avigdor Shinan, "Le-torat ha-petiḥta," *Jerusalem Studies in Hebrew Literature* 1 (1981), 133–44; Marc Bregman, "Circular Proems and Proems Beginning with the Formula 'Zo hi shene'emrah beruaḥ hakodesh,'" in *Studies in Aggadah, Targum and Jewish Liturgy in Memory of Joseph Heinemann* (eds. Ezra Fleischer and Jacob Petuchowski; Jerusa-

While PRK is a product of the *beit midrash*, it is intimately linked to the public recitation of scripture because it is a collection of exegeses of biblical texts in their role as lectionary texts. Each chapter comments on the opening verses of a lectionary text and the chapters are ordered according to the calendar. In addition, many of the exegeses of lectionary verses in PRK explore themes which may or may not be relevant to the verses in their biblical contexts, but are unquestionably relevant to the festival or season for which they are the designated texts.[5] As I will demonstrate below, many of the exegeses contained in the chapters on the Tisha b'Av haftarot invoke the theologies of sin, punishment, and consolation that are articulated in the lectionary sequence itself. Thus, it is the lectionary—the texts and context of the popular synagogue Bible—which provides the occasion for the rabbinic reflections contained in PRK's commentaries. While the commentaries in PRK are not synagogue texts like the lectionary sequence or the piyyutim, they are, nevertheless, generated and informed by the popular, lectionary function of the target texts.

The identification of PRK as a text of the academy which comments on the biblical texts in their popular, lectionary context suggests that PRK, along with the other homiletical midrashim, might have functioned as a sort of bridge text. Although he rejects the identification of the *petiḥta* as a transcript of a live sermon, Richard Sarason has agreed that some of the *petiḥtot* might have originated as sermons; David Stern has recently suggested that the collections of homiletical midrashim might have been rabbinic source books for preachers.[6] While there is currently no definitive evidence regarding the compositional history or use of the homiletical

---

lem: Magnes Press, 1981), 34–51. It was based on several factors: the target verses of *petiḥtot* in Gen R. and Lev R. are attested elsewhere as the opening verses of lectionary readings; b. Meg 10b–11a and b. Mak 10b seem to use "*pataḥ*" as a technical term that may refer to preaching. However, the identification of the *petiḥta* as a sermon or oral sermon rests largely on intuitions regarding the nature of rhetorical discourse. See Heinemann, "Proem," 101. Richard Sarason ("The *Petiḥtot* in Leviticus Rabba: 'Oral Homilies' or Redactional Constructions?" *JJS* 33 [1982]: 557–67) has argued persuasively for the latter view. He bases his evaluation on the fact that many of the exegeses contained in *petiḥtot* in Lev R. appear in other contexts as well. In addition, many of the exegeses are attached to the target verses by a stereotyped transition phrase. These two features suggest that the *petiḥtot* are constructed out of pre-existent exegetical units that are integrated into the *petiḥtot* for literary and thematic purposes.

5. See pp. 87–107 for a discussion of the combination of local exegetical concerns and larger thematic concerns in the chapters of PRK.

6. Sarason, "*Petihtot*," 564; David Stern, "Anthology and Polysemy in Classical Midrash," in *The Anthology in Jewish Literature* (ed. David Stern; New York: Oxford University Press, 2004), 124–128.

midrashim, the hypotheses of Stern and Sarason reflect the combination of synagogue orientation and academic form that characterizes PRK and the other homiletical midrashim.

Poetics

In many ways, the midrashic collection is the ideal case study for exploring the intersection of theology and exegesis that I described in the Introduction. At each level of composition, the midrash manifests both exegetical and thematic concerns. The individual units in the chapters of PRK are ostensibly exegetical units which interpret particular details of a biblical verse. However, in many cases the exegesis of the verse serves as a means to introduce and explore themes which are not present in the plain sense of the verse itself. Thus, each unit is simultaneously an interpretation of a verse and a means by which the midrashist can introduce and explore particular theological ideas. While the individual units articulate a variety of exegetical and thematic concerns, the selection of units and their arrangement within the chapters create coherent thematic units which define and explore the themes of the lectionary season. While not all of the units deal with the themes of the season, I will demonstrate that a critical mass of the units participate in the thematic coherence.

Individual Units

The individual exegetical units in PRK serve a dual purpose. They interpret features of a particular biblical verse, and at the same time define for the audience the themes which, according to the midrashist, are relevant to the target verse of the unit. The expansive nature of midrashic exegesis facilitates this dual function. According to the assumptions of midrashic hermeneutics, the Torah is a fundamentally multivalent text. Because each verse of Torah is theoretically endlessly significant, any given verse can become the vehicle for the discussion of a number of themes.[7] For example, in PRK 13, Jer 1:1 becomes the vehicle for the discussion of subjects as diverse as Jeremiah's lineage (PRK 13:4, 5 and 12) and the permanence of the prophetic word (PRK 13:3). Midrash's atomistic approach to exegesis also contributes to the multiplication of themes. In midrashic exegesis,

---

7. Midrash has been touted as a free and radically multivalent genre in which any given word in Torah can be interpreted endlessly—even to the point of self-contradiction. While this might be true in theory, in practice, midrash is a more bounded genre. Particular biblical verses become prooftexts for a limited number of assertions and reappear in different contexts as proof for these assertions.

84   *From Rebuke to Consolation*

verses, phrases, words, and occasionally individual letters serve as exegetical subjects. Consequently, the exegesis of a verse often is accomplished through the exegesis of its constituent parts. In PRK 13, for example, units 7 and 8 interpret the word דברי (words of) while units 11 and 12 interpret the name ירמיהו (Jeremiah). Within these units, the words are considered completely independently of one another. As a result, the midrash identifies the themes of the verse as a whole as the aggregate of the themes of its constituent words.

Finally, the intertextual assumptions of midrashic hermeneutics also lead to the multiplication of thematics. In midrashic exegesis, the interpretation of a verse will often invoke or encompass the exegesis of another biblical verse. The *petiḥta* form serves as a case in point. It opens with a biblical verse which seems unrelated to the target verse and then interprets this *petiḥta* verse. This interpretation might be simple or complex. It might be an interpretation of the verse as a whole or it might be an atomistic interpretation which breaks the verse down into its constituent parts and interprets each part separately. Ultimately, at the end of the exegesis of the *petiḥta* verse, a connection is made to the target verse which, theoretically, illuminates the target verse in a new way for the audience or reader. While the *petiḥta* is presented as a commentary on the target verse, the bulk of the unit is an exegesis of the *petiḥta* verse. Thus, the meanings generated by the exegesis of a distant verse, which might be completely foreign to the plain sense of the target verse, are imported into a discussion of the target verse.[8] As I will discuss in more detail below, the *petiḥta* is a particularly powerful exegetical device. Through the strategy of the *petiḥta*, a verse such as Jer 1:1, which does not discuss any of the issues raised by the Tisha b'Av season, can be transformed into a vehicle for the exploration of issues such as the theology of sin and punishment and the nature of the prophetic word.

Chapters

Joseph Heinemann's work provides the starting point for the scholarly discussion regarding the coherence of the midrashic chapter. Heinemann asserted that the chapters of Leviticus Rabbah were highly crafted literary compositions. He argued that the fixed structure of the chapters (*petiḥta*, *gufa* [body], messianic peroration) proves that the redactor did not assemble his material randomly. At the very least, he organized his materials according to genre and arranged his composition according to a conventional structure. The question remains, however, as to whether the

---

8. See pp. 89–91, 98–104 for extended analyses of the poetics of the *petiḥta*.

chapters of Leviticus Rabbah manifested signs of further compositional crafting.

Heinemann found that while all of the chapters of Leviticus Rabbah were comprised of individual (according to Heinemann, pre-existent) units, 22 of the 37 chapters were homogenous with regard to theme.[9] Consequently, Heinemann asserted that the redactor strove to create thematically coherent compositions out of pre-existing exegetical traditions culled from both live sermons and academic expositions of scripture. Each individual chapter is shaped by two, occasionally conflicting, motivations; the redactor wanted to explore a particular theme from a variety of angles while preserving the integrity of the pre-existing traditions. The redactors of the midrash chose pre-existent exegetical traditions that focused on a particular theme and wove them together into an integrated composition which explored that theme from different perspectives. Even in those chapters that were heterogeneous with regard to theme, Heinemann saw evidence of a high degree of compositional intentionality. The individual units were redacted in an ordered, structured way which both preserved the integrity of the pre-existent units and created a coherent anthology. Heinemann posits that the juxtaposition of contrasting and often contradictory texts and the multiplication of perspectives on any given topic are devices for integration. Through these strategies, the redactor "integrated" discrete, divergent traditions into a single coherent composition.

While Heinemann's observation regarding the high degree of thematic homogeneity, or at least of thematic focus, in many of the chapters of Leviticus Rabbah is quite perceptive, his descriptions of the techniques of "integration" are less persuasive. The presence of conflicting texts and entire blocks of pre-existent traditions can be seen as evidence that the redactor was more intent on preserving earlier traditions than on creating a unified composition. Nevertheless, Heinemann's pioneering work has been quite influential in midrashic scholarship. In recent decades, other scholars have attempted to further nuance his notion of integration by exploring the strategies through which the redactors of the midrash combined and juxtaposed discrete exegetical units.[10]

---

9. Joseph Heinemann, "The Art of Composition in Midrash Leviticus Rabbah," *Hasifrut* 2 (1971): 820 (Heb.).

10. Lewis Barth, "Literary Imagination and the Rabbinic Sermon: Some Observations," in *Proceedings of the Seventh World Congress of Jewish Studies* (Jerusalem: World Union for Jewish Studies, 1981), 29–36; Lou Silberman, "A Theological Treatise on Forgiveness: Chapter Twenty-Three of Pesiqta Derab Kahana," in *Studies in Aggadah,* 95–107; David Stern, "Midrash and the Language of Exegesis," in *Mid-*

In his essay "Midrash and the Language of Exegesis," David Stern amends Heinemann's description of thematic coherence:

> Instead of viewing that coherence as deriving from unity of theme, however, I wish to suggest that each chapter consists of an extended exegesis of the scriptural verse that serves as its prooftext. This exegesis develops progressively, albeit discontinuously, through the homily, and though it is nowhere stated explicitly in the chapter, it becomes clear to the reader by the homily's conclusion. The coherence of the homily consequently results from the logic by which the redactor allows the exegesis to unfold before the reader.[11]

Stern agrees with Heinemann's assertion that a theme emerges by the end of the chapter. He differs from Heinemann in his description of how that theme is generated. For Stern, midrash in general and the homiletical chapter in particular are primarily exegetical genres:

> In midrash the activity of exegesis is more powerful than the statement of theme. To be sure, the balance between the two is delicate . . . But what finally gives the Midrashic text its coherence, or semblance thereof, is not thematic unity but the pursuit of interpretation of the scriptural verse . . .[12]

For Stern, the *petiḥta* provides the model for the coherence of the chapter. Just as the *petiḥta* is an exegesis of the *petiḥta* verse that arrives at its "destination" in the target verse, so too is the chapter an atomistic interpretation of the target verse that arrives at its destination: the messianic peroration and a subtle articulation of the midrashically derived "message" of the target verse. In his reading of Lev R. 1, Stern demonstrates how the interplay of theme and exegesis works. He asserts that by the end of the chapter, "the language of *havivut*" (intimate companionship) has emerged as the theme of the chapter. He is careful to note, however, that the development of this theme never fully subverts or overshadows the individual exegetical processes that comprise the chapter.[13]

---

rash and Literature (eds. Geoffrey Hartman and Sanford Budick; New Haven: Yale University Press, 1986), 105–24; Stern, "Midrash and Poetics."

11. Stern, "Midrash and the Language," 107.
12. Ibid., 112.
13. I agree with Stern's description of the interplay of exegetical and thematic concerns in the homiletical chapter. However, his reading of Lev R. 1:1 overlooks the explicit thematics of the unit in an attempt to uncover and articulate a deeper thematic unity. It is clear from a close reading of the chapter that the redactor has chosen a cluster of texts that deal with levels of divine speech and encounter and with levels of prophetic experience. Stern overlooks this obvious thematic field in order to assert that the chapter has a deeper thematic focus which is derived subtly through exegesis and never stated explicitly.

Stern's modification of Heinemann's theory of thematic unity applies to PRK's chapters on the haftarot of the Tisha b'Av cycle. While a chapter might articulate a particular thematic field, the individual units of the chapter consist of the atomistic exegeses of either a *petiḥta* verse or the lemma. These exegeses each contribute to the articulation of the theme. The larger exegetical projects—namely, the exegesis of the *petiḥta* verse or lemma in its entirety—provide the framework for integrating the individual exegetical units and their articulations of theme into a complex, integrated composition. As Stern asserts, the individual units are bound together as elements of a complex exegetical process rather than as elements of logical-thematic exposition. The final result is one in which exegetical and thematic concerns are intertwined and interdependent. PRK 13 and 22 demonstrate this interdependence. In these chapters, the issues raised by the individual exegetical units participate in an overall thematic coherence which addresses the issues raised by the individual texts in their lectionary contexts as well as by the lectionary cycle as a whole.

Analysis

In the two case studies which follow, I will show how the individual units serve both as local exegeses and vehicles for the exploration of themes which are absent from the plain sense of the target verse but relevant to either its biblical or lectionary context. I will then demonstrate how the redactors of PRK use the strategies of selection and arrangement to shape each chapter into a coherent thematic unit which focuses on the particular function of the text within the lectionary sequence. Chapter 13, which comments on the opening verses of the first haftarah of rebuke, mirrors the central functions of the first haftarah within the lectionary cycle. It outlines the narrative of sin-punishment-restoration and explores the nature and reliability of the prophetic word. In addition, the chapter offers an ambiguous portrayal of the exilic experience which is entirely absent from the first haftarah of rebuke, but reflected in the lectionary cycle as a whole. The final chapter in the cycle, chapter 22, interprets the opening verses of the final haftarah. This chapter is a thematically coherent unit which, like the final haftarah itself, asserts that God's love for Israel is redemptive and will inevitably cause God to intervene in history on Israel's behalf.

Chapter 13

Chapter 13 is structured as an interpretation of Jer 1:1, the opening verse of the first haftarah of rebuke. To the casual reader, Jer 1:1 would not seem a terribly fruitful candidate for exegesis. It states, "The words of Jeremiah, son of Hilkiah of the priests who are in Anatoth in the land of Benjamin." In its biblical context, the verse is a straightforward identification of the prophecies to follow as the words of Jeremiah. Within the midrashic context, the verse is read and interpreted at three levels. Units 7, 8, 12 and 13 deal with the details and peculiarities of the verse itself. Units 7 and 8 interpret the word דִּבְרֵי ("words of"). While not *sui generis*, the formulation "The words of X prophet" is rare in the biblical corpus. Only the books of Micah and Jeremiah introduce the prophetic speech as the words of the prophet himself. This irregularity provides the exegetical motor for the exploration of the nature of the prophetic word in the chapter. Units 12 and 13 offer various midrashic etymologies of the name "Jeremiah." While some of the resulting interpretations dovetail with larger thematic concerns, these units are strongly exegetical. They are launched by features of the lectionary verse itself.

While these units are launched by individual features of the verse, units 4–6 and 12–14 are generated by the subject of the verse as a whole: the prophet Jeremiah. Units 4, 5 and 12 discuss Jeremiah's descent from Rahab and spin out the moral and theological implications of that descent. Units 6, 13 and 14 assert analogies between Jeremiah and Moses and Benjamin in order to articulate particular features of Jeremiah's identity and role. While the biblical text does not mention Jeremiah's descent from Rahab or his similarities to Moses and Benjamin, the midrash uses the introduction of the prophet within the biblical text as a frame for elaborating on his identity and his career. In other words, these midrashic units elaborate on the function of the verse within its biblical context.

A third set of units interprets the verse within the context of the lectionary cycle. Within the cycle, the first haftarah introduces the three haftarot of rebuke as well as the cycle as a whole. As discussed above, the three haftarot of rebuke decry Israel's sins and bear witness to the sin portion of the sin-punishment-redemption paradigm. These three haftarot provide the "evidence" that the catastrophes lamented on the ninth of Av are just punishment for Israel's sins, not capricious divine fury. Despite the fact that Jer 1:1 mentions none of these themes, several units of chapter 13 use the verse as a framework for invoking them. Units 2, 4, 5, 8–11 and 13 invoke Israel's sins. Jeremiah's prophecy is identified or portrayed as rebuke in units 2, 5–7, 10 and 14. The exile and/or destruction of Jerusalem is invoked or described in units 8–11 and 15. Finally, the sin-punishment paradigm is invoked in units 2, 5, 8, 10 and 11. Thus the chapter sets up the themes and modes of the haftarot of rebuke.

Finally, the over-arching shape of the chapter articulates the narrative of rebuke, punishment and consolation which undergirds the cycle. The strategic selection and placement of units 1, 9, 10 and 15 provide the anchors for this narrative structure. Unit 1 introduces the themes of sin, rebuke, and punishment. Units 9 and 10 describe the destruction itself. Unit 15 describes the restoration of Jerusalem and the redemption of the exiles.

Unit 1

The opening *petiḥta* sets the thematic stage for the Tisha b'Av cycle by situating the opening verse of the first haftarah in a larger context of exile, rebuke and punishment.[14] In so doing, it mirrors the function of the first haftarah within the cycle. Because of its importance to my analysis, I will cite the text in full.[15]

> R. Abba bar Kahana opened: *Give a shrill cry, O Bat-gallim! Hearken, Laishah! Take up the cry, Anatoth!* (Isa 10:30). *Give a shrill cry*: shout with your voice. *O Bat-gallim*: Daughter of the waves. Just as the waves are distinguished in the sea, so are your ancestors distinguished in the world. Another interpretation: *Bat-gallim*: Daughter of exiles (גולים); daughter of exiles (ברתהון דגילוליא).[16] Daughter of Abraham. What is written about him? *The Lord said to Abram, "Go forth from your native land . . ."* (Gen 12:1). Daughter of Isaac. What is written about him? *And Isaac went to Abimelech, king of the Philistines, in Gerar* (Gen 26:1). Daughter of Jacob. What is written about him? *Jacob [had] obeyed his father and mother [and gone to Padan-aram]* (Gen 28:7). *Hearken!* (Isa 10:30): Hearken to my commandments, hearken to words of Torah, hearken to words of prophecy. If not, *Laishah*: A lion will arise against you—this is the evil Nebuchadnezzar, of whom it is written: *The lion has come up from his thicket* (Jer 4:7).[17] *Take up the cry* (עֲנִיָּה): Poor in righteous people, poor in words of Torah, poor in commandments and good deeds.[18] If not, *Anatoth*: The one from Anatoth will come and prophesy against you words of rebuke. For this reason, scripture had to say *The words of Jeremiah, son of Hilkiah, of the priests of Anatoth*.

The bulk of the *petiḥta* consists of an extended exegesis of Isa 10:30. The midrash breaks the verse into three clauses; it translates the first clause into Aramaic and then offers two readings of *"Bat-gallim"* which identify Israel as the daughter of distinguished and exiled ancestors. The

---

14. This *petiḥta* is also the first unit of Lam R., a collection of midrashim which is closely linked to both the liturgy and thematics of Tisha b'Av.

15. Versions of this text appear in Lam R. Proem 1 and Yal Isa 416. For a detailed comparison of the versions, see Buber, *Pesikta*, 110–11.

16. גילוליא comes from the root גלל (to roll). However, the text glosses it as גולים as though it were derived from the root גלה (to exile).

17. לַיִשׁ means lion. The midrash is reading the place name לַיְשָׁה (Laishah) as a pun on לַיִשׁ (lion).

18. The midrash is punning on the word עֲנִיָּה. If it is derived from the root ענה, it means "cry out" or "answer." If it is derived from the root עני, it means "poor."

rest of the *petiḥta* transforms the last part of the verse from an exhortation of alarm and distress to a statement of the deuteronomic ideology of sin and punishment. The midrashist reads "Hearken, Laishah! Take up the cry, Anatoth" to mean: If Israel does not obey Torah, it will be punished with the invasion of Nebuchadnezzar. If Israel does not cry out, Jeremiah, the prophet from Anatoth, will come with words of chastisement.

This unit demonstrates how the *petiḥta* form serves as a strategy for expanding the themes and messages of a given biblical verse. Even though the themes of exile, sin, and punishment are absent from the plain sense of both the *petiḥta* verse (Isa 10:30) and the target verse (Jer. 1:1), the *petiḥta* format allows the midrashist to import these themes into the framework of the target verse.

First, the midrashist uses the strategy of atomistic reading to locate these themes within Isa 10:30. The re-reading of בַּת־גַּלִּים (bat-Gallim) as בַּת־גּוֹלִים (daughter of exiles), the puns on the words לַיְשָׁה (Laishah/lion) and עֲנִיָּה (cry out/poor), and the transformation of the exhortations "Hearken, Laishah" and "Take up the cry, Anatoth" into the conditional phrases "Hearken . . . If not, a lion" and "Take up the cry . . . If not, Anatoth," transform the verse of exhortation into a verse of deuteronomic warning.

Then, by linking Isa 10:30 to Jer 1:1, the midrashist imports the themes of exile and deuteronomic warning into the framework of the target verse. By reading "Anatoth" in Isaiah 10:30 as a reference to Jeremiah, who is "from the priests of Anatoth," the midrash establishes a connection between the two verses. Through this connection, the midrash asserts that the themes that arise in the exegesis of Isa 10:30 are relevant to our understanding of Jer 1:1. Thus, the *petiḥta* form gives the midrashist the freedom to import a midrashic reading of a foreign verse into the framework of the lectionary text without violating the exegetical structure which shapes the chapter. Even though the bulk of the *petiḥta* is an exegesis of Isa 10:30, the conventions of the *petiḥta* form identify this exegesis as part of the exegesis of Jer 1:1. Throughout the chapters on the lectionary cycle, the redactors of PRK capitalize on this form to raise issues that are integral to the Tisha b'Av season, but absent from the target verses.

While the primary thrust of the *petiḥta* is the articulation of the sin-punishment paradigm, the text also resonates strongly with the haftarot of consolation. Like the haftarot of consolation, Isa 10:30 is perched in anticipation of the divine advent. The exhortation "Give a shrill cry" echoes the various exhortations to cry out in joy at the divine advent which are voiced in the haftarot of consolation (Isa 40:9; 52:7–9; 54:1; 62:11–12). In addition, the direct address to *Bat-Gallim* resonates with the direct addresses to Jerusalem as a female personification in the haftarot: the word עֲנִיָּה (Cry out/unhappy/impoverished) also occurs in Isa 54:11, the opening verse of the third haftarah of consolation. Within the biblical context of Isa 10:30, these correspondences to scattered Second Isaianic texts are not significant to the meaning of the verse. When the verse opens a collection of exegeses of the haftarot of the lectionary cycle, however, these correspondences are underscored; they become vehicles for the optimism which is essential to the cycle. The very verse which launches the themes of rebuke hints at the texts and moves of consolation that conclude the cycle. At the same time, the correspondences between the biblical context of the *petihta* verse and the Tisha b'Av cycle inform the *petihta* with both a deep symmetry and a deep irony. In its biblical context, Isa 10:30 is part of a description of the approach of the Assyrian enemy. As the invader approaches Jerusalem, the settlements along the way are instructed to cry out. However, the invader's approach halts abruptly in Isa 10:33–34, which announces that God will appear at the last moment to repel and conquer the invader. The happy ending of Isaiah 10 constitutes a strong contrast to the tragic absence of divine salvation in the Tisha b'Av events.

Units 9–11

Units 9–11 deal with the destruction and exile.[19] In units 9–11, the *davar aher* (another interpretation) strategy is used to suggest two radically different interpretations of the exilic experience. Like the *petihta* form, the *davar aher* is a powerful redactional strategy which provides an exegetical framework for the introduction of material into the exegesis of a verse. Specifically, the *davar aher* allows for the assertion of competing interpretations of a single utterance or historical event. In units 9–11, two exegeses of the name "Jeremiah" yield contrasting interpretations of the exilic experience: In 9–10, the exile is the locus for the simultaneous experience of divine punishment and divine compassion; in 11, the exile is the site of divine absence.

Unit 9 begins by recounting a conversation between God and Jeremiah which is not found in the biblical text:

> God said to Jeremiah, "Either you go down with them to Babylon and I will remain here or you remain here and I will go down with them." Jeremiah replied to God, "Master of the Universe, if I go down what benefit will I be to them? Rather, let their creator go down with them, for he will be of benefit to them."

---

19. The material in units 9 and 10 appears in different orders in Lam R. proem 34 and Yal Jer 327. Parallel sources for individual traditions within the pericopes will be cited in the notes.

In this passage, the midrash introduces a portrait of the exile which is radically different from that of Lamentations, in which the events of 587 BCE were marked by an overwhelming sense of both God's enmity and God's absence. Here, the midrash asserts that God accompanied Israel into exile. Thus, although the exile is tragic, it does not signify a separation between God and Israel. Instead, it provides the opportunity for God to manifest great compassion and devotion by accompanying the Judeans into exile.[20]

The text goes on to give an expanded version of the episode recounted in Jer 39–40. Two questions generate this expansion. In Jer 39:12 Nebuchadnezzar says to his chief guard, Nebuzaradan, "Take him, look after him, and do him no harm, but grant whatever he asks you." Jeremiah 40:1 states:

> The word that came to Jeremiah from YHWH, after Nebuzaradan, the chief of the guards, set him free at Ramah, to which he had taken him, chained in fetters, among those from Jerusalem and Judah who were being exiled in Babylon.

These two verses seem to present a contradiction. If Nebuzaradan was told to do Jeremiah no harm, how did the prophet end up in chains? The midrash resolves this contradiction through an expansion of the biblical narrative in which Jeremiah insists on joining in with the shackled prisoners:

> Nebuchadnezzar gave Nebuzaradan three orders concerning Jeremiah. *Take him, look after him, and do him no harm* (Jer 39:12). But when Jeremiah saw a band of young men tied by neck chains one to the other, he went and cast in his lot with theirs. Then again when he saw a band of old men tied together by neck chains, he went and cast in his lot with theirs.[21]

Although Nebuzaradan was ordered not to harm Jeremiah (39:12), Jeremiah insisted on being shackled with the other prisoners. That is how he ended up in fetters in Jer 40:1.

Jeremiah 40 raises another question for the midrash. In vv. 4–5 Jeremiah refuses Nebuzaradan's offer to go free and to go wherever he pleases in the land. However, v. 6 states that Jeremiah went to Gedaliah at Mizpah. The conjunction of these two verses raises the question: "Why did Jeremiah change his mind?"

---

20. The notion that God accompanies Israel both to Egypt and into exile appears in several places in the rabbinic literature (e.g., Exod R. 15:17; Num R. 7:10; j. Taan 1:1, 64a; j. Suk 4:1, 54c; b. Meg 29a). The idea is associated exegetically with Jer 40:1 here and in the parallels in Lam R. proem 34 and Yal Jer 327.

21. Lam R. proem 34; Yal Jer 327; Pes R. 29.

> *But he [Jeremiah] still did not turn back* (Jer 40:5) until God revealed himself to him. Thus it is written: *The word that came to Jeremiah from* YHWH, *after Nebuzaradan, the chief of the guards, set him free . . . and he was chained in fetters* (Jer 40:1). What is *and he*? R. Aha said, as if it were possible to say: He and he.

The midrash reads "and he" as a reference to God—meaning that in addition to Jeremiah, God was bound in shackles with the exiles. This is a further radicalization of the trope of divine compassion and identification articulated above. God not only accompanies the Judeans into exiles, he even submits himself to their enchainment. The text then continues:

> What was the word [that came to Jeremiah]? . . . R. Lazar said: *He who scattered Israel will gather them and guard them as a shepherd his flock* (Jer 31:10). R. Yohanan said: *For the Lord will ransom Jacob, redeem him from one too strong for him* (Jer 31:11).

Once Jeremiah sees that God is committed to "shepherding" Israel and to redeeming them from their oppressors, he is willing to leave the exiles and return to Judea.[22] Unit 9 ends with a poignant description of Jeremiah's return to Judea:

> [Having been released by Nebuzaradan] and on his way back [to Jerusalem], Jeremiah saw fingers and toes [of captive Israel] that had been cut off and flung on the roadways. He picked them up, clasped them close, kissed them, and put them in his cloak, saying to them, "O my children, did I not say to you, *Give glory to the Lord your God, before it grows dark, and before your feet stumble,* etc. (Jer 13:16)—before words of Torah grow dark for you, before words of prophecy grow dark.[23]

---

22. Lam R. proem 34; Yal Jer 327. The version of this story which appears in Lam R. proem 34 is presented within the frame of a commentary on Jer 9:9. In this version, the narrative begins with the conversation between Nebuchadnezzar and Nebuzaradan regarding Jeremiah. The conversation between God and Jeremiah is inserted into the biblical narrative between Nebuzaradan's offer of freedom in 40:4 and Jeremiah's refusal in 40:5. The placement of the invented conversation between God and Jeremiah in Lam R. makes better narrative sense because it explains why Jeremiah changes his mind and goes to join Gedaliah. Perhaps it appears at the beginning of the PRK version so that it can serve as an immediate gloss on the name Jeremiah, reading it as ירם יה ("God arose"), meaning that God got up and left Jerusalem with the exiles. In Yal Jer 327, the conversation between God and Jeremiah appears after the interpretation of Jer 9:9 which occurs in PRK 13:10.

23. See the sources in n. 22.

94 *From Rebuke to Consolation*

Unit 10

The next unit begins with the citation of Jer 9:9.[24] This verse provides the springboard for the articulation of various traditions about the supernatural affects of the exile:

> *For the mountains I will lift up weeping and wailing and for the pastures in the wilderness, a lament* (Jer 9:9). For the tall and lofty mountains that were made into a wilderness, I will raise a lament. *They are laid waste, no man passes through, and no sound of cattle* (מִקְנֶה) *is heard* (ibid.). It was not enough for you that you did not listen to his voice, rather, מְקַנֶּה: You make me jealous with your idolatry.[25] In spite of this, *birds of the sky and beasts as well have fled and are gone* (ibid.).[26] For as R. Jose bar Halafta said: For fifty-two years [after the temple's destruction], not a bird was seen flying over the land of Israel, thus fulfilling the prophecy: *Both the fowl of the heavens and the beast are fled and gone.*[27] Nevertheless, said R. Hanina: [God saw to it that] forty years before Israel were exiled into Babylon, palm trees were planted in Babylon, because Israel craves sweet kinds of fruit which accustom the tongue to the sweetness of Torah.[28] As taught in the name of R. Judah: [Not only did the bird and the beasts flee, but] for seven years in the land there was fulfilled the prophecy, *The whole land thereof is brimstone, and salt, and a burning* (Deut 29:22).[29]

This account of the exile reflects the same ambiguity as the midrashic narrative which precedes it. The exile is simultaneously a catastrophic devastation—the land itself burned for seven years—and an opportunity for God to manifest his sweet devotion to Israel. Even though they were to be punished with exile, God made sure that they would have dates to eat in Babylon. This ambiguity recurs in the rest of the pericope. Even the seven-year conflagration could not squelch the tenacious fertility of the land of Israel. "R. Ze'era said: Come and see how brazen [in plenty] is the land of Israel! [Even as it burned] it produced fruits." The pericope ends with the assertion that

> There are seven hundred species of kosher fish, eight hundred kinds of kosher grasshoppers, and countless birds; they all went into exile with

---

24. Unit 10 seems to be a continuation of the preceding unit. In the Lam R. version, the entire narrative is imbedded in the exegesis of Jer 9:9.

25. This comment is based on a pun on the word מקנה, which can be vocalized to mean either "cattle" or "make jealous."

26. Lam R. proem 34; Yal Jer 281.

27. Lam R. proem 34; Yal Jer 281; Seder Olam ch. 27; j. Taan 4:8, 69b; b. Shab 145b; b. Yom 54a.

28. Lam R. proem 34; j. Taan 4:8, 69b; Yal Jer 281.

29. Lam R. proem 34; Yal Jer 281; Pes R. 1; Yal Pss 474; Yal Dan 1066; j. Kil 9:4, 32b; j. Ket 12:3, 35b; b. Yom 24a; Seder Olam 27.

the children of Israel to Babylon, and when the children of Israel came back, all returned with them except for the fish known as *sibutta*.[30]

Although God is not mentioned as the agent here, one can assume that he engineers the exile of the kosher animals. Once again, God is creatively attentive to the needs of the exiled Judeans.[31]

While units 9 and 10 portray the exile as a time of devastation and dislocation as well as divine attention and presence, unit 11 portrays the exile as a time of divine absence. The text is framed as a *davar aḥer*: "Another interpretation: Jeremiah: God ascended."[32] This interpretation introduces a stylized account of the retreat of the *shekhinah* from the temple.[33] The text recounts its stages of retreat and offers prooftexts for each stage. The litany is interrupted by a parable which compares the retreating *shekhinah* to a king who, when leaving his palace, kisses and embraces the pillars and walls and wishes peace on his house. The *shekhinah*'s itinerary is interrupted again at the final stage:

> There, on the Mount of Olives, for three and a half years—so said R. Jonathan—the *shekhinah* lingered, crying three times a day, *Return, you backsliding children, I will heal your backslidings* (Jer 3:22). But when they did not repent, the *shekhinah* soared up into the atmosphere and spoke this verse: *I will go and return to My place, until they acknowledge their guilt, and seek My face; in their trouble they will seek Me earnestly* (Hos 5:15).

Within the chapter, this unit serves as a companion piece to the unit which precedes it. Both readings are generated by the name, "Jeremiah," and both assert that God leaves Jerusalem at the destruction. However, here God's departure is a retreat from Israel, not an act of solidarity. God will return to the supernal abode until Israel repents. Through the strategy of the *davar aḥer*, the name "Jeremiah" comes to describe two radically different possibilities of divine behavior. These possibilities in turn suggest two radically different interpretations of the exilic experience. In the first, the

---

30. Lam R. proem 34; j. Taan 4:8, 69b; Yal Jer 281.

31. These two final traditions not only assert the tenacity of the land and God's providential care for Israel in exile, they also insist that despite the exile, both the people and land of Israel survived with their national and geographic identities intact. Despite devastation, the land of Israel retains its edenic fertility and despite exile, the Jews retain their Jewish identity, as mainfest through their observance of the dietary laws.

32. This interpetation is based on a parsing of ירמיהו (Jeremiah) as יה רם[י] ("God arose").

33. The account of the *shekhinah*'s retreat from the temple appears in Lam R. proem 25; Yal Jer 257; Yal Ezek 350; ARN 34 (version A); MHG *Tazria* 13:59; b. RH 31a.

exile is the locus for the simultaneous experience of divine punishment and divine compassion. In the second, the exile is the site of divine absence.

The particular force of the *davar aḥer* is made apparent when units 9–11 are compared to the lectionary sequence. Like the midrashic units, the lectionary presents a double-edged vision of the exilic experience. Lamentations asserts that the exile is a sign of enmity and divine alienation; the consolatory dialogue during the seven weeks of consolation asserts that the exilic present of the worshiping community is a time of divine presence and attention. Similarly, the midrash asserts that God is both absent (unit 11) and present and attentive (unit 9–10) during the exile. Whereas the lectionary cycle presents these interpretations sequentially, the *davar aḥer* strategy presents them as simultaneous and equally valid interpretations of the exilic experience.

Unit 15

Chapters in the homiletical midrashim conventionally end with a "messianic peroration," a final unit which deals with the messianic future.[34] In some chapters, the messianic peroration is closely linked to the themes and tropes of the other units; in others, it seems to be a formal addendum to the chapter. In chapter 13, the messianic peroration concludes the narrative of sin-punishment-redemption articulated by the chapter and serves as a summary unit to the chapter as a whole:

> To whom the word of God came in the days of Josiah, king of Judah until the end of the tenth year of Zedekiah, son of Josiah, king of Judah, until the exile of Jerusalem in the fifth month (This is a paraphrase of Jer 1:2–3). R. Abun said: A lion arose in the astrological sign of the lion and destroyed Ariel.[35] A lion arose: This is Nebuchadnezzar the wicked. It is written about him: *A lion arose from his thicket* (Jer 4:7). In the astrological sign of the lion: *Until the exile of Jerusalem in the fifth month* (Jer 1:3). And destroyed Ariel: *Ah Ariel, Ariel the city where David camped* (Isa 29:1). On that account a lion will arise in the astrological sign of the lion and will rebuild Ariel. A lion will come: This is God. It is written about him: *A lion roars, who will not fear* (Amos 3:8). In the sign of the lion: *I will turn your mourning into joy* (Jer 31:13). And will rebuild Ariel: *God builds Jerusalem; He gathers in the exiles of Jerusalem* (Ps 147:2).

---

34. For a detailed discussion of the messianic peroration, see Marc Bregman, "The Triennial Haftarot and the Perorations of the Midrashic Homilies," *JJS* 32 (1981): 74–84.

35. This interpretation hinges on the two meanings of the word "Ariel" (אריאל), which means "lion of God" and is also an epithet for Jerusalem.

The unit conforms to the conventions of the messianic peroration by foretelling the restoration of Jerusalem and the return of the exiles. This prediction of restoration also completes the narrative begun in the first unit and continued in units 9–11. Here, at the end of the chapter, the account of sin, rebuke and punishment culminates in redemption. The unit also serves as an *inclusio* to the chapter as a whole. In the first *petiḥta*, Nebuchadnezzar is referred to as a lion and his attack on Jerusalem is forecast. Here in the final unit he is once again referred to as a lion, but this time his moment of conquest is in the past and the text looks forward to its reversal. The correspondence between the first and last units supports the argument for the coherence of the chapter. The catastrophe is foretold in particular terms in the first unit and is reversed in identical terms in the final unit.

Unit 15 also resonates strongly with the lectionary cycle as a whole. On the level of plot, this text tells the same story as the cycle. Nebuchadnezzar destroyed the temple; God will rebuild it. Like the lectionary cycle, this text pictures a symmetry between the destruction and the restoration. In the cycle, the haftarot of consolation articulate precise reversals of the woes lamented in Lamentations. Here too, the restoration precisely reverses the catastrophe. Just as the destruction was wrought by a "lion" during the sign of Leo, so will the restoration be wrought by a "lion" during the sign of Leo.

Summary

In PRK chapter 13, various midrashic structures and strategies are employed to articulate and develop the themes which are familiar from the lectionary cycle. In unit 1, the *petiḥta* structure provides the vehicle for the introduction of ideas of sin and rebuke into the rather innocuous framework of Jer 1:1. In units 9–11, the *davar aḥer* strategy transforms the name "Jeremiah" into a framework for the simultaneous assertion of two radically different interpretations of the exile. In unit 15, the messianic peroration provides the framework for introducing the future restoration of Jerusalem and the return of the exiles. While each of these units explores a particular theme of the Tisha b'Av lectionary and season, the arrangement of the pericopes within the chapter articulates the narrative of sin-rebuke-punishment-redemption.

Chapter 22

Like chapter 13, PRK chapter 22 articulates the themes and mirrors the function of the haftarah on which it comments. In many ways, the final haftarah serves as a summary to the haftarot of consolation. It invokes many of the tropes of consolation which appear in the previous haftarot and reiterates the dynamic relationship between the two discourses of consolation which recur throughout the cycle. The disjunctive redaction of the haftarah highlights the differences between the consolation rooted in God's intimate relationship with Israel and the consolation rooted in God's powerful and often violent acts of intervention in history. At the same time, the redaction of the haftarah suggests that there is an intimate relationship between the two consolatory discourses. God's devotion to Israel motivates his redemptive acts on her behalf. In addition, the final haftarah underscores a consolatory strategy which was articulated earlier in the cycle in Lam 3. This strategy, which is also familiar from Psalms, suggests that human lament and prayer has power to move God to attention and intervention.

Chapter 22 articulates and underscores each of these themes. It asserts that God's romantic love for Israel is the fact that ultimately consoles her and causes her to rejoice. It also asserts, in terms far stronger than those of the haftarah, that God's love for Israel is inextricably entwined with Israel's redemption. God's love has motivated his redemptive acts in the past and will necessarily motivate his redemptive acts in the future. Finally, the midrash asserts that Israel's persistent faithfulness and romantic devotion to God will move him to intervene miraculously and redemptively on her behalf.

The chapter consists of two *petihtot* followed by four exegetical units which interpret segments of Isa 61:10–11. It ends with a messianic exegesis of Isa 61:11. With the exception of the messianic conclusion, each of the units deals with themes of romantic love, marriage, barrenness, and fertility.

Unit 1

1. Scripture says elsewhere: *Will you not revive us again so that your people will rejoice in you?* (Ps 85:7). R. Aha said: Your people and your city will rejoice in you.

2. *And Sarah said, "God has brought me laughter; [all who hear will laugh with me]"* (Gen 21:6). R. Yudan, R. Simon, R. Hanin, R. Shmuel b. Isaac (said): If Reuben is happy, why should Simeon care? For here Sarah our mother says, "All who hear will laugh with me." Rather, the verse teaches that when Sarah our mother gave birth to Isaac, all the barren women conceived, all the deaf gained hearing, all the blind gained sight, all the mute gained speech, and all the mentally incompetent became sound; and everyone said, "if only Sarah would conceive (תפקד) again so that we might be attended to (ניפקד) with her."

3. R. Berechiah in the name of R. Levi: [Isaac was born] to add to the heavenly lights. For here it speaks of doing (עשיה): *And God did* (עשה) *to*

Sarah as he had spoken (Gen 21:1). And it says there: *And God made* (ויעש) *the two heavenly lights* (Gen 1:16). Just as the "doing" there gives light to the world, so too the "doing" which is spoken of here gives light to the world.

4. It is said here "he did" (עשה) and it says elsewhere "And he made (עשה) a dispensation for the countries." Just as there "he did" means to give a gift to the world, so here "doing" means to give a gift to the world.

5. R. Berechiah in the name of R. Levi: You find that when our mother Sarah gave birth to Isaac, the nations were saying—God forbid to even think it!—"Sarah did not give birth to Isaac. Rather, Hagar, Sarah's maid, is the one who gave birth to him." What did God do? He dried up the breasts of the women of the nations of the world and their noblewomen came and kissed the dust of Sarah's feet and said to her, "Do us a good deed and suckle our children." So Abraham said to Sarah, "Sarah, this is no time to be modest. Sanctify the name of God and sit in the marketplace and suckle their children." Thus it is written: *Sarah suckled children* (Gen 21:7). "Child" is not written here, rather "children." And are not these things a case of a conclusion *a minori ad majus* (קל וחומר)? Just as when a human being receives joy, he becomes happy and makes everyone happy, so when God makes Jerusalem happy [this will happen] all the more so. *I will greatly rejoice in YHWH* (Isa 61:10).[36]

PRK 22:1 is a complex composite pericope. Unit 1.1 consists of a brief comment in which Ps 85:7 is used to explain the double locution שׂוֹשׂ אָשִׂישׂ ("I will greatly rejoice") in Isa 61:10. The unstated question of the midrash is, "Who are the two subjects indicated by the doubling of the verb שׂושׂ?"[37] The midrash seems to assume that the obvious rejoicer in Isa 61:10 is Jerusalem. Psalm 85:7, which speaks of the rejoicing of "your people," pro-

---

36. The narrative expansion of the birth of Isaac appears in five other sources without any reference to Isa 61:10. In Gen R. 53:8–9 and Yal *Vayera* 93, the material is introduced in the context of the interpretation of Gen 21:7. In PRE 51, the unit is included within a list of seven divine miracles. In Pes R., the material is divided between two chapters. The material about the miraculous healings which accompanied Isaac's birth and the gift/light material appear in chapter 42, which interprets Gen 21ff. The material about the gentile women's mockery and the nursing of their children occurs in chapter 43, which interprets 1 Sam 2:22ff. In MHG *Vayera* 21:8, the pericope ends with the same *kal vaḥomer* that appears in PRK, but the Isaiah verse is not invoked. In b. BM 87a the material appears in an aggadic section regarding the manners of the patriarchs. These parallels suggest that the attachment of the Sarah material to the Isaiah verse is a secondary development. The material itself is generated internally by the Genesis pericope.

37. The midrashic question is contrived. The double locution שׂוֹשׂ אָשִׂישׂ represents a case of the infinite absolute followed by the *kal* imperfect. It is a common grammatical construction which serves to strengthen the verb.

vides the identity of the second speaker. Thus, the midrash concludes that the doubled verb refers to the rejoicing of both Jerusalem and the people.

Units 1.2 and 1.3 transmit traditions related to Isaac's birth. Unit 1.2 opens with a quotation of Gen 21:6: "God has brought me laughter; all who hear will laugh with me." The midrash addresses the question, "Why does Sarah's laughter make other people laugh?" by relating an extra-biblical tradition which states that when Sarah gave birth, people suffering from various handicaps were miraculously cured. This miracle explains why Sarah's joy caused others to rejoice.

Units 1.3 and 1.4 use the device of the *gezerah shavah* (analogy based on verbal correspondences) to identify Isaac as both a light and a gift to the world.[38]

Unit 1.5 explains an irregularity in Gen 21:7. The verse states: "Who would have said to Abraham that Sarah would suckle children?" Why does the verse say "children" when Sarah only bore one child? The midrash resolves this problem by relating another miracle related to Isaac's birth. When Sarah gave birth, the nations of the world did not believe that the baby was hers and claimed that he was Hagar's son. As punishment for their disbelief, God dried up the breasts of the foreign women, who were then forced to beg Sarah to nurse their children. This tradition explains why Gen 21:7 says that Sarah nursed *children* rather than *a child*.

The section ends by connecting the traditions about the birth of Isaac to the target verse (Isa 61:10) through a *kal vahomer* construction. The situation of Isaac's birth, in which God caused Sarah to rejoice and her joy caused others to rejoice, is both paralleled and amplified when God brings joy to Jerusalem. The midrash connects the target verse to the preceding unit by re-reading the double locution שׂוֹשׂ אָשִׂישׂ as an intransitive form followed by a transitive form: "I will rejoice, and I will make others rejoice."[39]

This unit demonstrates once again the power of the *petiḥta* form. There is no organic connection between the bulk of the *petiḥta* and Isa 61:10.[40] PRK 22:1 is comprised of a series of traditions about the birth of

---

38. These traditions occur together in Gen R. 53:8, Pes R. 42, and Yal *Vayera* 93. The "gift" tradition does not appear in Pes R.

39. This reading of שׂוֹשׂ אָשִׂישׂ is also contrived. While אָשִׂישׂ can be read as a *hiphil* form, שׂוֹשׂ can only be read as an infinite absolute. It cannot be read as a first person *kal* form.

40. The parallel sources support this assertion. The traditions regarding Isaac's miraculous birth appear five other times in the rabbinic corpus with no mention of Isa 61:10. In addition, the other midrashic references to Isa 61:10 which comment on the significance of the double locution do not mention Gen 21:7 (e.g. Lev R. 10:2; Deut R. 2:37; Song R. 1:1, 2; PRK 16:4; Pes R. 37). Finally, in Yal Isa 505, the Sarah

Isaac which are generated exegetically within the midrashic context by the irregularities in Gen 21:6–7 and by the use of the word עשה (do/make) in v. 6. Within the midrash, Isaac's birth is a case of miraculous fertility which catalyzes a scene of miraculous physical healing and restoration and a scene in which the foreign nations pay obeisance to Israel. These traditions are not intrinsically connected to Isa 61:10; they are connected only by the *kal vaḥomer* construction. Nevertheless, the conventions of the *petiḥta* form allow the midrashist to introduce the themes of the unit into the framework of the target verse. In so doing, the midrashist expands the message of Isa 61:10 to include central themes of the lectionary cycle. Like the final haftarah, this *petiḥta* invokes the cycle's central images of restoration: miraculous fertility (cf. Isa 49:21; 54:1; 62:4), physical restoration (cf. Isa 52:1–2), and the obeisance of the nations (cf. Isa 49:23; 55:5; 60:5–16). Within the midrash, these are elements of Isaac's miraculous birth and, by extension, of the future redemption which it parallels. The midrash also creates a hierarchy among the tropes of consolation and restoration. In PRK's version of Isaac's birth, Sarah's miraculous fertility generates the other miracles. If Isaac's birth is a paradigm for the redemption, then there too the tropes of renewed fertility, which arise from the discourse of the intimate relationship between God and Israel, assume center stage.

Unit 2

The second unit of the chapter is also a complex *petiḥta*. This unit introduces the theme of romantic love and its redemptive power. While the bulk of the unit deals with human love, the midrash draws an analogy between this human love and the love between God and Israel which it sees expressed in Isa 61:10:

> 1. *This is the day that YHWH has made; rejoice and be glad in it* (בו) (Ps 118:24). R. Abun said: We do not know in what we are to rejoice—in the day or in the Holy One Blessed be He.[41] So Solomon came and interpreted it: *We will rejoice and be glad in you* (בָּךְ) (Song 1:4): in you and in your Torah, in you and in your salvation. R. Isaac said בָּךְ, in the 22 letters that you wrote for us in the Torah. *Bet* equals two and *kaf* equals twenty.
>
> 2. As it is taught: If a man marries a woman and he is with her ten years and she does not bear children, he is not permitted to forsake the commandment "Be fruitful and multiply." When he divorces her, she is permitted to marry another man. The second one is permitted to stay with

---

material is absent from the interpretation of Isa 61:10. This absence suggests that at least in the eyes of the later (prob. thirteenth century) redactor of Yalkut Shimoni, the Sarah material was not germane to a running commentary on Isaiah.

41. בו can either mean "in him" or "in it."

her ten years (without her bearing children). If she miscarries, they count from the time of the miscarriage. The man is obligated to fulfill the commandment, "Be fruitful and mulitply," but not the woman. R. Yohanan ben Barukah said: He said about both of them: *And God blessed them, saying, "Be fruitful and multiply . . ."* (Gen 1:28).

3. An incident occurred in Sidon to a man who had married a woman and stayed with her ten years but she did not bear a child. They went before R. Shimon ben Yohai for a divorce. He [the husband] said to her [the wife]: "Every pleasurable thing that I have in my house, take it and go to your father's house." R. Shimon ben Yohai said to them, "Just as you were united amid food and drink, so you can only separate amid food and drink." What did she do? She made a great feast and she made him drink too much. She whispered to her maidservants and said to them, "Take him to my father's house." In the middle of the night, he awoke from his sleep; he asked them, "Where am I?" She said to him, "Didn't you say to me, 'Every precious thing that I have in my house, take it to your father's house?' Isn't it the case, that I have nothing more precious than you?" When R. Shimon ben Yohai heard this, he prayed for them and they were attended to (conceived). God attends to barren women and the righteous ones attend to barren women. The situation is *kal vahomer*. When a human being is happy, he causes others to rejoice; when God causes Jerusalem to rejoice, all the more so. And Israel who awaits God's salvation, all the more so. *I will greatly rejoice in my God* (Isa 61:10).

The unit is comprised of three independent traditions. The opening unit is a comment on Ps 118:24 which seeks to identify the referent of the word בו in the verse. The midrash brings Song 1:4 as an intertext and, through it, identifies the referents of בו as God, God's Torah and God's salvation. Within the context of the *petiḥta*, this unit serves as a bridge from the *petiḥta* verse to Song 1:4, which serves as the rationale for the inclusion of the next two units.

Unit 2.2 is a legal principle first recorded in m. Yeb 6:6, which states that a man must divorce his wife if she has not borne him children within ten years of their marriage.[42] This legal dictum is followed by the story about the barren couple who go before R. Shimon b. Yohai for a divorce. The story poignantly describes the mutual love of the man and the woman, and, particularly, the tenacity of the woman's affection. As a reward for her loyalty, R. Shimon b.Yohai prays for them and, through the agency of his prayer, they conceive. The body of the *petiḥta* is connected to

---

42. The legal material appears in a variety of both halakhic and aggadic contexts (Gen R. 45:3; Song R. 1:4; Yal *Lekh lekha* 79; MHG *Lekh lekha* 16:3; m. Yeb 6:6, and t. Yeb 8:4).

the target verse through the stereotyped *kal vaḥomer* which is copied from the first unit.[43]

This *petiḥta*, like the one before it, serves as a vehicle for importing themes which are foreign to the lectionary verse into the framework of that verse. The opening move of the *petiḥta* introduces Song 1:4. By introducing this verse as an intertext to Isa 61:10, the midrash associates the joy which is expressed in Isa 61:10 with the romantic love expressed in Song of Songs. It also provides a bridge between Isa 61:10 and the narrative of the barren couple. Once Isa 61:10 is linked to Song 1:4, then this narrative, which is part of a tradition of exegesis of Song 1:4, can also be read as applying to Isa 61:10. By importing the narrative into the exegesis of Isa 61:10, the midrash boldly suggests that the relationship between the husband and wife in the midrash can shed light on the relationship between God and Israel. In the narrative, the woman's tenacious love for her husband saves their marriage and leads to an end to her barrenness. If this relationship is an analogy to the relationship between God and Israel, then the story suggests that Israel's tenacious love for God can preserve their relationship and lead to the renewal of fertility which has been asserted as a central trope of redemption. This pericope, then, further develops the theme of miraculous fertility which was introduced in the first *petiḥta* by asserting that it is the consequence of deep and tenacious love. Through the strategy of the *petiḥta*, the midrashists have imported the themes of

---

43. The narrative appears only in Song R. 1:4, MHG *Lekh lekha* 16:3, and Yal *Bereishit* 16. In Yal *Bereishit* 16 it appears in the context of Gen 1:28. In MHG, it appears in the context of a commentary on Gen 16:3, which states, "So Sarai, Abram's wife, took her maid Hagar the Egyptian—after Abram dwelt in the land of Canaan ten years—and gave her to her husband Abram as a concubine." This incident is used as support for the legal principle. The MHG version ends with the penultimate line of the PRK version, which states that both God and righteous people can cause barren women to conceive. Within the context of Gen 16, the narrative may function as a critique of Abraham and Sarah. Unlike the biblical couple, the couple in the midrashic narrative is able to solve the barrenness problem through the woman's love and the consequent intervention of R. Shimon b. Yohai. Abraham and Sarah willingly accede to the law and their acquiescence causes much future strife. In Song R., the narrative appears in the context of the exegesis of the verse, "We will rejoice and be glad in you" (Song 1:4). The logic of the *kal vaḥomer* is stronger in the version of this tradition which appears in Song R. than in PRK:

> Behold, it is a case of *kal vaḥomer*. When a human being says to one who is human like him, "I have no precious possession in this world apart from you," he is paid attention to. When Israel, who is awaiting salvation from God every day, says "We have no precious possession in this world apart from you," [they will be attended to] all the more so. Thus: *We will rejoice and be glad in you* (Song 1:4).

miraculous fertility and redemptive love into a verse whose plain sense merely asserts that the speaker rejoices in God.

Unit 3

The third unit begins the running exegesis of Isa 61:10:

> [This can be compared] to a noblewoman whose husband, son and son-in-law went on a journey to the nations of the sea. They said to her, "Your sons are coming." She said to them, "Let my daughters-in-law rejoice!" They said to her, "Your sons-in-law are coming." She said, "Let my daughters rejoice!" When they said to her, "Behold, your husband!" she said, "Joy, this is perfect joy." Thus, the prophets say to Jerusalem, *Our sons will come from afar* (Isa 60:4) and she says to them, *Let Mount Zion rejoice* (Ps 48:12). *They will bear your daughters on their sides* (Isa 60:4) and she says to them, *Let the daughters of Judah rejoice* (Ps 48:12). When they say to her, *Behold! Your king will come to you!* (Zech 9:9), she says to them, *I will greatly rejoice in YHWH* (Isa 61:10).[44]

This pericope explicitly asserts that Zion rejoices because God is coming. Furthermore, the force of the parable asserts that Zion's joy is so great because God, in his role as husband, is returning to her. It is the restoration of the intimate, erotic relationship between God and Israel that gives Zion joy. This assertion resonates strongly within the lectionary cycle. In both the midrashic pericope and the haftarot of consolation, the renewal of divine espousal is identified as the most effective consolation.

Unit 4

This unit, which interprets the phrase "For he has dressed me in garments of salvation, he has wrapped me in a cloak of righteousness" (Isa 61:10), compares the situation of Israel to that of an orphan.[45] The unit identifies the garments of salvation and the cloak of righteousness as the merit which Israel has inherited from her ancestors. This is the only unit in the chapter which does not relate directly to the theme of romantic love.

---

44. This tradition also appears in Song R. 1:4, where it follows a parallel to the preceding unit in PRK and ends with a reference to Isa 61:10. The occurrence of these two units together in Song R. suggests that Isa 61:10 and the tradition regarding the barren couple become linked through their shared exegetical connection to Song 1:4. The tradition also appears in Deut R. 2:37 and Yal Isa 505 in the context of the exegesis of Isa 61:10.

45. The only parallel appears in Yal Isa 505, also in the context of an exegesis of Isa 61:10.

Unit 5

The final pericope of chapter 22 explicitly states that God's love for Israel is salvific and will inevitably lead to Israel's redemption.[46]

> In ten places Israel is called "bride": six times by Solomon, three times by Isaiah and once by Jeremiah. Six times by Solomon: *Come with me from Lebanon, my bride* (Song 4:8); *You have ravished my heart, my sister, my bride* (Song 4:9); *How sweet is your love, my sister, my bride* (Song 4:10); *Your lips drip nectar, my bride* (Song 4:11); *A garden locked is my sister, my bride* (Song 4:12); *I come to my garden, my sister, my bride* (Song 5:1). Three times by Isaiah: *You shall put them all on as an ornament; you shall bind them on as a bride does* (Isa 49:18); and this one, *As a bridegroom decks himself with a garland and as a bride adorns herself with her jewels* (Isa 61:10); and *As a bridegroom rejoices over the bride* (Isa 62:5). And once by Jeremiah: *The voice of mirth and the voice of gladness, the voice of the bridegroom and the voice of the bride* (Jer 33:11). And in correspondence to these, the Holy One Blessed be He donned ten garments. On the day of the creation of the world, the first garment that the Holy One Blessed be He donned was of glory and majesty. As it is written: *You are clothed in glory and majesty* (Ps 104:1). The second garment, which the Holy One Blessed be He wore to destroy the generation of the flood, was of majesty. As it is written: *YHWH reigns; he is robed in majesty* (Ps 93:1). The third garment, which the Holy One Blessed be He wore to give Torah to Israel, was strength. As it is written: *YHWH is robed, he is girded with strength* (ibid.). The fourth garment, which the Holy One Blessed be He wore to destroy the kingdom of Babylon, was white. As it is written: *His raiment was white as snow* (Dan 7:9). The fifth garment, which the Holy One Blessed be He wore to destroy the kingdom of Media, was vengeance. As it is written: *He put on garments of vengeance for clothing, and wrapped himself in fury as a mantle* (Isa 59:17)—this [verse counts as] two. The seventh garment, which the Holy One Blessed be He wore to destroy the kingdom of Greece, was righteousness. As it is written: *He put on righteousness as a breastplate and a helmet of salvation upon his head* (ibid.)—this [verse also counts as] two. The ninth garment, which the Holy One Blessed be He will wear in the future to destroy the kingdom of Edom, is red: *Why is your apparel red* (אָדֹם)*?* (Isa 63:2)[47] The tenth garment, which the Holy One Blessed be He will wear in the future when he destroys the kingdoms of Gog and Magog, will be glory. As it is written:

---

46. This pericope is a combination of two separate traditions. The first part of the unit, which identifies the "bride" texts, appears in Deut R. 2:37 and Yal Isa 506 as comments on Isa 61:10. In addition, it appears in Song R. 4:10 and Yal Song 988 as comments on Song 4:10 ("How lovely are your breasts, my sister, bride"). The "garments" section appears in these texts as well as in four additional texts in the context of commentaries on Ps 93:1 (Pes R. 38; Midr Pss 93:1; Yal Pss 847; and MHG Bereishit 1:30).

47. This reading is based on a pun between Edom (אֱדוֹם) and red (אָדֹם).

> *Glorious in his apparel* (Isa 63:1). The congregation of Israel says to God: Of all the garments, this one is the most wonderful, as it is written: *This is the most glorious of his apparel.*[48]

This pericope is generated by a series of exegetical innovations. First, the author asserts that there is a correspondence between the ten places that Israel is called "bride" and the ten places that God gets dressed. Although this announcement is made with little fanfare, it is a bold move. There is no contextual relationship between the "bride" texts and the "dressing" texts. The texts themselves do not assert that God gets dressed when Israel is called bride or that God gets dressed because Israel is called bride.[49] The argument for thematic correspondence is based only on the parallel number of occurrences.[50] The second innovation is the identification of each act of garbing with a particular moment of divine intervention in history. In three out of the six cases, this identification is motivated by the prooftexts themselves. These verses speak both of clothing and divine acts of power. Psalm 104 speaks of creation; Ps 93 mentions the rising up of floods and God's power over the waters; Isa 63:2 mentions Edom and implies a bloody encounter there. Although Ps 93:1 does not explicitly mention revelation, the correspondence is generated by the powers of midrashic association. The verse is identified with the giving of Torah because "strength" is a common rabbinic epithet for Torah. In six out of ten cases, however, there is no apparent connection between the verse and the event with which it is identified.[51] These identifications are based solely on the assertion of the paradigm of correspondence. The "extra" references to divine dressing provide a space for the identification of additional acts of divine redemptive intervention.

---

48. The final comment is based on a punning reading of Isa 63:1: "he (זֶה) that is glorious in his apparel." In its biblical context, the referent of זֶה is God. The midrash reads the referent as "the garment" so that the verse means, "the garment that is the most glorious of his garments."

49. Isa 61:10 does invoke both bridal imagery and dressing imagery. However, in this verse God clothes Israel "as a bridegroom decks himself with a garland, and as a bride adorns herself with her jewels." God does not clothe himself. Nevertheless, the conjunction of bridal and clothing language in this verse might have served as the inspiration for the midrash.

50. Even this parallelism is a rabbinic contrivance. The number of "dressing" references depends on how one counts two references in a single verse.

51. Braude and Kapstein (*Pesikta*, 348) suggest that the eighth verse (Isa 59:17) is associated with Greece because Greek soldiers wore helmets. They suggest that Dan 7:9 is associated with Babylon because white symbolizes the forgiveness which will be marked by the end of the exile. I find these suggestions unconvincing.

These two innovative moves lead to the conclusion that God's love for Israel is essentially redemptive. Each act of dressing corresponds to an act of divine intervention. With the exception of creation and the giving of Torah, each intervention is a divine defeat of an enemy of Israel. These acts of redemptive intervention, in turn, correspond to Israel's status as a bride. Thus the midrash asserts that there is an essential connection between Israel's status as a bride and God's redemptive acts in history: because God loves and espouses Israel, he defeats her enemies.

While the first eight cases of dressing correspond to past acts of redemption, the ninth and tenth cases, which are selected from the final haftarah of consolation, represent the defeat of Edom/Rome and the defeats of Gog and Magog. Thus, the midrash identifies the final haftarah as the locus of two powerful consolations. The first is paradigmatic: God's love for Israel is redemptive. The second is messianic: the particular acts of dressing described in the final haftarah correspond to the future acts of divine intervention which will both free Israel from her current subjugation and will insure her eternal, messianic redemption. The midrash explicitly states the message which is indicated implicitly by the redacted form of the final haftarah. Through the redaction of the haftarah, the creators of the lectionary cycle bring together the romantic language of Isa 61:10–11 and 62:3–5 and the bellicose, messianic language of Isa 63:1–7. The redaction of the haftarah asserts that even though these pericopes seem quite disjunctive, they in fact belong together. PRK 22:5 makes the same point through the paradigm of correspondence. It identifies Isa 61:10 as a "bride" verse and identifies Isa 63:1 and 63:2 as "dressing" verses. According to the logic of the midrash, they belong together because there is a causal relationship between the espousal of God and Israel and God's acts of redemption. Thus the pericope serves to underscore and make explicit the theology which is expressed through the redaction and structure of the lectionary sequence.

Summary

PRK chapter 22 expands and elaborates on the trope of the erotic, romantic relationship between God and Israel. In the first unit, the *petiḥta* structure is used to import a series of traditions regarding Isaac's miraculous birth into the context of the final haftarah of consolation. Through this strategy, the redactors of the chapter assert that the themes of renewed fertility, miraculous birth and healing, and the obeisance of the nations are imbedded within Isa 61:10. Thus the verse serves as a vehicle for a summation of central themes of the lectionary cycle. This summary, though, is not a mere catalogue of consolatory and redemptive themes. In the midrashic pericope, miraculous fertility and birth are identified as the central causes for rejoicing. When this pericope is associated with the final haftarah, it serves to identify these themes as the primary causes for rejoicing in the lectionary context as well.

The next unit of chapter 22 adds another valence to the fertility theme: Here, miraculous fertility is a result of the tenacious love of a woman for her husband. Within the context of the lectionary cycle, this assertion resonates with the trope of exhortation. In the *petiḥta*, the woman's tenacity leads to reconciliation and fertility. The inclusion of this pericope suggests that Israel's tenacious expressions of love for God will also lead to reconciliation and restoration.

While the second *petiḥta* deals with the redemptive power of human love, the final unit describes the redemptive power of divine love. In this pericope, God's acts of dressing, which correspond to divine interventions in history, are correlated to the times Israel is called bride. This assertion of correspondence suggests that there is a relationship between God's love for Israel and God's intervention in history. If God and Israel are married, then God will inevitably intervene in history on Israel's behalf. The final unit makes explicit the causal connection that is expressed more subtly in the lectionary cycle itself.

Theology of Consolation and the Culture of the Synagogue

Thus far, I have demonstrated that the relationship between chapters 13 and 22 of PRK and the lectionary cycle itself is largely complementary. The midrashim highlight and develop themes that are articulated more subtly by the lectionary cycle and introduce additional themes that are relevant to the Tisha b'Av season. Reflection on the midrashim in relation to the culture of the synagogue both underscores areas of overlap and highlights some of the rabbinic specificity of the midrashim.

When read in light of the material culture of the synagogue, the final pericope of PRK chapter 22 serves as a masterful link between the synagogue representations of God as cosmic, mythic creator and the rabbinic representation of God as Israel's intimate lover. The midrashic pericope quotes from Pss 93 and 104, which describe God in terms which resonate strongly with the images of God as Helios enthroned in the synagogue mosaics. Ps 104:1–2 states, "YHWH, you are clothed in glory and majesty / wrapping light like a garment / you spread the heavens like a tent cloth." Subsequent verses of the psalm refer to the clouds as God's chariot and the winds as his messengers. Ps 93 invokes God's eternal throne and God's majesty over the waters. These images are all echoed in the synagogue images of *sol invictus* in the center of the zodiac. By invoking these verses, the midrash aligns itself with a cosmic, mythic strand of theology which echoes that of the synagogue art. In the midrash, however, these verses and the images that they invoke are linked to the "bride" verses, which in turn invoke the theology of intimate reconciliation which is the focus of the seasonal theology of consolation. The midrashic yoking of the "bride" and "clothing" verses also serves to link the rabbinic theology of the season to the ongoing mythic theology which is evidenced by the synagogue iconography.[52]

As I mentioned in chapter 1, it is difficult to discern the precise significance of the iconography of late antique synagogues. Scholars have posited conflicting readings of the layout of several synagogue mosaics in which the central mosaic panel is flanked by panels representing biblical scenes, temple images and a Torah niche. Zvi Weiss and Ehud Netzer have argued that the Sepphoris mosaic represents a stance toward the temple and temple times that is nostalgic and eschatological; Seth Schwartz has argued that it communicates a sense of the ongoing sacrality and efficacy of the post-destruction Jewish community and its ritual.[53] The two perspectives on exile in PRK chapter 13 provide an interesting analogue to these possibilities. In the midrash, the exile is presented both as a site of divine absence and as a site of intense divine presence and attention. The midrash's artful presentation of the paradox of exile invites us to think about the mosaic floors as icons that granted access to different, potentially contradictory stances toward the relationship between the contemporary community and the defunct temple.

Comparison to the synagogue setting also highlights the striking absence of the temple in PRK's commentaries on the haftarot of the Tisha b'Av season. Since, for the rabbis, Tisha b'Av was a day of mourning for the destroyed temples, one might expect that the Tisha b'Av season would provide the opportunity for reflection on the temple and expression of whatever sentiments its absence engendered. This expectation would be strengthened both by the importance of the temple elsewhere in rabbinic ideology and its significant presence in both the material culture of the late antique synagogues and the synagogue liturgy developed and codified by the rabbis themselves. Instead of using the Tisha b'Av season lectionary as an occasion to talk about the temple, however, the authors of PRK use it as an occasion to reiterate the narrative of sin-punishment-repentance-redemption and to develop a theology of consolation and of di-

---

52. I am not arguing that this pericope was composed for the synagogue setting or that its purpose was the linking or appropriation of a popular, mythic theology. Rather, I am suggesting that the pericope's midrashic linkage can be seen as being in conversation with the theology of the synagogue.

53. Weiss and Netzer, "Sepphoris Synagogues"; Schwartz, *Imperialism*, 252–59.

vine presence that is not at all hindered by the absence of the temple. Obviously, this latter notion is not unique to the midrashic commentaries of the Tisha b'Av season. The rabbinic development of functional substitutes for the temple cult is well documented.[54] However, other rabbinic texts, most importantly the statutory liturgy, express some nostalgia for the temple. It is the absence of this nostalgia, or of related fantasies of the eschatological rebuilding of the temple, that is striking. It is difficult to know how to read this silence. It may have been an attempt to deflect preoccupation with the temple in a season when it might have been particularly intense, or it might represent an attempt to offer a counterpoint to the ever-present concern with the temple expressed in the daily liturgy and the synagogue setting.

Conclusion

My analyses of PRK chapters 13 and 22 have demonstrated how the redactors of PRK use the arrangement of pericopes within chapters, and the strategies of the *petiḥta* and the *davar aḥer* to highlight and expand on themes which are articulated within the lectionary cycle. The redactors of PRK use these midrashic strategies to express these themes in didactic terms which are far more explicit than those of the lectionary cycle itself. In addition, while the midrashic strategies identify the themes of sin-punishment-redemption and the redemptive power of divine love with the texts of the lectionary cycle, the strategies also locate the lectionary texts and themes within the larger complex of written and oral Torah. By importing *petiḥta* verses and prooftexts along with their interpretations into the framework of the lectionary texts, the redactors of PRK assert that the themes which are appropriate to the Tisha b'Av lectionary cycle are parts of larger thematic currents which recur in other texts of Torah. The consideration of PRK in relationship to the iconography of the synagogue demonstrates that although the midrashim in PRK are products of the rabbinic academy, they resonate with the theological expressions of synagogue

---

54. Baruch Bokser, "Rabbinic Responses to Catastrophe: From Continuity to Discontinuity," *PAAJR* 50 (1983): 40–47; Michael Fishbane, "Substitutions for Sacrifice in Judaism," in *The Exegetical Imagination: On Jewish Thought and Theology* (Cambridge: Harvard University Press, 1998), 123–35; Nahum Glatzer, "The Concept of Sacrifice in Post-biblical Judaism," in *Essays in Jewish Thought* (University, AL: University Press, 1978), 48–57; Judah Goldin, "Three Pillars of Simeon the Righteous," *PAAJR* 27 (1958): 43–58; Jacob Neusner, "Map Without Territory: Mishnah's System of Sacrifice and Sanctuary," in *Method and Meaning in Ancient Judaism* (Missoula, MT: Scholars Press, 1979), 133–53.

culture. At the same time, however, comparison with the synagogue art highlights the striking absence of the temple from the Tisha b'Av season midrashim.

4

Eleazar Kallir's *Kedushtot* for the Sabbaths of Consolation

In the past several years, liturgical poetry has emerged as an important source of evidence for the study of Judaism in late antiquity. The piyyutim are among the few surviving Jewish texts of late antique Palestine that were not authored by rabbinic sages.[1] As a result, they provide rare testimony to the theology and thought-world of Jews other than the sages themselves. At the same time, the theological overlaps between the classical piyyutim and rabbinic literature, as well as the many cases of payyetanic (a *payyetan* is a liturgical poet) allusion to rabbinic traditions, attest to the significant influence of the rabbinic movement on Palestinian synagogue culture from as early as the fifth century CE. Eleazar Kallir's *kedushtot* for the Sabbaths of consolation, which were composed during the late sixth or early seventh century CE, provide examples of this mediating role.[2] As I will demonstrate, these poems echo the rabbinic material in their emphasis on the redemptive nature of God's romantic love for Israel and in their interest in, and expansion of, the dialogue between God and Israel. At the same, the piyyutim diverge from the lectionary and the midrashim in PRK in their expressions of desire for the imminent restoration of the temple and the ingathering of the exiles.

---

1. See chapter 1, n. 22 (p. 8).
2. For Seth Schwartz, who has articulated one of the most minimalist evaluations of the influence of the rabbinic movement, the piyyutim provide the first major evidence of rabbinic influence in the synagogue (Schwartz, *Imperialism*, 263).

Sitz im Leben

The piyyutim were composed as substitutions for, or insertions into, the statutory prayers of the sabbath and festival liturgies.[3] The relationship of the poems to the liturgy is clear from the poetic texts themselves. Each type of piyyut corresponds to a particular form and section of the liturgy. For example, the piyyutim of the *yotzer* genre were appended to, or replaced, the first blessing before the *shema*. The *kedushta* genre was appended to, or replaced, the first three blessings of the *amidah* on occasions when the *kedushah* prayer was recited. In both manuscript and printed versions, the piyyutim often end with the closing lines of the prayers to which they correspond, thus identifying clearly their place within the service. While the texts of the piyyutim themselves identify their place in the liturgy, the actual manner of recitation is more difficult to discern. According to general synagogue practice, each individual recited the seven benedictions of the sabbath and festival *amidah* silently and then the prayer leader repeated them. Ezra Fleischer suggests that prayer leaders began to recite piyyutim instead of repeating the fixed texts of the statutory prayers. Thus, the practice of piyyut developed in order to avoid the boredom of repetition and to integrate thematic material from the lectionary or from the life of the congregation into the *amidah*.[4]

While Fleischer's hypothesis explains when the piyyutim were recited and gives a pragmatic reason for their recitation, few scholars have investigated the liturgical function of the piyyutim.[5] What religious or communal need did they address? What liturgical function did they fulfill? While these questions lie outside the scope of my project, I will address them insofar as they relate to my analysis of the piyyutim and to the history of

---

3. For comprehensive surveys of the function and form of the piyyutim, see Shulamit Elizur, *Ha-piyut ha-Ivri be-Erets Yisra'el uva-mizraḥ* (Jerusalem: Hebrew University Press, 1991); Fleischer, *Hebrew Liturgical Poetry*; Abraham Habermann, *Ha-piyut: mahuto ve-hitpatḥuto* (Tel Aviv: Mifal hashikhpul, 1967); idem, *Toldot ha-piyut veha-shirah* (Ramat Gan: Masada, 1972); Aaron Mirsky, *Hapiyut: The Development of Post-biblical Poetry in Erets Yisrael and the Diaspora* (Jerusalem: Magnes Press, 1990) (Heb.); idem, *Reshit ha-piyut* (Jerusalem: Jewish Agency, 1965); Yehuda Ratzaby, *Texts and Studies in Orient Liturgical Poetry* (Jerusalem: Misgav Yerushalayim, 1991) (Heb.); Leon Weinberger, *Jewish Hymnography: A Literary History* (London: Littman Library of Jewish Civilization, 1998); Yahalom, *Poetic Language*.

4. Fleischer, *Hebrew Liturgical Poetry*, 57.

5. Shulamit Elizur discusses the aesthetic experience of the *kedushta*'s audience in "The Congregation in the Synagogue and the Ancient Qedushta," in *Knesset Ezra* (ed. S. Elizur, et al.; Jerusalem: Yad Izhak Ben-Zvi, 1994), 171–90) (Heb.).

scholarship thus far. The myths of origin of the practice of piyyut give some clues to later authorities' views regarding the function of piyyut. Pirqoi b. Baboi (eighth century) states that "they [the rulers of Palestine] decreed that the Jews could not recite the *shema* or pray [the *amidah*], but they did allow them to enter on sabbath morning to speak and to sing *ma'amadot*."[6] This view is echoed by Samau'al ibn Yahyā al-Maghribī, a twelfth-century Jewish convert to Islam, in his polemical *Ifḥām al-Yahūd* (The Silencing of the Jews): "When the Jews saw that the Persians persisted in obstructing their prayer, they invented invocations into which they admixed passages from their prayers, and they called these *hizana*."[7] While Samau'al ibn Yahyā al-Maghribī's version identifies the Persians as the persecutors, the substance of these two accounts is the same: piyyutim originated as substitutes for prohibited prayers. By suggesting that the piyyutim were composed as substitutions for statutory prayers, the myths imply that they perform the same function as these prayers.

R. Judah b. Barzilai of Barcelona (twelfth century) offers a different version of the myth of origin in his *Sefer ha'itim*. He states that piyyut was

> only introduced at a time of persecution because they were not able to speak of the words of the Torah, for the enemy decreed that Israel might not study the Torah. Therefore the sages among them introduced as part of the prayer service the practice of reciting and teaching to the ignorant the laws of each festival in its time and the laws of the holy days and the Sabbaths and the details of the commandments in the form of songs of praise and thanksgiving and rhymes and piyyut.[8]

According to Judah b. Barzilai, piyyut replaces prohibited Torah study, not prohibited prayer. Consequently, this text suggests that piyyut's function is primarily pedagogical, not liturgical. The discrepancy among the sources accurately reflects the multifaceted nature of piyyut. As substitutes for the statutory prayers, piyyutim are certainly prayer. As meditations or commentaries on the lectionary texts of the day, they are

---

6. Louis Ginzberg, *Ginze Shekhter* (New York: Jewish Theological Seminary, 1929), vol. 2, 551–52. This myth of origin resembles the myth of origin of the haftarah cited by Abudarham (fourteenth century). He states that the haftarah came into being during the period of Syrian persecution, when the Jews were prohibited from reading Torah. Both myths of origin communicate discomfort with perceived liturgical innovation. Piyyut and haftarah are justified as responses to outside pressures which made innovations necessary rather than as manifestations of internal desires for change.

7. Elbogen, *Jewish Liturgy*, 223.

8. Ibid., 222.

also works of biblical interpretation. At the same time, they are also poetry and participate in the functions of poetic language.[9]

The multifaceted nature of piyyut has important repercussions for Jewish worship. While there was certainly overlap between biblical and liturgical texts, the mishnaic and talmudic sources treat prayer and the ritual recitation of the Bible as distinct activities which are governed by distinct sets of rules and assumptions.[10] The recitation of piyyutim which dealt with the themes of the lectionary served to blur the boundary between prayer and Torah. Through the recitation of the piyyutim, the themes of the lectionary texts became, in effect, themes of the day. The issues of the lectionary texts, as they were translated into the language of prayer and poetry by the liturgical poets, came to permeate the entirety of the worship service, not just the ritual recitation of the biblical texts. This function is particularly relevant to the Tisha b'Av season. As I mentioned above, with the exception of the penitential rituals of the three weeks and the ninth of Av itself, the season is not marked by any particular practices. Through the piyyutim, the liturgical poets transformed the statutory prayers into a season-specific ritual. In so doing, they contributed to the differentiation of the ten weeks surrounding Tisha b'Av as a discrete season with its own theological meaning.

In the case studies that follow, I will focus on the way piyyut functions as a nexus of prayer, poetry and exegesis. In particular, I will focus on the ways in which rhyme and allusion function both as poetic devices and as strategies for the interpretation of the lectionary texts.

Piyyut as Prayer

In many ways, the piyyutim which I analyze below bear little relationship to the statutory prayers to which they correspond. Unlike the first blessings of the *amidah,* the bodies of the piyyutim are not devoted to praise of God, rehearsal of God's saving deeds, or supplication. The first poem consists of God's consolatory words to Zion. The second consists of Zion's

---

9. The medieval debates over piyyut further reinforce the genre's location at the intersection of prayer, Torah study and poetry. See, for example, the critique of R. Natronai (ninth century) cited in Lawrence Hoffman, *The Canonization of the Synagogue Service* (Notre Dame: University of Notre Dame Press, 1979), 68, and Abraham Ibn Ezra's comment in his commentary on Eccl 5:1.

10. The rules governing the Torah reading ritual appear in m. Meg and the talmudic commentaries on it as well as in the post-talmudic tractate Soferim. The subject of prayer is discussed primarily in m. Ber and the commentaries on it.

complaint against God, and the third consists of more divine consolation.[11] Despite these differences, the piyyutim do manifest prayer-like attributes:

1. The final verses of each of the poems are verses of supplication which correspond to the themes of the statutory prayers. These verses represent the most straightforward accommodation of the piyyutim to the genre of statutory prayer.

2. The stance of the poet is that of a prayer leader. He speaks in the voice of the community, not in his own individual voice.[12]

3. Unlike the recitation of scripture or midrash, the piyyutim are not didactic. Rather, they are lyrical, emotional texts which seem more concerned with the emotional tenor invoked by a theological idea or liturgical moment than with the content of the idea itself. This lyricism and emotional expression echo the psalms, which probably originated as liturgical compositions and were eventually introduced into the standard liturgy.

4. As I will discuss below, the themes and concerns of the prayers which the piyyutim parallel are present in the piyyutim, albeit in more indirect forms.

5. As Raymond Scheindlin has noted, the litanies of biblical verses which appear between the third and fourth stanzas of the first three poems of the piyyutim of the *kedushta* genre resemble the *malkhuyot, zikhronot,* and *shofarot* liturgies. These liturgies, which are recited during the *amidah* of Rosh Hashanah, are comprised of strings of biblical verses which make reference to the themes of divine kingship, divine remembrance or attention, and the blowing of ram's horns. Scheindlin also suggests that the liturgies for fast days described in m. Taan 2:1–4 are related as well. There, the *zikhronot* and *shofarot,* as well as a series of Psalms, are identified as blessings. From the evidence of the mishnaic text and the Rosh Hashanah liturgy, Scheindlin hypothesizes that one form of early Jewish prayer consisted of the recitation of biblical verses which were linked by a word or

---

11. Aaron Mirsky (*Reshit ha-piyut,* 59) identifies divine address as one of the central features of piyyut. While the piyyutim do often address God, these poems demonstrate that the generalization is not absolute.

12. Ibid., 60.

theme. He suggests that the litanies of verses which appear in the piyyutim might be examples of this genre of prayer which became incorporated into the piyyut genres.[13]

Piyyut as Poetry

While the midrashim discussed in chapter 3 and the poems discussed below correspond to the same set of lectionary texts and are designated for the same lectionary season, their roles in the Tisha b'Av complex are quite distinct. The midrashim are didactic texts whose *raison d'être* is the interpretation of the biblical text and the articulation of rabbinic theology and ideology. They argue for a particular understanding of a prooftext or assert a particular notion about God, Israel, or the relationship between them. In contrast, the piyyutim are essentially poetic texts. They are not primarily concerned with making an argument.[14] Rather, the poems are dominated by the emotive, conative (vocative), and poetic functions of language.[15] The poems articulate the emotions of the speaker, supplicate and exhort the listener, and use the features of the poetic composition itself to evoke moods and images. While the midrashim are interpretations of the biblical texts, the piyyutim are meditations on them; they are poems which articulate the emotions and moods of the lectionary text and the lectionary moment.

Kedushtot for the Sabbaths of Consolation by Eleazar Kallir

Kallir worked in Palestine during the late sixth to early seventh century. He wrote poems for all of the festivals, special sabbaths, festive weekdays,

---

13. Raymond Scheindlin in conversation, August 1998.

14. Some piyyutim did serve a didactic function. L. Weinberger (*Jewish Hymnography*, 7) notes that both Yannai and Pinhas Hacohen (seventh century) incorporated laws regarding festivals in their piyyutim.

15. The terminology is used by Roman Jakobson in "Linguistics and Poetics," in *Style in Language* (ed. T. A. Sebeok; Cambridge: MIT Press, 1967), 350–77. Jakobson argues that while most instances of language are dominated by the referential function of language, poetry is dominated by the poetic function—a focus on the nature of the message itself. He describes the poetic function as a "set toward the message as such, focus on the message for its own sake" ("Linguistics," 356). In poetry, as in prose, various functions of language operate simultaneously. However, the poetic function becomes dominant while the referential function recedes.

and fasts. His work was disseminated widely, and the structure and style of his poems became the definitive model for generations of poets. Poem cycles by Kallir are extant for six of the sabbaths of consolation.[16]

* * *

The *kedushta* is one of the most elaborate piyyut forms. *Kedushtot* were composed for the morning liturgies of sabbaths and festivals during which the *kedushah* prayer is recited. While there are differences among the extant *kedushtot*, the general structure is as follows:

1. The first three poems of the *kedushta* form a discrete unit. The poems are connected to one another through their symmetrical structures, use of acrostics, biblical litanies, and explicit connection to the first three blessings of the *amidah* and the first three lines of the lectionary text.

2. The fourth and fifth poems also comprise a discrete unit. According to Ezra Fleischer, this part of the *kedushta* structure is mysterious. It is not clearly liturgically linked nor does it seem to be motivated by particular structural conventions.[17] In the *kedushtot* that I analyze here, this unit serves to further expand on the themes articulated more precisely in the first three poems.

3. Fleischer describes the final unit of the *kedushta* as the "pericopes of expansion." This unit consists of two or more poems and ends with a transition to the *kedushah* itself.[18]

A comprehensive analysis of the entire corpus of Kallir's *kedushtot* for the sabbaths of consolation is beyond the scope of this chapter. I have chosen to analyze three poems from two *kedushtot*: the first poem (*magen*) for the first sabbath of consolation, and the first and second poems (*magen* and *meḥayeh*) for the second sabbath of consolation. I have limited my study to poems from the first sections of the *kedushtot* because these are the poems which are most explicitly linked to the lectionary texts both through their opening lines and through the inclusion of the lectionary verses in the litanies of biblical verses. I chose these three poems because

---

16. The kedushtot have been edited, annotated and published by Shulamit Elizur in *Kedushah ve-shir: kedushta'ot le-shabtot ha-neḥamah le-Rabbi El'azar bi-Rabi Kilir* (Jerusalem: Magnes Press, 1988). The cycle for the final sabbath is missing. In addition, the cycle for the sixth sabbath is quite fragmentary.
17. Fleischer, *Hebrew Liturgical Poetry*, 145–47.
18. Ibid., 147–51.

they contain interesting treatments of the theme of the romantic love between God and Israel, and because they represent rich examples of the use of rhyme and allusion.

Rhyme

Rhyme is one of the salient features of the *kedushtot*. It serves as a structuring device for individual stanzas and serves to distinguish stanzas from one other. In addition, rhyme is one of the strategies through which poets communicate meaning.

In "One Relation of Rhyme to Reason," W. K. Wimsatt writes:

> The words of a rhyme, with their curious harmony of sound and distinction of sense, are an amalgam of the sensory and the logical, or an arrest and precipitation of the logical in sensory form; they are the icon on which the idea is caught.[19]

Rhyme is based on the similarity of sound between words that are distinct in meaning. Even though two words mean different things and are separated spatially/temporally and grammatically within a poem, rhyme brings them together in the mind/ear of the reader.[20] Rhyme then leads the reader to give "logical" sense to a "sensory" similarity or relationship between the rhymed words. In other words, in the case of a rhyme, your ear tells you the words belong together and then your brain has to figure out the meaning of the conjunction. The meaning generated by the rhyme stands in a particular relationship to the meanings generated by the non-poetic functions of the text or utterance. Wimsatt suggests that verse and rhyme "impose upon the logical pattern of expressed argument a kind of fixative counterpattern of alogical implication."[21] While his language of "logic" and "alogic" has become outmoded in literary studies, Wimsatt's description of rhyme as a counterpattern of implication which exists alongside the "logical" meaning or "content" of a poem is quite apt.[22]

---

19. William K. Wimsatt, *The Verbal Icon: Studies in the Meaning of Poetry* (Lexington: University of Kentucky Press, 1954), 165.
20. While the relationship between words on the page is a spatial one, the reader often experiences the distance between words in temporal terms. Similarly, in the case of poetry, a reader will often experience the text aurally by hearing the words in his/her head.
21. Wimsatt, *Verbal Icon*, 154.
22. For lack of a better term, I will use the phrase "content meaning" to connote the meaning communicated by the plain grammatical and syntactic arrangement of the words. I differentiate "content" meanings from the meanings and messages

In some cases, the relationship between the rhymed words proves to be exclusively one of sound. In these cases, attention to the poetic counterpattern articulated by the rhyme does not enhance the meaning of the poem. In other cases, however, the rhyme pattern articulates a message independent of that of the "content" message of the poem. In the analyses which follow, I will describe the rhyme patterns of the three poems and will analyze the ways in which they contribute to the meanings of the texts.

Allusion

Like rhyme, allusion is a central feature of classical piyyut in general, and Kallir's *kedushtot* in particular. In the *kedushtot*, Kallir employs a wide range of intertextual references. The litanies of biblical verses which separate the penultimate and final stanzas are verbatim quotations of complete verses. In the poems themselves, Kallir will, at times, quote fragments of biblical verses. At other times, he will opt for a paraphrase which is a near-quotation of a biblical phrase. In still other cases, Kallir will not use biblical language at all but will evoke a common biblical image or trope.[23] These allusions serve as a powerful strategy for enhancing and nuancing the "referential" or "content" meaning of the poem.

While rhyme works by activating relationships among separate words in a poem, allusion functions by activating a connection between a feature of the alluding text and a feature of a separate, prior text. Ziva Ben-Porat describes a four step process of allusion: The reader

1. recognizes the marker as a feature from another text;

2. identifies the evoked texts;

3. brings certain features of the evoked text to bear in his/her reading of the alluding text. In this stage, the recognition of the role of the marker in the alluded text affects the reader's understanding of the alluding text;

---

which are generated by strategies such as rhyme, meter, sound patterns and allusion.

23. See John Hollander, *The Figure of Echo: A Mode of Allusion in Milton and After* (Berkeley: University of California Press, 1981), and Richard B. Hays, *Echoes of Scripture in the Letters of Paul* (New Haven: Yale University Press, 1989) for discussions of various degrees and types of intertextual reference and the allusive force of each.

4. not only reads the alluding marker in light of the alluded text but makes broader connections between the alluding text and the alluded text.[24]

John Hollander describes this final, most comprehensive form of allusion, as metalepsis. He describes metalepsis as follows: "When a literary echo links the text in which it occurs to an earlier text, the figurative effect of the echo can lie in the unstated or suppressed (transumed) points of resonance between the two texts . . ."[25] Or, as Richard Hays describes it,

> Allusive echo functions to suggest to the reader that text B should be understood in light of a broad interplay with text A, encompassing aspects of A beyond those explicitly echoed . . . Metalepsis . . . places the reader within a field of whispered or unstated correspondences.[26]

According to Ben-Porat, Hollander, and Hays, allusion—in its most powerful form—enables the invocation of the entire range of meaning and significance of the invoked text. Whether or not this potential is actualized depends on the power of the connection and the ear of the reader. In some cases, the reader will not recognize the marker as an allusion at all or will recognize the marker as an allusion but not know its source. In other cases, the recognition and identification of the alluded text might not change the reader's interpretation of the alluding text significantly. Even in cases where the full activation of the alluded text does not occur, however, allusion still serves several functions: it bolsters the authority of the author; it keeps older words alive and relevant; it creates a link between the author and the audience on the basis of shared knowledge; it shows the erudition of the author and locates him/her within a tradition; it is fun; and in some cases it makes up for the linguistic poverty of the alluding text.[27]

In the case of piyyut, metalepsis, or the fullest activation of the alluded text, invokes the alluded texts in both their biblical and midrashic contexts. Often, a particular epithet or allusion will make sense only if the reader is aware of the underlying midrashic tradition.[28] Thus, it is legitimate and even necessary to be sensitive to the midrashic resonances of

---

24. Ziva Ben-Porat, "The Poetics of Literary Allusion," *PTL: A Journal for Descriptive Poetics and Theory of Literature* 1 (1976): 110–11.
25. Hollander, *Figure*, 115.
26. Hays, *Echoes*, 20.
27. Sommer, *Prophet*, 18–20.
28. For the use of midrashic traditions in the piyyutim, see Zvi Meir Rabinowitz, *Halakhah ve-agadah be-fiyute Yanai: mekorot ha-payetan, le-shono u-tekufato* (Tel Aviv: Keren Alexander Kahut, 1965); Joseph Yahalom, *Poetry and Society in Jewish Galilee of Late Antiquity* (Tel Aviv: ha-Kibbuts ha-meuhad, 1999) (Heb.).

biblical allusions invoked within the poems. At the same time, not all midrashic valences enhance the meaning of the allusion. In the case studies that follow, I will analyze the various levels of allusion that occur within the poems. In the footnotes, I will indicate intertextual echoes which seem to be low-level allusions. These references perform the rhetorical functions of allusion in general but do not significantly enhance the meaning of the poem. In my analyses, I will focus on those cases in which the activation of the alluded text within both its biblical and rabbinic contexts enhances the meaning of the poem. To a certain degree, my judgment as to the power of an allusion and the relevance of midrashic context is subjective. As a rule, I focus on those midrashic traditions which are articulated in the midrashim relating to the Tisha b'Av season.[29] These allusions are more likely to be relevant because they appear elsewhere in the same lectionary context that generates the piyyutim. In addition, multiple iterations of, or allusions to, particular midrashic traditions within the larger corpus of Tisha b'Av season literature might suggest that these traditions were part of the public discourse of the season.

Case Study 1
Magen for *Kedushta* to Shabbat Naḥamu[30]

אִתִּי מִלְּבָנוֹן לֹא תֵבוֹשִׁי
בִּגְדֵי עוֹזֵךְ בְּכָבוֹד לִבְשִׁי
גּוֹיִים בְּרַגְלַיִךְ תִּדְרְכִי וְתָדוּשִׁי
דְּגָלַיִךְ אֲעַדֶּה שֵׁשׁ וָמֶשִׁי

הִתְנַעֲרִי בַּת צִיּוֹן מֵעָפָר
וְקוּמִי עֲטִי מַלְבּוּשׁ שַׁפָּר
[ז]רֶךְ הָאַחֲרוֹן מִן הָרִאשׁוֹן יְשׁוּפָּר
חֶטְאֵךְ יוּתַם וּכְעָב יְכוּפָּר

טִירוֹתַיִךְ אֲשֶׁר בְּאַפִּי הוּעָמוּ
יָקְדוּ בְחֵמָה וּבְכָלָה הֻזְעָמוּ
כָּבוֹד יַעֲטוּ וּמִפִּי יְרֻחָמוּ

---

29. Lam R., Lam Z., PRK 113–22 and Pes R. 28–37.

30. I have reproduced the Hebrew texts of this and the next case study from Elizur, *Kedushah*, 13–14, 32–34. The English translations are mine. I have translated the poems as literally as possible but have not preserved the rhyme or meter of the Hebrew.

לָהֶם הַשְׁמִיעוּ נַ[חֲמוּ] נַ[חֲמוּ]

ככ[תוב] (יש׳ מ, א): נ[חמו] נ[חמו] עמי [יאמר אלהיכם]
ונא[מר] (תה׳ צד, יט): ברב שרעפי בקר[בי תנחומיך ישעשעו
נפשי]
ונא[מר] (איוב ו, י): ותהי זאת (!) נחמתי ואסלדה בחילה לא יחמל
כי לא כיחדתי אמרי קדוש
ונא[מר] (יש׳ סו, י): שמחו א[ת] ירוש[ל]ם וגילו בה כל אהביה
שישו אתה משוש כל המתאבלים עליה]
ונא[מר] (שם יא): למען ת[ינקו] וש[בעתם] מ[שד] תנחמיה
[למען תמצו והתענגתם מזיז כבודה]

כְּבוֹדָהּ עַל כֹּל יִתְעַלֶּה
וּכְבוֹדָךְ בָּהּ כְּאָז תִּגָּלֶה
יָמֵינוּ כִּימֵי קֶדֶם תְּמַלֵּא
וּבְעוֹז מָגִנָּךְ בְּכָבוֹד [נ]תְעַלֶּה

ב[רוך . . . מגן אברהם]

With me from Lebanon[31] you will not be ashamed,[32]
Don in glory your garments of strength,
You will trample and you will tread nations with your feet,[33]
I will adorn your banners[34] with silk and fine linen.

Shake yourself free from dust, daughter Zion,
And rise.[35] Wrap [yourself in] a garment of beauty,

---

31. Lebanon is an epithet for Israel which derives from Song 4:8.

32. The exact phrase in the f.s. impf. appears in Isa 54:4 and Zeph 3:11. Isa 54:4 is part of the fifth haftarah of consolation.

33. Vocabulary from the prophecy of restoration and redemption in Mic 4:13 ("Arise and trample, daughter Zion, for I will make your horns iron and your hoofs bronze") appears throughout the first two stanzas. Kallir may have alluded to this verse both because of its theme and because of the use of the epithet, "daughter Zion."

34. Banners are often an epithet for the tribes in piyyut.

35. This verse alludes heavily to the lectionary texts of the Tisha b'Av cycle. Isa 52:2 states, "Shake yourself free from dust! Rise! Sit! Jerusalem." The epithet "daughter Zion" appears eight times in the Tisha b'Av lectionary cycle: Isa 52:2; Lam 2:1, 4, 8, 10, 13, 18; 4:22. The piyyut verse is a direct reversal of Lam 2:10 ("Sit on the ground and be silent, elders of Daughter Zion. Raise dust upon your heads . . .").

Your last crown will be more beautiful than your first.
Your sin will be finished and atoned for like a cloud.[36]

Your towers that were darkened in my anger,[37]
They burned in anger and were utterly destroyed in fury.
They will wrap (themselves) in glory and will be comforted
    from my mouth.
To them announce: Comfort! Comfort!

As it is written (Isa 40:1): *Comfort, comfort my people, says your God.*
And it is said (Ps 94:19): *When my inner cares are many, your consolations soothe my soul.*
And it is said (Job 6:10): *And this [sic][38] will be my consolation as I writhe in pain that will not be soothed; I did not deny the words of the Holy One.*
And it is said (Isa 66:10): *Be glad over Jerusalem and rejoice in her, all who love her! Rejoice in her joy, all who mourn over her!*
And it is said (Isa 66:11): *That you may suck and be satisfied from the breast of her consolations, so that you may suck and take pleasure from the breast/abundance of her glory.*

Her glory will rise up over all,
And you will reveal your glory in her as before.
You will fill our days like the days of old,
And in strength and in glory your shield will be raised up.

Blessed . . . shield of Abraham.

Within the liturgical setting, this poem would have served as the initial marker of the seven-week period of consolation. Since the *amidah* precedes the Torah service in the order of the liturgy, the recitation of this poem would have preceded the recitation of the haftarah itself and, consequently, would have been the first season-specific text of the consolatory period. The poem serves as an introduction to the period by providing a preview of the consolations which will be proffered during the seven

---

36. This verse is a paraphrase of Isa 44:22 ("I have erased your transgressions like a cloud and your sins like a cloud"), which appears in the literature of the Tisha b'Av season in Lam R. 1:1. There, the verse is a prooftext for the assertion that Isaiah responded to all of Jeremiah's words of doom with words of consolation.

37. In a poem by R. Judah b. Rabbi Benjamin (a Babylonian poet of the tenth century), "towers" is an epithet for the temple (Shulamit Elizur, *Piyute R. Yehudah bi-Rabi Binyamin* [Jerusalem: Nirdamim Press, 1988], 218). This association makes sense here as well.

38. The biblical verse reads "also" instead of "this."

sabbaths of consolation. At the "content" level, the poem consists of a catalogue of consolatory tropes common to rabbinic literature that are, for the most part, recurrent themes in the haftarot of consolation.[39] In the poem, Kallir focuses on tropes of consolation which are reversals of Lamentations' tropes of destruction. In so doing, Kallir underscores the dialogic and "antidote" relationship between Lamentations and the haftarot of consolation. By using tropes of consolation which remind the audience of Lamentations' tropes of despair, Kallir asserts that Tisha b'Av and the weeks of consolation are integral parts of a single spiritual journey from despair to consolation.

The first stanza announces four images of consolation: Israel will come with God from "Lebanon" (line 1). She will don garments of strength in glory (line 2). She will trample her enemies (line 3). God will adorn her banners/tribes (line 4). The first three images occur repeatedly in the haftarah cycle and are among the "measure-for-measure" reversals of Lamentations' woes. The first image collapses two of the central consolatory tropes of the Tisha b'Av cycle. God will bring Israel back from exile (Isa 40:10–11; 49:16–20, 22; 52:11–12; 60:4; 62:11) and God is with Israel and has not abandoned her (Isa 49:15; 50:1; 54:5–10; 51:12). This image serves as a reversal of Lamentations' lament over Zion's isolation (Lam 1:1, 2, 9, 16, 17, 21).[40]

The second image echoes the images of dressing in the lectionary texts. In the haftarot, Zion will don the exiles like an ornament (Isa 49:18); she is told to put on strength and to don garments of glory (Isa 52:1). In the final haftarah, the speaker states that God has clothed him with garments of salvation and has wrapped him in a cloak of righteousness just as a groom puts on a turban and a bride adorns herself with jewelry (Isa 61:10). In addition, the image of donning garments of strength reverses the tropes of soiled clothing and sackcloth and ashes which appears in Lam 1:9 and 2:10. The image of trampling one's enemies both echoes the tropes of vengeance and reverses the tropes of oppression and subjugation within the cycle.[41] The final image is the least allusive. God does not adorn

---

39. It is important to note that the level of explicit content is not necessarily the most accessible to piyyut audiences. Because much of the language and syntax of the poems is obscure, and because the piyyutim were sung, the audience may not have followed the "plot" of the poems easily. The message conveyed by rhyme patterns and melody might have been more accessible. See Elizur, "Congregation."

40. This image also parallels the return of God and the exiles to Zion in Isa 40:3–4.

41. Isa 51:23, 63:3; Lam 1:15.

the tribes anywhere in the haftarot but he does adorn the personified city (Isa 54:11–12).

The next stanzas add to the consolatory catalogue. In the second stanza, Zion is commanded to shake herself free from the dust (line 5), to arise and to don redemptive garments (line 6). She is also told that her sins will be forgiven (line 8). These themes are present in the haftarot of consolation where they function as reversals of Lamentations' tropes of destruction and despair. The first verse of the second stanza is a paraphrase of Isa 52:2: "Shake yourself free from the dust! Rise! Sit! Jerusalem." Within the Tisha b'Av lectionary cycle, this verse serves as an antidote to Lam 2:1 and 10, in which Zion and her inhabitants sit on the ground in despair. The second and third verses expand on the redemptive clothing theme while the third verse articulates the idea that the second "crown" or redemption will be more beautiful than the first. This assertion conflates two tropes from the haftarot of consolation. Throughout Second Isaiah, the prophet asserts that the return from Babylon will be a second exodus which will be more glorious than the first (Isa 52:12; 55:12).[42] In addition, the prophet uses dressing as a trope for restoration and redemption. Here the assertion that the second redemption will supersede the first is translated into the language of dressing and crowning. The final verse of the stanza asserts the complete forgiveness of Israel's sins. This theme, which occurs in Isa 40:2, 51:22, and 54:4 and 7, counters the descriptions of ongoing divine fury in Lamentations.

The third stanza introduces the themes of the rebuilding of the city itself. God acknowledges that he himself destroyed the city in his anger, and promises to restore it in mercy. These verses echo Isa 54:11–12, in which God promises to rebuild the ruins of the city. In addition, these verses serve as a "measure-for-measure" response to Lam 2:1–9, in which God reduces the city to ruins.

The litany of verses consists of five verses which contain the root נחם (comfort). The first is the opening verse of the haftarah and the last forms a bridge to the last stanza of the poem. The repetition of the root נחם serves to underscore the central theme and mode of the poem.

The final stanza continues the preview of consolation. The first two verses refer to the rising and revelation of God's glory. They echo the opening lines of the sixth haftarah of consolation: "Arise and shine! For your light is coming and the glory of God shines on you . . . and God will shine on you and his glory will appear over you" (Isa 60:1). The third line of the stanza is one of the poem's most obvious responses to Lamenta-

---

42. See chapter 2, n. 86 (p. 65).

tions: "Fill our days as the days of old."[43] In the context of the lectionary season, this line echoes the penultimate line of Lamentations: "Return us to you, YHWH, so that we may return. Renew our days as of old." While the "content" of the poem serves as an introduction to the themes of the seven weeks of consolation, the rhyme patterns and allusions of the poem elaborate on the emotional tenor of the target verse, Isa 40:1. Within the lectionary cycle, this verse introduces the trope of God as comforter and asserts that Zion's sins have been forgiven. Through the poetic devices of rhyme and allusion, Kallir elaborates on these tropes. The poetic features of the poem depict the dynamics of relation that ensue when God is portrayed as divine comforter; Zion is portrayed as personified mourner; and Zion's misfortune is understood as divine punishment.

Rhyme Patterns

The rhyme patterns of the poem articulate both the dynamics of the comforter/mourner relationship and the journey from sin to forgiveness. Through the repetition of certain grammatical forms, Kallir communicates information about the dynamics of power and connection which are imbedded in the assertion that God comforts Israel. Through sequences of rhymed words, Kallir reproduces the journey from sin to atonement.

The rhyme pattern of the first stanza asserts both the femininity of Zion and God's power over her. The first stanza is structured around the rhyme שִׁי (*shi*). With the exception of the last verse, each of the rhyming words is a verb in the feminine imperative or imperfect: תֵבוֹשִׁי־לִבְשִׁי־וְתָדוּשִׁי (*teivoshi*/you will [not] be ashamed—*livshi*/don—*vetadushi*/you will tread). The repeated occurrence of these verbal forms serves several functions. The repetition of the feminine forms reinforces the female personification of Zion/Israel. At the same time, the rhyme pattern succinctly communicates the power differential that exists between the divine speaker and the addressee. Through the series of imperatives and imperfects, Kallir asserts that God has the authority to command Zion and the power to predict her future.[44]

The second stanza is built on the rhyme פַּר (*par/far*). Unlike the ending שִׁי (*shi*) which has a distinct grammatical meaning, פַּר is grammatically insignificant. The phoneme itself does not communicate information. How-

---

43. According to the conventions of the kedushta form, the last line of the fourth stanza forms a bridge to the poem's corresponding blessing. In the kedushtot for the sabbaths of consolation, these verses rarely relate specifically to the themes of the rest of the poems. Consequently, the third line of the final stanza is, in effect, the last line of the poem.

44. In Hebrew, the imperative and the imperfect have overlapping valences.

ever, the movement from the first rhymed word, מֵעָפָר (*me'afar*/from dust) to the last rhymed word, יְכוּפָּר (*yekhupar*/will be atoned) expresses in shorthand the spiritual transformation which begins at Tisha b'Av and ends on Yom Kippur. The movement from מֵעָפָר (from dust) to יְכוּפָּר (will be atoned for) testifies to a journey from ashes, which are a sign of mourning and repentance, to complete forgiveness and atonement.[45] Although the words are separated syntactically within the poem, the rhyme brings them together in the ear of the audience. Consequently the sequence which extends from "dust" to "atonement" coexists alongside the syntactic sequence of words which continues to express the catalogue of consolation.

While the second stanza describes Israel's transformation, the rhyme pattern of the third stanza encapsulates the divine experience which is articulated during the Tisha b'Av cycle. It also reinforces the power relationship between God and Israel. Here, the structuring rhyme is more extensive than in the first two stanzas. Each word ends with the syllable מוּ־ (*amu*): הוּעָמוּ־הוּזְעָמוּ־יְרוּחָמוּ־נָחֲמוּ (*hu'amu*/were darkened—*huzamu*/were angrily destroyed—*yeruhamu*/will be comforted—*nahamu*/comfort). In addition, the first three rhyme words are either *pual* or *hophal* forms. Consequently, the vowel patterns of their final three syllables is identical: ־ֻ־ְ־מוּ. This rhyme pattern, like the one in the first stanza, is grammatically significant; it is the sign of the passive voice. The insistent repetition of the passive forms communicates the utter passivity of Zion/Israel. The people and their fate are at the mercy of God and are utterly subject to divine action.

The progression of rhymed verbs also recounts God's journey from anger to compassion, which is narrated by the Tisha b'Av cycle as a whole and underscored by the midrash. The first two verbs describe destruction and fury. The final two verbs describe compassion and consolation. Just as the second stanza narrates Israel's journey from lament and repentance to forgiveness, so too does the third stanza testify to God's journey from fury to compassion.

The rhyme scheme of the fourth verse is based on the syllables, ־ֶּה. While this phoneme is not grammatically significant, the roots of the rhymed words, יִתְעַלֶּה־תְּגַלֶּה־תְּמַלֵּא־נִתְעַלֶּה (*yitalleh*/will rise—*tegalleh*/you will reveal—*temalle*/you will fill—*nitalleh*/it will be raised up), are all common components of the consolatory lexicon. Ascension, redemptive

---

45. The movement imbedded in the rhymed words also resonates with Isa 40:1b which states that Zion's time of service is over and her sin has been forgiven.

revelation and fullness are all ingredients of Second Isaiah's vision of the time of redemption.[46]

The counterpatterns articulated by the rhyme schemes of the poem complement the "content" meaning of the poem in two ways. First, while the "content" of the poem describes *what* the consolation will be, the rhyme patterns describe *how* the consolation will be. The rhyme patterns place the poem's consolatory tropes and events within the context of the God-Israel relationship. God is the sole agent of both Zion's past punishment and her future redemption. The consolations take place alongside the simultaneous transformations that God and Israel undergo during the course of the Tisha b'Av cycle. As Israel travels from grief and repentance to atonement, God travels from fury to compassion. Both of these journeys are fitting narratives for the period between Tisha b'Av and Rosh Hashanah. They both describe the necessary changes that must occur before Israel and God are ready for reconciliation and renewal. The "content" meaning of the poem and its poetic meaning also complement each other liturgically. The explicit content of the poem seems to function more as an introduction to the weeks of consolation as a whole than as a meditation on Isa 40:1. The rhyme patterns, however, seem to relate more closely to the content of the verse.

Allusion

Like the rhyme patterns, the allusions deepen and nuance the "content" of the poem. Allusions within the piyyutim function like *petiḥtot* within the midrashim. They serve as vehicles for the importation of texts, images and themes into the body of the text. An effective allusion activates the alluded text in the mind of the reader. That text, along with its attendant associations, then becomes part of the reader's understanding of the alluding text. Within the *kedushtot,* there are many degrees of allusion. Certain allusions within the poems activate specific prior texts while the most powerful allusions activate entire constellations of images and ideas. In the discussion which follows, I will focus on a few potent allusions within the first poem.

Kallir opens the poem with a particularly powerful allusion: "With me from Lebanon" alludes to Song 4:8. For a hearer who recognizes the words as a quotation from Song of Songs, the phrase immediately situates the poem within the context of the romantic relationship between God and Israel.[47] The evocation of the love relationship between God and Israel

---

46. See Isa 40:1–23.
47. Gerson Cohen suggests that Song of Songs was understood as a text about the relationship between God and Israel even before it was included in the biblical

is particularly powerful at this point in the Tisha b'Av season. As I noted above, this *kedushta* is situated liturgically between Lamentations and the first haftarah of consolation. By opening the season of consolation with an allusion to Song of Songs, Kallir indicates a radical sea change in the description of the relationship between God and Israel. God was last described on Tisha b'Av as Zion's furious adversary. Suddenly, God speaks as her lover. Thus, the allusion to Song of Songs is simultaneously a strong rebuttal to Israel's accusations of divine abandonment and a signal to the synagogue audience that they have entered a new stage in the relationship with God.

For the hearer who not only recognizes the source of the allusion but can also fill in the rest of the verse, "With me from Lebanon, bride; come with me from Lebanon," the first line of the piyyut, which appears to be a grammatical fragment, now makes grammatical sense. Instead of reading, "With me from Lebanon, do not be ashamed," the verse reads, "[Come] with me from Lebanon, do not be ashamed." The rest of the alluded verse also reinforces the romantic trope. Not only does God summon Israel, he addresses her as his bride.

The allusion is most potent, however, if we read the verse with its midrashic valences. From as early as the tannaitic period, Song 4:8 was used as a prooftext to support the idea that God went into exile with Israel and would return with them. In the Mekhilta de-Rabbi Ishmael, *Pisḥa* 14, the midrashist reads Exod 12:41 ("On that very day all the hosts of YHWH went out of the land of Egypt") as evidence that God went to Egypt with Israel and also accompanied the people out. As part of the commentary on this verse, the midrash states:

> Thus you find that in every place that Israel was exiled, the *shekhinah*, as it were, was exiled with them. . . . And it says: *With me from Lebanon, bride.* Was she coming *from* Lebanon? Was she not going up *to* Lebanon? What does scripture mean by *With me* from *Lebanon*? Rather, this: I and you, as it were, were exiled from Lebanon, and I and you will go up to Lebanon.

This reading is generated by the preposition, "from" (מִ-). In rabbinic literature, Lebanon is a frequent epithet for the temple. Thus, the Song of Songs verse seems to mean, "Come with me from the temple, my bride."[48] The midrash asks why God is calling Israel *from* the temple. Shouldn't God be calling Israel *to* the temple? The midrash concludes that Song 4:8

---

canon ("The Song of Songs and the Jewish Religious Mentality," in *Studies in the Variety of Rabbinic Cultures* [Philadelphia: Jewish Publication Society, 1991], 3–18). The assumption that the God-Israel relationship is the subject of the Song underlies most midrashic interpretations of the biblical text.

48. See Song Z. 4:8 for an explanation of the epithet.

signifies that God and Israel were exiled from the temple and would also return together to the temple. In *Beshallaḥ* 7, the author of the Mekhilta interprets the verse as a reference to the future return from exile:

> And so you find that in the future, the exiles will only be gathered in as a reward for faith. As it is written: *With me from Lebanon, my bride; Look down from the top of Amana.*[49]

In the amoraic midrashim, Song 4:8 is interpreted in several ways. Most of these readings are compiled in Song R., where the verse is interpreted a follows:

> *With me from Lebanon, bride; Come with me from Lebanon.* The Holy One Blessed be He said: *Come with me from Lebanon.* There it teaches: They give a maiden twelve months from when her husband claims her to prepare herself. But I did not do this. Rather, when you were still busy with mortar and bricks, I leapt and redeemed you . . . The Holy One Blessed be He said to them, "When I exiled you to Babylon, I was with you." As it is written: *For your sake I will send to Babylon* (Isa 43:14). When you return to the chosen house in the future, I will be with you. As it is written: *With me from Lebanon, bride.* R. Levi said: Didn't scripture mean to say instead, "With me *to* Lebanon, my bride?" But you say *from* Lebanon! Rather, at first he will arise from the temple and afterwards he will vanquish the nations of the world. R. Berechia said: Within three hours, the Holy One Blessed be He will vanquish the evil Esau and his captains. What is the proof? *Now I will arise, says God. Now I will rise up, now I will lift up* (Isa 33:10).[50] Every time that Israel is oppressed in the dust, as if it could be said, he is also. And this is what Isaiah said: *Shake yourself free* (הִתְנַעֲרִי) *from dust, arise! Sit! Jerusalem* (Isa 52:2). At the same hour: *Be silent, all flesh, before YHWH* (Zech 2:17). Why? *For he rouses* (נֵעוֹר) *himself from his holy dwelling* (ibid.).[51] R. Aha said: Like a rooster which shakes its wings free from the ashes.

The first reading is generated by a pun between לְבָנוֹן (Lebanon) and לְבֵנִים (*levenim*, bricks). The midrash read Song 4:8 as "Come with me from *the bricks*, my bride." It explains this (new) verse by saying that unlike a human king who gives his bride a year to prepare herself for marriage, God took Israel to be his bride directly from the brickworks of slavery.[52] The implications of this reading are twofold. First, the midrash asserts that

---

49. אמנה (Amana) is being read as אמונה (faith). A parallel text appears in Mekhilta de-Rabbi Shimon bar Yochai 14:31.

50. Each occurrence of the word "now" is read as a reference to an hour.

51. The reading is based on the use of the root נער (to shake) in Isa 52:2 and Zech 2:17.

52. A parallel text appears in Exod R. 23:5.

espousal is the appropriate metaphor for the Exodus—romance is an appropriate trope for redemption. Second, the text asserts that God is so gracious and loves Israel so much that he married her even though she was still a slave.

The next reading of the verse is generated by the same "problem" which generated the reading in the Mekhilta. Here, the midrash explains the use of the preposition "from" by saying that after God returns to the temple, he will go out from the sanctuary and punish Israel's enemies. Song 4:8 refers to this mission of vengeance when it says "With me *from* Lebanon." This comment expands the midrashic valence of the verse to embrace the notion of divine vengeance on Israel's enemies. Thus far, Song R. has read Song 4:8 to be a prooftext for God's presence in exile, God's gracious romantic love for Israel which is manifest in his intervention on her behalf, and God's vengeance on Israel's enemies.[53]

The last unit of Song R. 4:8 brings together Song 4:8 and Isa 52:2, the verse which is alluded to in line 5 of the poem. According to the midrash, these two verses are synonymous—they both serve as prooftexts for the idea that God's experience parallels that of Israel. When Israel is in exile and wallowing in the dust, God too wallows in exile. When God rises up, Israel too arises in redemption.[54]

Song 4:8 also appears in the final pericope of PRK 22. There, the verse serves as one of the prooftexts for the assertion that Israel is called "bride" ten times. As I discussed in the previous chapter, this pericope asserts that God's romantic love for Israel is intimately linked to God's redemptive acts of intervention in history.[55]

The midrashic valences of Song 4:8 seem quite relevant to the poem. First, the verse is invoked in the Tisha b'Av midrashic complex in PRK 22. Second, the theme of God's presence in exile and God's loving devotion to Israel are central to the lectionary cycle and the midrashim which comment on it. By opening the cycle of *kedushtot* with a citation of Song 4:8, Kallir brings the theological notions which are associated with the biblical verse to bear on the poem itself. "With me from Lebanon" is not merely a divine summons to return from exile, it is also an avowal of the intensity of God's love for Israel and testimony to God's ongoing presence with Israel in exile. In addition, when read with the valence ascribed to it in PRK, the phrase "with me from Lebanon, my bride" invokes the idea that God's

---

53. Song 4:8 is also used as a prooftext for the idea that God accompanies Israel into exile, in Num R. 7:10, Exod R. 23:5, and Song Z. 4:8.
54. This reading of Isa 52:2 also appears in Gen R. 65:1.
55. See pp. 105–7 for an extended analysis of this pericope.

love for Israel is not only ongoing and intense, it is also ultimately redemptive.

This analysis demonstrates how an allusion to a "potent" biblical verse can serve as a means to introduce a range of themes into the meaning of the poem. When read as an allusion to Song 4:8 in its midrashic context, "With me from Lebanon" is no longer just an erudite epithet for Israel; it is a compact code which imports into the poem radical notions of divine sympathy, love and presence *vis-à-vis* Israel. While the plain sense content of the poem consists of rather prosaic tropes of consolation, the allusion activates the romantic consolation which, I have argued, undergirds the cycle.[56]

Litany of Biblical Verses

The litanies of verses which appear after the third stanzas in the first two poems of the *kedushtot* provide an interesting case study for the exploration of allusion in the piyyutim. In some cases, attention to the biblical and midrashic contexts of the verses enhances the meaning of the poem. However, in many cases the verses do not seem relevant to the surrounding poem. Their selection and inclusion seem to be based entirely on the presence of the theme word of the litany. These verses still fulfill certain literary functions. Within the poem, they serve to underscore the theme word. In addition, they fulfill the functions of all low-level allusions: they invoke the authority of the biblical text and place the poem and its poet within the biblical tradition. In the *magen* of the first *kedushta*, the verses of the litany all contain a form of the root נחם (comfort/console). The first verse is Isa 40:1, the opening verse of the haftarah. The second and third verses seem

---

56. The degree to which understanding of this allusion enhances the meaning of the poem raises the question of the original audience of the poem. Did Kallir expect that the majority of his audience would understand the midrashic allusions, or did he compose the poem to speak on two levels—an explicit level directed at the congregation as a whole, and an encoded level directed at the knowledgeable members? Ezra Fleischer suggests the latter. He argues that the poems operate on many levels simultaneously and that each poem contains enough accessible material to hold the attention of a lay audience (Fleischer, *Hebrew Liturgical Poetry*, 273–75). Shulamit Elizur has elaborated on this argument by suggesting that the kedushtot, including those of Kallir, move from more difficult poems to easier poems. She argues that the terse midrashic allusions that pepper the first and second poems of the kedushtot are often spelled out in later poems—most frequently in the fifth poems of the cycle ("Congregation," 184–89). While the kedushta for the first sabbath of consolation does conform linguistically and stylistically to the "hard to easy" pattern, the allusions in the first poems are not spelled out more explicitly later in the cycle.

to be relevant only because they include the root נחם.⁵⁷ The fourth and fifth verses are consecutive (Isa 66:10–11), and the root only appears in the second verse. However, the plain sense of both verses is relevant to both the themes of the piyyut and of the lectionary moment:

> Be glad over Jerusalem and rejoice in her, all who love her!
> Rejoice in her joy, all who mourn over her!
> That you may suck and be satisfied from the breast of her consolations,
> So that you may suck and take pleasure from the breast/abundance of her glory. (Isa 66:10–11)

These verses underscore the feminized and sexualized portrait of Zion which has been central to the lectionary cycle, the midrash, and the piyyut. Here, Zion is portrayed as a nursing mother and the addressees are her suckling children. The verses also underscore the shift from the grief of Tisha b'Av to the joy which will come at the end of the seven weeks of consolation. In the lectionary cycle, the exhortation to rejoice first occurs in the fifth week. The inclusion of these verses during the first week of consolation both foreshadows and hastens that exhortation.

The midrashic valences of Isa 66:10–11 are also relevant to the piyyut and to the lectionary cycle. In Song R. 1:4, Isa 66:10 appears with Isa 61:10 and 54:1 as an example of one of the ten expressions for joy used with regard to Israel.

In Lam Z. 1:28, the verse is used to redefine Tisha b'Av as a day of future rejoicing. In addition, the midrash identifies lamenting over Jerusalem as a precondition for participation in the messianic age:

> God will turn the ninth of Av into [a day of] joy, as it is said: *Thus says YHWH of hosts, the fast of the fourth and the fast of the fifth and the fast of the seventh and the fast of the tenth will become joy and gladness and good festivals for the house of Judah* (Zech 8:19). And he himself will build Jerusalem and gather the exiles within it, as it is said: *YHWH builds Jerusalem, he will gather the scattered of Israel* (Ps 147:2). R. Yohanan said: All who mourn over Jerusalem are worthy and will see her in joy, as it is written: *Be glad over Jerusalem and rejoice in her, all who love her! Rejoice in her joy, all who mourn over her!* (Isa 66:10). Everyone who does not mourn over her will not see her in her joy.

This midrash applies the trope of reversal, which undergirds the relationship between Lamentations and the haftarot of consolation, to Tisha

---

57. Ps 92:19 only appears twice in the midrashic literature: Mid Pss 92:6 and 119:38. In these cases, "consolations" is read as a reference to the sabbath (92:6) and to Torah (119:38). Neither comment is relevant to the themes of the piyyut. The third verse, Job 6:10, does not appear in the midrashic literature.

b'Av itself. Just as Lamentations' complaints are reversed in the haftarot of consolation, so too will Tisha b'Av itself be "reversed" in the messianic redemption. The day of mourning will be turned into a day of joy. In addition, the midrash identifies mourning over Jerusalem as a salvific religious act. Those who mourn for Jerusalem will participate in her messianic restoration. Those who don't, won't. This assertion represents a new attitude toward the value of exhortation and petition. Whereas the lectionary cycle itself, as well as PRK 22, asserts that lament and supplication can influence divine action and hasten redemption, this text asserts that participation in the lament will benefit the lamenter. Although this message is absent from the rest of the poem, it is certainly relevant to the themes of the Tisha b'Av season. The invocation of Isa 66:10–11 in the litany of verses not only serves to reinforce the message of consolation, it also serves to underscore the importance of participation in the liturgical season itself.

Relationship to the Kedushta *as a Whole*

While the first part of the *kedushta* resonates with the lectionary cycle and the interpretations of it in PRK, the rest of the poem cycle diverges from these other texts in two significant ways. Unlike PRK, Kallir identifies Jerusalem and the temple cult as central foci of his consolatory discourse. The fourth poem uses the mention of Jerusalem in Isa 40:1 as the trigger for a vision of the imminent restoration of Jerusalem as the seat of the temple, the site of pilgrimage and the dwelling place of God. Several of the other poems invoke the defunct sacrifices with great nostalgia and eagerly proclaim their restoration. For example, the final poem uses the language of Song of Songs to articulate a vision of God's return to the temple and the restoration of the cult. "When you return in mercy to the hills of spices to restore the altar of the incense spices, there you will comfort the mournful children." In addition, in the rest of the *kedushta* the disjunction between reconciliation and redemption, which characterized both the lectionary sequence and its midrashic treatment, is absent. These poems announce acts of salvation and restoration in dynamic and immediate language. For example, in the fourth poem, God announces that he *has* returned to Jerusalem in mercy to rebuild and re-establish its walls, etc. In the sixth poem, God announces that he will *quickly* return the exiles.

Summary

The first poem of the *kedushta* for the first sabbath of consolation underscores many of the central ideas and motifs of the haftarot of consolation in general and the first haftarah in particular. The "content" of the poem consists of a catalogue of consolations which both reverses the complaints of Lamentations and serves as a preview of the ensuing lectionary texts. The rhyme patterns of the poem articulate the dynamics of the God-Israel relationship and hint at the transformations that both God and Israel will undergo during the weeks of consolation. At the same time, the allusions within the poem underscore the romantic nature of the God-Israel relationship and hint at the redemptive potential of the romance. Finally, the litany of verses reinforces the themes of consolation and future redemption while underscoring the importance of continued participation in the liturgical season.

Case Study 2
Magen and *Meḥayeh* to Shabbat *Vatomar Tzion*

My second case study consists of the first two poems of the *kedushta* for the second sabbath of consolation. In liturgical terms, the poems correspond to the first two benedictions of the *amidah* and the first two verses (Isa 49:14–15) of the second haftarah of consolation. On the content level, these poems are treatments of the plain sense meanings of the biblical verses. The first poem elaborates on the trope of lamenting Zion and expands on her lament. The second poem elaborates on God's consoling response. The poetic features of the poems articulate a second layer of meaning which echoes the theology of the lectionary as a whole and the midrashim of PRK. The rhyme patterns and allusions of the first poem emphasize the pathos of Zion's condition. The poetic features of the second poem assert that God and Israel are partners in an intense romantic relationship which is essentially redemptive and consolatory.

Poem 1 (Magen)

אֵם הַבָּנִים כַּיּוֹנָה מְנַהֶמֶת
בְּלֵב מִתְאוֹנֶנֶת וּבְפֶה מִתְרַעֶמֶת
גּוֹעָה בִּבְכִי וּבְמַר נוֹאֶמֶת
דְּמָעוֹת מַזֶּלֶת וְדוֹמֶמֶת וְנִדְהֶמֶת

הִשְׁלִיכַנִי בַּעְלִי וְסָר מֵעָלַי
וְלֹא זָכַר אַהֲבַת כִּילוּלָיי
זֵרַנִי וּפִיְּזְדַנִי מֵעַל גְּבוּלָיי
חִידָה עָלַיי כָּל תּוֹלָלַיי

טְרָפַנִי כַּנִּידָה וּמִפָּנָיו הֲדִיחַנִי
יְקָשַׁנִי בְּכוֹבֶד וְל[א] הֱנִיחַנִי
כָּלוּ עֵינַיי בְּתוֹכָחוֹת וְיִכְּחַנִי
לָמָּה לָנֶצַח עֲזָבַנִי שְׁכֵחַנִי

ככתוב (יש׳ מט, יד): ותאמר ציון עז[בני] יי [ויי שכחני]
ונ[אמר] (איכה ה, כ): למה לנצח תש[כחני תעזבנו לארך ימים]
ונאמר (תה׳ לא, יג): נשכחתי כמת מל[ב הייתי ככלי אבד]
ונ[אמר] (תה׳ עט, ד): היינו חרפה לש[כנינו לעג וקלס לסביבותינו]
ונ[אמר] (איכה ה, כב): כי אם מאוס מאסתנו קצ[פת] על[ינו]
עד מאד

עַד מְאֹד אַל תִּזְנָחֵנוּ
וּמִנֶּגֶד עֵינֶיךָ אַל תַּד[י]חֵנוּ
יוֹצֵר אַתָּה וְחוֹמֶר אֲנַחְנוּ
בְּעֹז יְמִינְךָ גּוֹנְנֵנוּ

ב[רוך . . . מגן אברהם]

The mother of children moans like a dove,[58]
In her heart she mourns and in her mouth she is troubled.
She wails in weeping and in bitterness she speaks,
Tears flow and she is silent and struck dumb.

My husband cast me out and turned away from me;
He did not remember the love of my bridehood.[59]
He scattered me and dispersed me from my borders;
He causes all those who mock me to rejoice over me.

He cast me out like a menstruant and he pushed me away from before him,[60]
He trapped me heavily and did not give me rest.

---

58. "Mother of children" (אֵם הַבָּנִים) is a quotation of Ps 113:9.
59. This verse is an ironic reversal of Jer 2:1, the penultimate line of the first haftarah of rebuke ("I have remembered on your account the lovingkindness of your youth, the love of your bridal days").
60. Or, "He ravaged me like an unclean thing." The reference to Zion as a menstruant resonates with Lam 1:8: "Jerusalem sinned a sin, therefore she has become like a menstruant." In both the biblical text and the poem, the figure of the menstruant represents Zion, who is abused by God or her enemies.

My eyes overflow with rebuke; he has disputed against me.[61]
Why forever has he abandoned me, forgotten me?

As it is written (Isa 49:14): *And Zion said, "YHWH has forsaken me, and YHWH has forgotten me."*
And it is said (Lam 5:20): *Why have you forgotten us forever, abandoned us for all time?*
And it is said (Ps 31:13): *I have been forgotten like one who is dead, I have become like a broken vessel.*
And it is said (Ps 79:4): *We have become a disgrace to our neighbors, a laughingstock and a mockery to those that surround us.*
And it is said (Lam 5:22): *Rather, you have utterly rejected us, raged against us exceedingly.*

Do not despise us exceedingly,
And from before your eyes do not repel us.
You are [our] creator and we are [your] material,
With the strength of your right hand protect us!

Poem 2 (Meḥayeh)

מַה תִּתְאוֹנְנִי עָלַי יוֹנָתִי
נֶטַע חֶמֶד עֲרוּגַת גַּנָּתִי
שִׂיחַ פְּלוּלַיִךְ כְּבָר עָנִיתִי
עָטוּר בָּךְ כְּאָז חָנִיתִי

פָּנִיתִי אֵלַיִךְ בְּרַחֲמַיִּ הָרַבִּים
צָעוֹד בְּשַׁעַר בַּת רַבִּים
קָמַיִךְ אֲשֶׁ[ר] עָלַיִךְ מִתְרַבִּים
רִיעַשְׁתִּי הֱיוֹת כְּעָשָׁן כָּבִים

שְׁחוֹרְתִי לָעַד לֹא אֶזְנָחֵךְ
שֵׁינִית אוֹסִיף יָד וְאֶקָּחֵךְ
תַּמּוּ וְסָפוּ דְבָרֵי וִיכּוּחֵךְ
תַּמָּתִי לֹא אֶעֱזָבֵךְ וְלֹ[א] אֶשְׁכָּחֵךְ

ככת[וב] (יש׳ מט, טו): התשכח אשה עולה [מרחם בן בטנה
גם אלה תשכחנה ואנכי לא אשכחך]
ונ[אמר] (תה׳ קלז, ה): אם אשכחך ירושלם תש[כח] ימיני

---

61. "My eyes overflow" echoes Lam 2:11 ("My eyes overflow with tears").

ונ[אמר] (יש׳ נד, ז): ברגע קטון עזבתיך [וברחמים גדולים אקבצך]
ונ[אמר] (ש״א יב, כב): כי לא יטוש יי את עמו בע[בור] ש[מו]
הג[דול כי הואיל יי לעשות אתכם לו לעם]

לְעָם וּלְנַחֲלָה / לְשֵׁם וְלִתְהִלָּה
עֲשׂוֹתֵךְ כְּאָז בְּאַהַב חוֹלָה
הֱיוֹתֵךְ בְּגַנֵּךְ מִרְעֲנֶנֶת שְׁתוּלָה
טַלְלֵי חַיִּים לָךְ לְהַזִּילָה

ב[רוך . . . מחיה המתים]

Why do you lament about me, my dove,[62]
The precious planting of the bed of my garden?[63]
The petition of your prayer I have already answered,
I have encamped around you as before.

I turned to you in my great compassion,
Striding in the gate of *Bat-rabbim*.[64]
The enemies who multiplied against you
I have punished. They are extinguished like smoke.

My black one, forever I will not reject you,[65]
Again, I reach out my hand and I take you,
Complete and finished are the words of your dispute,

---

62. "My dove" is a term of endearment in Song 2:14, 5:2, and 6:9.

63. The reference to Israel as "precious planting" echoes the many uses of garden language in Song of Songs. In Song 4:12–16, 5:1, and 6:2, the garden is the site of, and metaphor for, the lovers' erotic encounters. The word "bed" appears in Song 5:13, which compares the male lover's cheeks to a bed of spices, and in Song 6:2, which uses the word as part of an extended sexual metaphor. The image of God as a gardener and Israel as a plant (vine, specifically) also appears in Isa 5 and Ezek 17. In Isa 5, God prepares the vineyard lovingly, but the grapes grow bad. In Ezek 17, the image of planting and re-planting is used to describe Israel's exile and return. Within the context of the Tisha b'Av cycle, the reference to God's garden resonates with Lam 2:6 in which God destroys his tabernacle "like a garden." Here, God's assertion that Zion is the precious planting of the furrow of his garden serves as a reversal of the scene of destruction in Lamentations.

64. Bat-rabbim is an epithet for Jerusalem that is based on Song 7:5 ("Your neck is like an ivory tower; your eyes are like the pools of Heshbon at the gate of Bat-rabbim").

65. The endearment, "my black one" is derived from Song 1:5, where the female lover describes herself saying , "I am black and comely."

> My perfect one, I will not abandon you and I will not forget you.[66]
>
> As it is written (Isa 49:15): *Can a woman forget her suckling child, not have compassion on the child of her womb? These may forget, but I will not forget you.*
> And it is said (Ps 137:5): *If I forget you, Jerusalem, let my right hand forget.*[67]
> And it is said (Isa 54:7): *For a brief moment, I forsook you; but with great compassion, I will gather you.*
> And it is said (1 Sam 12:22): *For YHWH will not cast away his people for his great name's sake; for God has determined to make you his people.*
>
> For a people and for a possession, for a name and for praise,
> Doing as you did before in lovesickness,[68]
> You are a shoot in your lovely garden.
> The dew of life will flow for you.
> Blessed . . . who gives life to the dead.

These poems echo the themes of complaint and consolation which recur throughout the texts of the Tisha b'Av season. The *magen* is an elaboration of the trope of lamenting Zion which appears in Isa 49:14. The first stanza of the poem describes the figure of Zion lamenting. The second and third stanzas relate her lament: God has abandoned her, cast her out, and caused her to suffer. The litany verses relate to the themes of forgetfulness and rejection. The final stanza of the poem implores God not to abandon the people, but to protect them with his right hand.

The *meḥayeh* consists of God's response to Israel's accusation of abandonment.[69] In the first stanza, God assures Israel that she need not complain because he has already answered her prayers. In the second stanza he vows to protect her and avenge her. In the third stanza, God addresses the issue of abandonment and assures Israel that her time of trial is over. He has taken her back and will never abandon or forget her. The litany of

---

66. The endearment "my perfect one" is an allusion to Song 5:2 and 6:9, where it is used by the male lover to address the female lover.

67. The plain sense of the Hebrew here is difficult. The Septuagint understands the Hebrew as a niphal (תִּשָּׁכַח). Other commentators emend the text to תִּכְחַשׁ, meaning "wither."

68. "In lovesickness" is an allusion to Song 2:5 and 5:8, where the female lover describes herself as "lovesick."

69. The thematic relationship between the two poems mirrors the thematic relationship between the first and second verses of the haftarah. Isa 49:14 is Zion's complaint; Isa 49:15 is God's response.

verses asserts God's faithfulness to Israel; the final stanza heralds a nostalgic return to an idyllic state of relationship between God and Israel.

In these poems, Kallir uses a wide range of semantic fields to describe the God-Israel relationship. He uses master/husband (בעל) language (line 5), language of exile (8), hunting (9–10), forensics (11), and creation (15). He also invokes the mythic language of God's right hand (16). In the second poem, he uses language of the garden (2, 15), prayer (3), the military and forensic realms(6–8, 11), compassion and forgiveness (4, 9–10, 11), and romantic love (14). While there are scattered uses of romantic, erotic language, this language does not dominate the "content" of the poem. Rather, the poems reflect the range of divine imagery which is familiar from the haftarot of consolation.[70] However, the rhyme schemes and potent biblical allusions underscore the intimate, romantic aspects of the God-Israel relationship and emphasize the redemptive potential of that romantic intimacy.

Rhyme Patterns

The rhyme scheme of the first poem underscores the portrait of Zion as a female victim. In the first stanza, the last word of each line ends in the syllables ־ֶמֶת (*emet*): מְנַהֶמֶת־מִתְרַעֲמֶת־נוֹאֶמֶת־וְנִדְהֶמֶת (*menahemet*/moans—*mitra'emet*/is troubled—*no'emet*/speaks—*venidhemet*/is struck dumb). The rhyme is echoed in the second and fourth lines of the stanza by the words מִתְאוֹנֶנֶת (*mit'onenet*/wails) and וְדוֹמֶמֶת (*vedomemet*/is silent). This rhyme scheme, which is based on the feminine singular form of the participle, serves to underscore the female identity of Zion.[71] In addition, the repetition of the rhyming syllable within related words of lament and distress (moans, is troubled, speaks [in bitterness], struck dumb) emphasizes Zion's despair. The rhymed words of lament stand out from the rest of the words of the poem, causing the reader/hearer to hear a litany of verbs of complaint and distress. The echoing of the rhyme in the words *mit'onenet* (mourns) and *domemet* (is silent) saturates the stanza with words of lament.

In the second stanza, the rhyme pattern again reinforces the personification of Zion and articulates her distress. The rhyme is based on the syllable ־ַי (*ay*; first person possessive suffix): מֵעָלַי־כִּלּוּלַיי־גְּבוּלַי־תּוֹלָלַיי (*me'alay*/from me—*killulay*/my bridehood—*gevulay*/my borders—*tolalay*/

---

70. Kallir may not be mirroring the haftarot in particular. Many of the images which he invokes appear throughout the biblical corpus.

71. Feminine grammatical forms do not always indicate female subjects. In this case, however, where the verbs are verbs of human action, the feminine verbal endings reinforce the female gender of the personified city.

those who mock me). This rhyme is echoed within the stanza in the word עָלַי (alay/me) in line 8. The repetition of the first person possessive suffix reinforces the personal, personified nature of the speaking Zion. In addition, the repeated *ay*-sound of the rhyme mimics the sound of wailing and creates a counter-current of keening within the stanza.

In the third stanza, the rhyme pattern emphasizes Zion's victimization by God. The rhyme is based on the syllables, חַנִי (*ḥani*): ־הִדִּיחַנִי־הֱנִיחַנִי־וִיכְּחַנִי־שְׁכֵחַנִי (*hiddiḥani*/pushed me away—*heiniḥani*/gave me rest—*vikkeḥani*/disputed against me—*shekheḥani*/forgotten me). The rhyme is echoed in the first, second and fourth lines by the words: טְרָפַנִי (*terafani*/cast me out), יְקָשַׁנִי (*yekashani*/trapped me) and עֲזָבַנִי (*azavani*/abandoned me). The persistent repetition of the first person object suffix (־נִי) reinforces Zion's description of her victimization throughout the stanza; she is the powerless object of another's (God's) actions. In the first three lines, she laments that God has rejected, entrapped, argued against, and forsaken her. The rhyme pattern culminates with the accusation of divine forgetfulness, "Why forever has he abandoned me, forgotten me (*shekheḥani*)," which is articulated by the opening verse of the haftarah (Isa 49:14).

The rhyme scheme of the final stanza marks a shift in speaker from Zion to the supplicating community.[72] The rhyme schemes of the first three stanzas underscored the solitude of the speaker. The grammatical forms of the rhymed syllables in these stanzas assert that the words are being spoken by a single individual. In the context of the lament, this grammatical marker of singleness is significant because it underscores Zion's isolation.[73] In contrast to these verses, the rhyme scheme of the final stanza is based on the first person plural ending, נוּ (*nu*): ־תִּזְנָחֵנוּ־תַּדִּ[י]חֵנוּ־אֲנַחְנוּ־גּוֹנְנֵנוּ (*tiznaḥenu*/despise us—*taddiḥenu*/repel us—*anaḥnu*/we—*gonenenu*/protect us). This rhyme scheme articulates a transition from isolation to communal expression, thereby indicating an end to Zion's isolation.[74]

The rhyme scheme of the *meḥayeh* foregrounds the conscientious, dialogic nature of God's response to Zion. This foregrounding mirrors the theology of the lectionary cycle itself, where God's meticulous response to Zion functions as a sign of God's devotion and reconciliation. In this

---

72. The shift to the first person plural in the final stanzas of the *magen* and *meḥayeh* occurs frequently in the Kallir's *kedushtot*. In the present case, the shift to the first person plural is emphasized through the rhyme pattern.

73. Zion's isolation is a central trope in Lamentations. See pp. 47–48.

74. This pattern also has echoes in Lamentations, in which chapters 1–4 are uttered by single speakers while the final chapter is articulated in the first person plural.

poem, Kallir uses rhyme patterns and echoes of Zion's complaint in the *magen* to assert that God is responding attentively to Zion's concerns. In the *magen*, the rhyme schemes of the first three stanzas underscore Zion's isolation. In the *meḥayeh*, the rhyme schemes of stanzas 1 and 2 counter this message by underscoring the ongoing relationship between God and Israel. The rhyme scheme of the first stanza is based on the syllables יתִָ (*ati*): יוֹנָתִי־גַּנָּתִי (*yonati-gannati*) and יתִָ (*iti*): עָנִיתִי־חָנִיתִי (*aniti-ḥaniti*). The repetition of the first person possessive ending in the first two verses—"my dove" (יוֹנָתִי), "my garden" (גַּנָּתִי)—which is echoed in the first person singular verbal endings of the third and fourth verses—"I have already answered" (עָנִיתִי), "I have encamped" (חָנִיתִי)—asserts that a relationship of possession exists between God and Israel. God considers Israel to be his dove and a planting in his garden. While Zion's speech in the first poem articulates her sense of abandonment, the repeated assertion of the possessive relationship in the second poem counters her concern.

The rhyme scheme of the third stanza, which is based on the syllable חֵךְ (*ḥekh*), also serves as a response to the first poem. There, the rhyme scheme of the third stanza underscored Zion's victimization. Here, the repetition of the second person object suffix, ךְ, also asserts that God is acting on Zion, but God's actions are redemptive, not destructive. In the first poem, Zion lamented that God rejected, opposed, abandoned and forgot her. Here God vows that he will not abandon or forget her (lines 9, 12). He promises that their argument is over (11) and that he will gather her back (10). The precise echoes between the third stanzas of the two poems reinforce the point. In the first poem Zion complains, "My eyes overflow with rebuke; he has disputed against me / Why forever has he abandoned me, forgotten me?" The second poem responds, "Complete and finished are the words of your dispute / My perfect one, I will not abandon you and I will not forget you." At the "content" level, God counters Zion's lament by telling her that the argument between them is over and that he will neither abandon nor forget her. On the poetic level, the reuse of the words "abandon," "dispute," and "forget" in the second poem reinforces the sense that God promises a precise reversal of Zion's complaints. In addition, the dialogic structure of the two poems resonates strongly within the lectionary cycle, where dialogue is a central trope of reconciliation and ongoing presence.

Allusion

The potent biblical allusions within these poems both underscore Zion's lament and introduce the theme of the redemptive, romantic love existing between God and Israel. The first poem opens with the phrase "the mother of children," which is an allusion to Ps 113:9: "He causes the barren woman to dwell in a house, the happy mother of children."[75] This allusion simultaneously underscores the horror of Zion's situation and evokes hope for her restoration and renewal. When read as an echo of Ps 113:9, the poem's reference to Zion as "the mother of children [who] moans like a dove" is deeply poignant because it not only paints a moving portrait of lamenting Zion, but also contrasts sharply with the joyful biblical text to which it alludes.

The allusion resonates more strongly if we read the verse with its midrashic valences as well. In the midrashic literature, Ps 113:9 is invoked as a prooftext in discussions of the miraculous onset or renewal of fertility. In Gen R. 53:5 and Pes R. 43 (180) it refers to Sarah. In Exod R. 1:23 it refers to Jochebed.

The verse is invoked twice within the Tisha b'Av complex. In Lam R. 1:16, the verse is invoked ironically and elegiacally in a martyrological narrative about a mother of seven sons who sees her children murdered by the Romans. The end of the unit states, "They say that after a while this woman went mad and went up to the roof and threw herself off and died and they cried over her, *the joyful mother of children.*"[76] In Lam R. 1, as in the poem, the exultant biblical verse is transformed into a lament for the mourning mother.

Psalm 113:9 is also invoked within the Tisha b'Av complex as a prooftext for Zion's restored fertility. In PRK 20:1 the verse launches a *petiḥta* to Isa 54:1:

> *He causes the barren woman to dwell in a house, the happy mother of children.* There are seven barren women: Sarah, Rebecca, Rachel and Leah, the wife of Manoah, Hannah and Zion.

Psalm 113:9 is then read as a reference to each of these barren women and their transformations into mothers of children. The pericope ends:

> *Another interpretation: He causes the barren woman to dwell in a house* (Ps 113:9). This is Zion: *Rejoice, barren one who has not given birth* (Isa 54:1). *The*

---

75. The form עֲקֶרֶת ("barren woman") is unusual and makes translation of the verse difficult. Other possible translations include: "He gives the barren woman a home" (RSV); "He sets the childless woman among her household" (JPS); "He founds a family for the sterile" (Mitchell Dahood, *Psalms 101–150* [AB 17a; Garden City: Doubleday, 1964], 130). The translation of the second stich depends on the degree of parallelism which is assumed. The RSV carries over the verbal aspect from the first stich into the second stich and translates, "Making her the barren mother of children." JPS preserves the verbless character of the stich and translates, "as a happy mother of children."

76. A parallel version of this text appears in Lam Z. 1:21.

> *happy mother of children.* [This corresponds to] *and you will say in your heart, "who caused me to bear these?"* (Isa 49:21).

Here Ps 113:9 is read as a reference to Zion's restoration as it is portrayed in reproductive terms. It is interesting to note that the midrash does not cite the end of Isa 54:1 ("for the children of her destruction will outnumber the children of her espousal") as a prooftext for Zion's renewed fertility. Instead, it cites Isa 49:21, a verse which subtly implies that God is the father of Zion's children. By citing Isa 49:21 instead of Isa 54:1b the midrash suggests that Ps 113:9 refers not only to Zion's renewed fertility but also to her romantic/sexual reunion with God. If we read the phrase "the mother of children," in the poem, as an allusion to Ps 113:9 as it is colored by this midrashic valence, then the reference injects a note of hope into the portrait of grieving Zion. At the moment of her lament she is the bereft mother, but her future re-espousal to God and her consequent fertility are already imbedded in the figure of despair.[77]

The uses of the word "dove" also function as powerful allusions. The first poem states, "The mother of children moans like a dove." The second poem opens, "Why do you lament about me, my dove?" Within the *kedushta,* this repetition is quite powerful. In the first poem, "dove" is a figure of isolation. In the second poem, it is a term of endearment. The transformation of the mourning dove in the first poem into God's dove in the second signals the transformation of Zion's isolation into her intimate relatedness to God. When read as allusions, the references to Zion as "dove" also signal God's ongoing presence and the redemptive natures of both prayer and divine love.

Unlike the phrase "the mother of children," the word "dove" in the *magen* is not an allusion to any particular biblical verse. However, since piyyut is so firmly situated within a tradition of biblical language and allusion, it is valid to read the term in light of its biblical meanings and uses. In the Bible, doves appear primarily in five rhetorical contexts. In Leviticus, they are designated as sacrificial animals (Lev 1:14; 12:6; 14:30). In the prophetic books, doves appear as figures of lament (Isa 38:14; 59:11; Ezek 7:16; Nah 2:8). Doves also appear as figures of fleeing or hiding (Ps 55:7; Jer 48:28) and as figures for the returning exiles (Hos 11:11; Isa 60:8). Finally, in Song of Songs the word "dove" is used as an epithet for the female lover (2:14; 5:2; 6:9) and as a simile for eyes (1:15; 4:1; 5:12). The plain sense of the poem resonates with the biblical uses of the dove as a figure of lament. When these prophetic texts are "activated" by the poetic allusion, Zion's lament in the poem becomes situated within an age-old tradition of

---

77. This mirrors the haftarot of rebuke, which foreshadow Zion's restoration as they prophesy her doom. See pp. 43–44.

mourning and despair. Zion, like generations of Israelites before her, mourns like a dove. While this resonance is the most straightforward, the other rhetorical contexts nuance the poem in more interesting and ironic ways. The references to doves as sacrificial animals in the priestly texts evoke a disturbing image of the lamenting Zion as a perverse sacrifice of atonement for the people's sins.[78] The dove as a trope of the returning exiles is also darkly ironic. Hosea 11:11 states, "They shall come trembling like birds from Egypt, like doves from the land of Assyria / And I will return them to their houses, says YHWH." Isaiah 60:8 states, "Who are these who fly like a cloud and like doves to their dovecotes?"[79] In the *magen*, this trope of return is inverted and used to portray Zion mourning over Israel's ongoing exile. Similarly, the use of the word "dove" as a term of endearment in Song of Songs makes the comparison of lamenting Zion to a dove all the more poignant. She, who was once the beloved dove of God, is now the lamenting, bereaved mother who suffers the consequences of divine anger. Thus, the invocation of the image of the dove serves a dual purpose. It situates Zion's lament in a tradition of dove-like lament and underscores the tragic distance between Zion's plight in the poem and that of the "doves" in Song of Songs, Hos 11:11 and Isa 60:8.

The ambiguous term "dove" in the *magen* is followed by the univocally positive allusion "my dove" in the *meḥayeh*. "My dove" is a verbatim quotation of Song 2:14, 5:2 and 6:9. By alluding to one of the signature terms of endearment in Song of Songs, Kallir identifies God's response to Israel as that of a lover to his beloved. Kallir reinforces this point by using two other endearments which allude to the Song of Songs: "my black one" (line 9) and "my perfect one" (line 12).[80] Kallir is certainly not the first to identify Song of Songs with the relationship between God and Israel. However, by alluding to Song of Songs in the context of the sabbaths of consolation, Kallir, like the authors of PRK, asserts that the romantic relationship between God and Israel is germane to the consolatory agenda of the weeks following Tisha b'Av.

At the level of biblical allusion, the uses of the terms "my dove," "my black one," and "my perfect one" serve to identify the God-Israel relationship as a romantic, erotic one. At the level of midrashic allusion, the terms "my dove" and "my perfect one" invoke the themes of God's redemptive love for Israel, Israel's singular status, and the redemptive power of

---

78. The trope of sacrifice is invoked in dark and disturbing ways in the context of the Tisha b'Av cycle in PRK 15:7.

79. This verse is part of the sixth haftarah of consolation.

80. While the precise term "my black one" (שְׁחוֹרָתִי) never appears in Song of Songs, the female lover refers to herself as "black" (שְׁחוֹרָה) in Song 1:5. The endearment תַּמָּתִי occurs in Song 5:2 and 6:9.

prayer. Within the midrashic literature, Song 2:14 is a prooftext for the redemptive power of prayer and obedience. In Mek *Beshallaḥ* 2, Mek *Baḥodesh* 3, and Gen R. 45:4, the first part of the verse, "My dove, who is in the clefts of the rock, in the covert of the cliff," is read as a reference to a perilous moment in Israel's history.[81] In Mek *Beshallaḥ* 2, the verse is identified with the Israelites at the shores of the sea, fleeing before the Egyptians. In Mek *Baḥodesh* 3 it describes the Israelites standing under Mt. Sinai, which has been uprooted from the earth. In Gen R. 45:4 the verse describes the barrenness of the matriarchs. In each of these cases, the second part of the verse, "let me see your face; let me hear your voice," is parsed as a reference to the prayer and obedience to Torah that is motivated by the experience of danger. Genesis Rabbah 45:4 states the connection most explicitly:

> Why were the matriarchs barren? R. Levi said in R. Shila's name and R. Helbo in R. Yohanan's name: Because the Holy One Blessed be He yearns for their prayers and supplications. Thus it is written: *My dove who is in the clefts of the rocks* (Song 2:14). Why did I make you barren? In order that [it would cause you to say] *let me see your face; let me hear your voice* (ibid.).

In these midrashic texts, Song 2:14 becomes a prooftext for the notion that danger and tribulation compel Israel to pray to God and obey the Torah. These acts in turn lead to Israel's redemption. Thus, the term "my dove" is associated with the idea that suffering leads to prayer which in turn leads to repentance.[82]

The midrashic interpretations of Song 6:9 focus on the singularity of Israel and her unique relationship to God. The verse states, "She is one, my dove, my perfect one; she is one to her mother..." In Gen R. 90:1, 94:1, and Song R. 6:9, the verse is read as a reference to Abraham, Jacob and the tribal ancestors. In Num R. 4:2, 9:14, 14:10, and Song R. 6:9 the verse is read with reference to Israel. According to these texts, Song 6:8 ("There are sixty queens and eighty concubines and maidens without number") refers to the nations of the world while the singular "dove" of 6:9 refers to Israel and her special relationship with God. Song Rabbah 6:9 also uses the verse to assert the singularity and unity of Torah. Song Rabbah 5:2 reads Song 5:2 similarly. There the verse ("Open for me my sister, my beloved, my bride, my perfect one") is interpreted as a reference to Israel, which is distinguished from the other nations by its precepts, virtues, and good deeds.

---

81. See also Song Z. 1:1, 2:14.
82. In an isolated case in Exod R. 21:5, the verse is cited as a prooftext for Israel's docility and devotion before God.

If we read the references to "my dove" and "my perfect one" in the *mehayeh* with their midrashic valences, then the terms serve to invoke several themes which are relevant to the theology of consolation which is articulated in the lectionary cycle and the midrashic commentaries on it: misfortune is an impetus to prayer, which then leads to divine attention and redemption. Israel has a unique and favored status in the eyes of God. Within the context of the poems, which reiterate Zion's lament over ongoing divine rejection, this midrashic valence serves as a powerful counter-argument. God has not rejected Israel; by calling her "my dove," he affirms that Israel is uniquely chosen and favored among all the nations.

Litany of Biblical Verses

The litanies of biblical verses manifest a concern with the status of Zion's complaint and God's response. The first three verses in the litany of the *magen* are linked by the root שכח (to forget). The final two verses, Ps 31:3 and Lam 5:22, do not contain this root, but they are linked to the other verses thematically by their descriptions of rejection. Of the four verses which follow the opening verse of the haftarah, only Lam 5:20 and 5:22 appear elsewhere in the literature of the Tisha b'Av season. In Lam R. 5:20, Lam 5:20 is invoked in a pericope which comments on Jeremiah's accusations of abandonment, forgetting, rejection, and fury and closes with a reference to Isa 49:14:

> Abandonment and forgetting: *Why have you forgotten us forever, abandoned us for all time?* (Lam 5:20). Rejection and fury: *Rather, you have utterly rejected us, raged against us exceedingly* (Lam 5:22). Rejection was already replied to in his days. As it is said: *Thus says YHWH, If heaven above can be measured and if the foundations of the earth below can be searched, then I too can reject the seed of Israel* (Jer 31:37). Fury was already replied to in the days of Isaiah. As it is said: *For I will not contest forever and will not be angry eternally* (Isa 57:16). But abandonment and forgetting have not been responded to. Therefore Zion complains and says: *And Zion says, YHWH has abandoned me, my Lord has forgotten me* (Isa 49:14).

A more elaborate version of this text appears in Pes R. 31:3 (chapter for the second sabbath of consolation). Here the distinction between anger and rejection on the one hand and forgetting and abandoning on the other is explored in a parable. God's treatment of Israel is compared to a king's punishment of his disobedient wife. When a member of the queen's family sees her being expelled from the palace, he says to the king:

> My master, the king, tell me something. Do you intend to return to her or not? If you do intend to return, a man has sovereignty over his wife [and

can treat her as he pleases]. If you do not intend to return to her, divorce her so that she may go and marry someone else.

Just as the king's abuse of his wife is a sign that he intends to take her back, so too is God's abuse of Israel a sign that he has not rejected her. The pericope ends by stating that although God has countered Israel's claim of rejection and fury, he has not countered her claim of abandonment and forgetting. Isaiah 49:14 serves as a prooftext for this assertion.[83]

Thus, in both Lam R. and Pes R. 31, Lam 5:20 is linked to Isa 49:14. The conjunction of verses is used to assert that while God has countered the claims that he has rejected Israel and is terminally angry with her, he has not countered the claims that he has forgotten and abandoned her. At the level of biblical allusion, the invocation of Lam 5:20 in the litany of verses highlights the correspondences between the laments of Lamentations and those of Zion. At the level of midrashic valence, the invocation serves to underscore the ongoing validity of Zion's accusation and to highlight the need for a divine response.

Lamentations 5:22 serves two functions within the complex of texts relating to the Tisha b'Av season. It is cited in Lam R. 5:20 as a prooftext for Jeremiah's accusations of anger and rejection. There, the midrash asserts that this rejection has already been countered by God. In Lam R. 5:22 a note of hope is injected into the verse. "Resh Lakish said: If it is rejection, there is no hope. But if it is anger, there is hope. For one who is angry may eventually be appeased."[84] By ending the litany with Lam 5:22, Kallir not only underscores the anxiety expressed in the verse but also capitalizes on its ambiguity. Because the verse, both in its biblical context and in its midrashic interpretation, expresses some doubt over the inevitability of divine rejection, it remains possible for the community to beg God not to reject it.

The verses of the litany of the *meḥayeh* are also bound by words related to the themes of forgetting and rejection. However, whereas the verses in the first poem resonated with Zion's sense of abandonment, the verses in this poem counter her complaints. Like the opening verse (Isa 49:15), which is the second verse of the haftarah, the second and third verses (Ps 137:5 and Isa 54:7) are present elsewhere in the Tisha b'Av season literature.[85] Isaiah 54:7 is a pivotal verse in the fifth haftarah of consola-

---

83. Lam 5:20 also appears in Mid Pss 119:30, but the comment is not relevant to the present context.

84. The comment also appears in Lam R. 1:1 and PRK 17:2.

85. The fourth verse, 1 Sam 12:22, is cited in Ruth R. 2:12 (6), Est R. 7:12, and Mid Pss 94:3 as a prooftext for the assertion that God can never abandon Israel. While this notion is thematically relevant to the sabbaths of consolation, the verse is not invoked as part of the literature of the Tisha b'Av season.

tion.⁸⁶ Psalm 137:5 ("If I forget you, Jerusalem, let my right hand forget") is invoked in six places within the Tisha b'Av literature: Lam R. 1:54; Lam R. (Buber) 2:3; PRK 17:5; Pes R. 28, 29 and 31. In addition, it appears in Mid Pss 121:3 and 137:5. In Lam R. 1:54, it is invoked as a prooftext for the importance of remembering the destruction of the temple. In the remaining texts, the verse is understood as an oath taken by God in response to the destruction of the temple. God vows, "If I forget you, Jerusalem, let my right hand forget." The version in Lam R. 2:3 states:

> *He put his hand behind in the presence of the enemy* (Lam 2:4): R. Azariah and R. Abbahu in the name of Resh Lakish: At the moment when the nations entered the palace [temple] they were capturing the young men and tying their hands behind their backs. The Holy One Blessed be He said, "I have already promised to my children, *I am with him in trouble* (Ps 91:15). It is by right that I should be with them in trouble." Thus it is written: *He put his hand behind.* And he said, *If I forget you, Jerusalem, let my right hand forget* (Ps 137:5).

This midrash serves several functions.⁸⁷ It explains the troubling verse in Lam 2:4: God put his hand behind his back, not out of malice or weakness, but out of solidarity with Israel. Psalm 137:5 is read as a divine utterance which explains the divine action in Lam 2:4. The midrash asserts not only that God acts in solidarity with Israel but also that God's fate is tied to Israel's. The version of the text in Pes R. 31:5 adds:

> And all the days that Israel is held in pawn in this world, so too is the right hand of the Holy One Blessed be He held in pawn with them. David said before the Holy One Blessed be He, "Master of the Universe: What do you think?—That there is no urgency for you to bring the endtime? Even if there is no urgency for us, do it for your right hand. How long will your right hand be held in pawn?" *In order that your beloved would be delivered. Save your right hand and answer me* (Ps 60:7). Thus when Zion says, "God has abandoned me and forgotten me," the Holy One Blessed be He says, "How could I forget you? My right hand is held in pawn for your sake—am I going to forget you? If I forget you, I forget my right hand." *If I forget you, Jerusalem, let my right hand forget* (Ps 137:5).⁸⁸

---

86. See pp. 65–66.

87. See Michael Fishbane, "Arm of the Lord: Biblical Myth, Rabbinic Midrash, and the Mystery of History" in *Language, Theology and the Bible: Essays in Honor of James Barr* (ed. Samuel Balentine and John Barton; Clarendon: Oxford, 1994), 271–92.

88. Here, the word תִּשְׁכַּח is being interpreted as a passive form. See n. 67. The beginning of Pes R. 31:5 also uses Ps 137:5 as a prooftext for the interdependency of God and Israel. Pes R. 31:6–7 is comprised of additional readings which join Isa

In this text, Ps 137:5 is invoked as a response to Isa 49:15, the target verse of the chapter. God responds to Israel's accusation of forgetfulness by reminding her that his fate is tied to hers. If he were to forget Zion, his right hand would remain bound forever. In the biblical text, God responds to Zion's accusation with the powerful assertion, "Can a woman forget her suckling child, not have compassion on the child of her womb? / These may forget, but I will not forget you / Behold I have engraved you on my palms, your walls are always before me" (Isa 49:15–16). The midrash, however, trumps the biblical response. God is not only deeply aware of and invested in Israel's well-being, his own fate and power are also tied to hers. By including Ps 137:5 in the litany of verses, Kallir imports this radical notion of divine sympathy and voluntary dependence into the framework of the second haftarah. While the rest of the poem underscores the romantic nature of the God-Israel relationship, the presence of Ps 137:5 in the litany introduces the even more radical notion of divine bondage and dependence. While the two notions are quite different, there are affinities between them. They are both ways of asserting a deep intimacy between God and Israel. In addition, both the "love affair" between God and Israel and God's participation in Israel's subjugation provide motivation for God to hasten the redemption. He should either make redemption come for the sake of his beloved Israel or for the sake of his own right hand.

Relationship to the Kedushta *as a Whole*

In the first case study, the rest of the *kedushta* did not develop some of the lectionary themes that were alluded to in the first poem. In contrast, the rest of the *kedushta* for the second sabbath of consolation expands upon and reiterates the themes that are activated by the rhyme schemes and allusions of the first poems. Unlike the *kedushta* for the first sabbath of consolation, this *kedushta* conforms to the pattern of allusion and explanation that Shulamit Elizur identified.[89] The rest of the *kedushta* continues the dialogic pattern of complaint and consolation, and reiterates the consolatory themes of the first poems. The fifth poem in particular offers a poetic version of the midrashic traditions alluded to in the first poem. God addresses Israel by quoting Song 2:14 ("My dove, who is in the clefts of the rock") and promises that he has returned to take her out of her suffering, restore her land, and insure the fertile increase of her offspring.

49:14 to Ps 137:5. However, the readings seem to be independent traditions about the future redemption which are inserted into this framework.

89. See n. 56.

Summary

The first two poems of the *kedushta* for the second sabbath of consolation explore the nature of Zion's complaint in Isa 49:14 and God's response in Isa 49:15. Like the lectionary cycle itself, the poems give full voice to Zion's voice of lament. At the same time, the poems respond to Zion's accusations by asserting that God has not forgotten Israel. Instead, he responds meticulously to her complaints. Both the assertion of ongoing relationship between God and Israel and the "measure-for-measure" nature of the divine response are articulated through the poetic features of the poems. The litanies of biblical verses also manifest Kallir's concern for the nature of Israel's complaint and God's response. Elsewhere in the Tisha b'Av midrashic complex, Lam 5:20, 22 and Ps 137:5 are linked to Zion's complaint in Isa 49:14. Lamentations 5:20 is invoked in texts that assert that God has not yet responded to Israel's accusation of abandonment. In contrast, Ps 137:5 is invoked to prove that God has not abandoned Israel. To the contrary, he has bound his fate to hers. While the rhyme scheme, word choice and biblical litanies address the call and response dynamic established in the biblical text, the multiple allusions to Song of Songs in the second poem address the nature of the God-Israel relationship. Through these allusions, Kallir identifies the relationship between God and Israel as a romantic one—Israel is God's only beloved.

Poetry, Prayer, and the Synagogue Context

While I have focused here on poems that further develop the consolatory strategies that I identified in the lectionary cycle and the midrashim of PRK, the entire set of *kedushtot* for the season also articulates a nostalgic yearning for the temple and a fervent desire for its restitution in the messianic age.[90] These concerns resonate with other artifacts from the late antique synagogue, and with the liturgy itself. As I mentioned earlier, the iconography of Palestinian synagogues from the fifth to sixth centuries testifies to the ongoing importance of the temple or temple symbolism for the worshiping community. It is not surprising that the poetry that was composed for these synagogues also articulates a nostalgia for the temple and sacrificial cult. However, piyyut's concern with the temple and the messianic redemption should not solely be ascribed to its synagogal status or its non-rabbinic origins. Piyyut is a form of prayer which is grounded in the rabbinic liturgical system. The piyyutim are structured around the rabbinic liturgy and invoke the language and themes of the rabbinically

---

90. See p. 136.

prescribed prayers. The restoration of the temple and the redemption of Israel are central themes of the rabbinic liturgy. In addition, rabbinic prayer acclaims God's power to redeem Israel and rectify her misfortunes and includes petitions for the restoration of Jerusalem, the return of the exiles, and the defeat of Israel's enemy. As prayer, piyyut participates in more urgent expressions of desire for redemption than are articulated in the lectionary sequence or the rabbinic commentaries on it. Thus, the contrast between the piyyutim's concern with the temple and the near absence of this concern in the lectionary cycle and the midrashim may be a consequence of generic, as well as authorial difference.

5

Targum Jonathan's Translation of the Haftarot of Consolation

Targum Jonathan (hereafter, TJ) is a highly literalist Aramaic translation of the prophetic books which was probably originally composed in Palestine as early as the first century CE, but underwent several stages of redaction in Babylonia in the ensuing centuries.[1] Targum (pl. *targumim*) was first identified by scholars as a synagogue genre.[2] They based this identification on tannaitic sources which both assume and prescribe the recitation of an Aramaic translation of the lectionary texts.[3] More recently, Anthony York has argued that the extant written targumim were pedagogical tools. He based this contention on the targumic inclusion of nonlectionary texts, and on Sifre Deut 161 and ARN 12, both of which refer to the use of targum for personal study.[4] Most contemporary scholars now agree that the targumim were used in both the academic and the synago-

---

1. For summaries of the debate over the dating and provenance of TJ, see Bruce D. Chilton, *The Isaiah Targum* (Wilmington: Glazier, 1987), xx–xxvii; Philip Alexander, "Jewish Aramaic Translations," in *Mikra: Text, Translation, Reading, and Interpretation of the Hebrew Bible in Ancient Judaism and Early Christianity* (ed. Martin L. Mulder; Philadelphia: Fortress Press, 1988), 243–50; Leivy Smolar and Moshe Aberbach, *Studies in Targum Jonathan to the Prophets* (New York: Ktav, 1983), xii–xvii.

2. Wilhelm Bacher, "Targum," *Jewish Encyclopedia* (New York: Funk and Wagnalls: 1905), 57–63.

3. See, for example, m. Meg 4:4, 6:10; t. Meg 4 (3):20, 21.

4. Anthony York, "The Targum in the Synagogue and the School," *JSJ* 10 (1979): 74–86.

gal settings.[5] While synagogue use may have been part of its original function, its scope and format suggest that it was composed largely for use in an academic setting. Unlike PRK and the other texts in this study, TJ does not deal with the biblical texts in their lectionary order, nor does it recognize lectionary divisions. Instead, the targum is a translation of the entire prophetic canon in its canonical order. This feature links TJ strongly to the academic setting. It was in the school, rather than in the synagogue, that entire prophetic books would have been the subject of study.

Within this study, then, TJ provides a marked contrast to PRK and the *kedushtot* of Kallir, which explicitly interpret the biblical texts in their popular, synagogal role as lectionary texts. Thus far, I have argued that the creators of the lectionary cycle created a new, second-order biblical text which articulates a theology of consolation which is different from that of its constituent parts. In the lectionary sequence, the discourse of redemption is unhitched from the discourse of reconciliation and the latter is elevated and underscored as an effective consolatory discourse. PRK and the poems of Kallir expand on this theology of consolation, rather than on the theology of the constituent texts in their biblical context. TJ, which interprets the texts within their canonical context, articulates an interpretation of the haftarah texts which contrasts sharply with those that I have discussed in the previous chapters. Throughout the translation of Isa 40–66, TJ consistently emends or eliminates texts that contribute to the portrayal of the personal, intimate relationship between God and Israel; at the same time, it enhances the tropes of divine transcendence and power. The contrast between TJ's tendencies and the theology of consolation articulated by the lectionary cycle, PRK, and the piyyutim is relevant to my larger study for several reasons: It articulates an alternative interpretation of Isa 40–66 that existed contemporaneously with the theology of consolation explored thus far. It also supports my assertion regarding the seasonal, liturgical, and contextual specificity of the theology of consolation. While this theology is articulated in those texts which comment on the biblical texts in their lectionary context, it is absent from TJ, which deals with the texts in their original biblical context. Finally, the contrast between TJ and the lectionary-specific texts supports the hypothesis that even though TJ

---

5. See, for example, D. M. Golomb, *A Grammar of Targum Neofiti* (Chico: Scholars Press, 1985); Alexander, "Jewish Aramaic Translations," 248; Rimon Kasher, "The Aramaic Targumim and their *Sitz im Leben*," in *Proceedings of the Ninth World Congress of Jewish Studies* (ed. M. Goshen-Gottstein; Jerusalem: World Congress of Jewish Studies, 1988), 75–83; Steven D. Fraade, "Rabbinic Views on the Practice of Targum, and Multilingualism in the Jewish Galilee of the Third–Sixth Centuries," in *The Galilee in Late Antiquity* (ed. Lee Levine; New York: Jewish Theological Seminary, 1992), 253–86.

was eventually used in synagogues, it was not composed explicitly for use in the synagogue context.

Targumic Function and Exegesis

Although the targumim are translations of the biblical text into Aramaic, they probably did not function as versions of a text for Aramaic-speaking audiences who could not understand the text in the original language. Evidence from the third to sixth centuries suggests that most Jews in Palestine during this period were bi-lingual.[6] Certainly the Jews who studied in the academies where targumim were used would have been able to understand the Hebrew of the biblical text. The targumim, therefore, were probably composed as explanatory texts which were designed to complement the Hebrew text and facilitate a particular understanding of it. Several tannaitic and amoraic texts attribute an explanatory function to both the practice and texts of targum, and describe a complementary relationship between the targum text and the original biblical text. For example, j. Meg 4:1 states:

> From where do we derive the practice of targum? R. Zeirah in the name of R. Hananel: *And they read from the book, from the Torah of God* (Neh 8:8): This is scripture. *Clearly* (ibid.): This is targum.[7]

There are other texts, however, which focus on the ways in which translations deviate from scripture. B. Meg 9a lists thirteen places in which the Septuagint deviates from a literalist translation of the Hebrew text. While it only offers an explanation for one of these deviations, the impetus behind many of the others is quite clear. Some of the cases alter Hebrew texts that appear to refer to a plurality of gods. Others protect the reputation of Israel, its ancestors and its leaders, while others emend embarrassing comments regarding God's activity on the seventh day and Israelite polytheism. A reasonable person listening to these biblical verses would derive a meaning which the translators felt was incorrect or inappropriate. In these situations, the translation deviates from literalism and emends the "misleading" Hebrew text in order to bring it into line with the central tenets of the translators' post-biblical theology.

TJ's deviations from literalist translation conform to the two views of targum articulated in the rabbinic literature. Many of TJ's deviations from

---

6. Fraade, "Rabbinic Views"; Avigdor Shinan, "Hebrew and Aramaic in the Literature of the Synagogue," in *Tura: Studies in Jewish Thought* (ed. Meir Ayali; Tel Aviv: ha-Kibbuts ha-meuhad, 1989), 224–32 (Heb.).

7. See also b. Meg 3a; b. MK 28b; b. San 94b; b. Ber 28b.

the literal are exegetical in nature. TJ replaces difficult Hebrew locutions with more comprehensible elements; it interprets poetic or metaphorical passages and incorporates these interpretive decisions into the translation. For example, TJ sometimes identifies speakers or addressees where the Hebrew text leaves them unnamed, or replaces a presumed metaphor with an assumed referent.

Other emendations, however, are ideologically or theologically driven.[8] In some of these cases, TJ replaces a (problematic) Hebrew element with an Aramaic element that deviates from it or even contradicts it. In other cases, TJ incorporates a prevalent interpretive tradition into its translation or uses a syntactic or thematic feature of the text as an occasion to insert a common targumic phrase or idea. Many of these content-driven emendations occur in TJ's translations of descriptions of God or divine action:

1. While TJ translates most anthropomorphisms literally, it does emend a significant minority of anthropomorphic locutions.

2. TJ frequently emends texts in which God is represented as the direct subject or object of action. In most cases the targumist transforms these texts into the passive voice through the inclusion of the preposition "before" (קדם).

3. TJ emends most references to divine movement.

4. TJ sometimes replaces references to God as YHWH with circumlocutions such as "*shekhinah*," "glory," or "glory of the *shekhinah*."

There is a wide range of scholarly opinion regarding the significance of this set of emendations. Michael Klein and Martin McNamara have argued that these emendations have little effect on the received meaning of the biblical text. According to McNamara, circumlocutions for YHWH "were merely other ways of saying 'the Lord.' They were reverential ways of speaking about the God of Israel."[9] Similarly, Klein argues that the "issue of anthropomorphism was not of theological import" to the targum-

---

8. The distinction between exegetical and content-driven emendations is, to some degree, heuristic. As the examples below will demonstrate, the two motivations probably intertwine in many cases. A theologically problematic verse is identified by the targumist as metaphorical discourse and consequently is translated in a way that represents the text's "true" referential meaning in the eyes of the targumist.

9. Martin McNamara, *Targum*, 98.

ists. If it had been, Klein argues, they would have emended anthropomorphisms more consistently and completely.[10]

In contrast, Bruce Chilton has argued that TJ's anti-anthropomorphisms are theologically significant: "Rather than being merely replacement words, designed to avoid anthropomorphism, such terms deliberately emphasize some aspect of God's activity . . ."[11] Leivy Smolar and Moshe Aberbach argue that the emendation of anthropomorphism radically changes the theology of the biblical text: "It was precisely because the Bible frequently expresses concepts and views which were later rejected by the rabbis that TJ . . . significantly changes the translation with a view to eliminating all traces of unorthodox theology."[12] While I disagree that TJ's theology can be identified as "orthodox" rabbinic theology, I agree that its emendations do have a significant effect on the portrayal of God in TJ. The aggregate effect of the reduced anthropomorphism, the circumlocutions, and the distancing of God from direct interaction with human subjects, results in the portrayal of a divine character which is significantly more transcendent and less imminent and intimate than that of Second Isaiah. This revised portrait of God differentiates TJ's interpretation of the texts of the haftarot of consolation sharply from those of PRK and Kallir. While the midrash and the piyyut underscore the discourse of divine intimacy and assert its consolatory power, TJ's typical emendations dilute this discourse while enhancing the discourse of transcendent power.

Analysis of Targum Jonathan to Isaiah 40:1–23

TJ to Isa 40:1–23 provides a representative example of the effects of TJ's typical emendations on the theology of the text. Within the biblical pericope, God commands unnamed addressees to comfort Jerusalem and proclaim the end of her time of punishment. The text goes on to announce the imminent advent of God and to praise his incomparable power as creator of the cosmos and master of history. TJ translates about half of the references to God and divine action in the pericope literally. In these translations, it preserves references to God as: the creator of the universe (vv. 22, 26),[13] a force which intervenes in history (v. 23), and a speaking entity (vv.

---

10. Michael Klein, *Anthropomorphisms*, xi.
11. Chilton, *Isaiah Targum*, xvi.
12. Smolar and Aberbach, *Studies*, 129–30.
13. In Isa 40:22, the description of God's creative acts is translated literally, but the reference to the heavens as "a tent for dwelling" is rendered, "as a dwelling of glory for his shekhinah."

1, 25). It also preserves three anthropomorphisms and a reference to divine movement (vv. 10–11).[14] Finally, it renders literally three verses which conform to conventional targumic discourse by referring to God's glory and God's word and by using the phrase "considered by him" (vv. 5, 8, 17).

The remaining theological references deviate from the literal. TJ emends most anthropomorphic references to God and most references to divine movement. TJ consistently emends references to God's hand, mouth, spirit/breath (רוח):

1. Isaiah 40:2: "She has received *from* YHWH*'s hand* double for her all her sins."

   TJ: "She has received a cup of consolations *from before* YHWH as if she had suffered two for one for all her sins."[15]

2. Isaiah 40:5: "For *the mouth* of YHWH has spoken."

   TJ: "For *by the memra* of YHWH it is decreed."[16]

3. Isaiah 40:7: "For the breath/spirit *of* YHWH blows on it."

   TJ: "For the breath/spirit *from before* YHWH blows upon it.

4. Isaiah 40:12: "*Who has measured* the waters in the hollow of his hand and marked off the heavens with a span . . ."

---

14. In Isa 40:10–11, the anthropomorphisms and reference to divine movement occur within a simile which compares God to a shepherd. While the verses attribute the anthropomorphisms and verbs of movement directly to God, and not to the shepherd to whom God is compared, the presence of the simile might have served as a softening factor which led the targumist to refrain from emending these features.

15. In addition to emending the anthropomorphism, TJ inserts a reference to the cup of consolations. It also softens the phrase, "has received from the hand of YHWH double for all her sins" by transforming the end of the verse into a simile: "as if she had suffered two for one for all her sins."

16. There is a scholarly debate over the precise function of the term *memra*. Some scholars identify it as a hypostatization of God while others see it as a means through which God communicates to humanity. See Klein, *Anthropomorphism*, 124–35 for a summary of the debate and analysis of the term. For discussion of the term in TJ to Isaiah, see Domingo Muñoz-León, "Memra in the Targum to Isaiah," in *Proceedings of the Ninth World Congress of Jewish Studies* (ed. M. H. Goshen-Gottstein; Jerusalem: World Congress of Jewish Studies, 1986), 135–42.

TJ: "*Before whom* all the waters of the world *are counted* as a drop in the hollow of his hand, and the expanse of the heavens *as if they had been* adjusted with a span."

5. Isaiah 40:13: "Who established/plumbed *the spirit of* YHWH?"

TJ: "Who established *the holy spirit in the mouth of all the prophets?*"

As I mentioned above, many critics are unwilling to see the targumic emendations of anthropomorphisms as significantly revisionist.[17] They describe these emendations as strategies for *avoiding misunderstanding* on the part of the lay public. This reading assumes that the Bible itself is essentially non-anthropomorphic and that to read the references to God's hands or mouth with any degree of seriousness (either literal or metaphorical) would be a misunderstanding. Theologians, however, have described the centrality of anthropomorphism to the theology of the Hebrew Bible. The portrayal of God as a character with anthropomorphic and anthropopathic characteristics is one of the defining features of the Bible's personalist theology. It is essential to the idea that God and Israel, as well as God and humanity, exist in meaningful and dynamic relationship to one another.[18] By diluting the anthropomorphic portrait of God in Second Isaiah, TJ preempts the theology of intimacy articulated by the lectionary cycle. In order to be Israel's lover, God must be invested with anthropomorphic and anthropopathic features. The discourse of divine power, however, is not diluted by these emendations. Rather, TJ's anti-anthropomorphic emendations render God more transcendent than in the biblical text.

TJ also emends most of the references to divine movement in the pericope:

1. Isaiah 40:10: Behold, the Lord, YHWH, *comes* in strength.

TJ: Behold, YHWH, God, *reveals himself* in strength.

---

17. See pp. 158–59.
18. For discussions of the theological role of anthropomorphism, see Sallie McFague, *Metaphorical Theology: Models of God in Religious Language* (Philadelphia: Fortress Press, 1982); David Stern, *Parables in Midrash: Narrative and Exegesis in Rabbinic Literature* (Cambridge: Harvard University Press, 1991); Renita J. Weems, *Battered Love: Marriage, Sex, and Violence in the Hebrew Prophets* (Minneapolis: Fortress Press, 1995).

2. Isaiah 40:22: "Who *sits* above the circle of the earth . . ."

TJ: "[He] who caused the *shekhinah* of his glory to dwell in the mighty height . . ."

Even implied references to divine movement are replaced:

1. Isaiah 40:3: "Prepare a way *for* YHWH; make straight in the wilderness a highway *for our God.*"

TJ: "Prepare a way *before the people of* YHWH; level in the wilderness roads *before the congregation of our God.*"

2. Isaiah 40:9: "Behold, your God."

TJ: "The kingdom of your God is revealed."

Both Michael Klein and Bruce Chilton have hypothesized about the impetus for these emendations. Klein addresses divine movement as a sub-category of anthropomorphism.[19] This identification suggests that the emendations of references to divine movement stem from a discomfort with the concrete nature of these references. If God can come and go, then God must have a defined and bounded physical presence. References to divine movement, like references to God's back or feet, give an incorrect impression of the physical nature of God. Chilton suggests that these emendations are part of a targumic theology of consolation. He argues that in TJ's version of Second Isaiah, the heavenly Jerusalem exists intact in the exilic present as the dwelling place of God. Consequently, God's return to Zion is no longer a necessary part of the redemptive picture, so references to it are emended.[20] These suggestions help to illuminate both the anxieties and theology of TJ, but they do not address the strong theological revisionism of the text.

Within Second Isaiah, references to God's coming and going communicate a dynamic sense of divine presence and absence. By stating "Behold, the Lord, YHWH comes in strength," Isa 40:10 communicates both that God is arriving and that God has been absent until now. The Aramaic rendering "Behold, YHWH, God, reveals himself in strength" does not negotiate God's presence or absence. Rather it merely speaks of the self-revelation of the ever-present deity. TJ's reluctance to speak of divine movement not only represents an emendation of the biblical text, it also stands in marked contrast to the haftarah cycle. In their lectionary context, the haftarot of consolation are a carefully calibrated response to the accusa-

---

19. Klein, *Anthropomorphisms*, 77–89.
20. Chilton, *Isaiah Targum*, xix–xx.

tions of divine rejection and abandonment voiced in Lamentations and by Zion in the second haftarah of consolation. In their lectionary context, the haftarot of consolation both announce and enact God's emotional and relational return to Israel. By emending the references to divine movement, TJ both denies the sense of divine abandonment articulated by Zion's voice in the cycle and nullifies the consolatory effects of the tropes of return. The patterns of literalist translation and anti-anthropomorphic emendation which occur in TJ's treatment of Isa 40:1–23 recur throughout its treatment of Isa 40–66. Thus, throughout TJ's treatment of the lectionary texts, the theology of redemption remains intact while the theology of intimate reconciliation is diluted significantly.

The Romantic Trope:
Isaiah 49:14–23; 50:1–3; 54:1–8; 62:1–5

As I discussed in the previous chapters, both PRK and the *kedushtot* of Kallir develop the trope of the erotic relationship between God and Israel. For both the midrash and the piyyut, the romance between God and Israel is a central vehicle for the expression of notions of divine presence, and divine devotion and attachment to Israel. In the lectionary cycle, the midrash and the piyyut, God's romantic love for Israel motivates God's intervention in history on Israel's behalf. Thus, the erotic trope is at once a figure of intimacy and of redemption. In contrast to the other three genres, TJ does not capitalize on the erotic trope. Instead, TJ consistently emends references to the erotic relationship between God and Israel. This persistent emendation does not mean that TJ rejects notions of redemption or divine intimacy. However, it does attest to TJ's rejection of the erotic trope as a vehicle for the expression of these theological ideas.

The gendered personification of Zion is central to the erotic trope. According to the heterosexual orientation of biblical and early Jewish culture, Israel must be imagined as a woman if she is to be the romantic partner of the male God. While the targumist does not manifest discomfort with the personification of Zion *per se*, he is less comfortable with texts which attribute gender and sexuality to the personification. TJ translates references to Zion's feet (49:23), hand (51:22), and eyes (60:4) literally. Verbs of movement and human action such as drinking and lying down (51:22–23), rising, sitting (52:2), singing (52:9), and dressing (52:1) are also rendered literally. However, the gendered representations of Israel as mother and lover are treated less consistently. TJ preserves references to Zion's children in Isa 49:22, 25; 51:18, 20; 54:1, 3; and 60:9. It also preserves a reference to Zion's young womanhood and widowhood in 54:4. However, the other depictions of Zion as mother and lover are altered in the targum. References to "the children of your bereavement" (49:20) and "your children" (60:4) are translated "the children of the people of your exiles."[21] These changes replace the representation of Zion as the mother of her inhabitants with representations of the city as the home of the exiled community. Similarly, in Isa 50:1, TJ replaces the reference to "your mother" with "your congregation." "Where is the bill of divorce of your mother whom I dismissed?" becomes "Where is the bill of divorce which I gave your congregation, that it is rejected?" Thus, while TJ still speaks of the (false) rejection of Israel by God, the Aramaic version is not as explicitly gendered as the Hebrew.

TJ also desexualizes the personified Zion by eliminating the paradoxical image of the barren mother in 49:20–21 and 54:1. While TJ's rendering of 49:20–21 is, in many respects, quite literalist, the few deviations serve to dilute the feminized and sexualized portrayal of Zion. Isa 49:20–21 states:

> The children *born in the time of your bereavement* will yet say *in your ears,*
> "The place is too narrow for me; make room for me to dwell in."
> And you will say in your heart, "Who *caused me to bear* these? I was bereaved and *barren,* exiled and put away, but who has *brought up* these?"

TJ renders these verses:

> Henceforth, the children *of the people of your exiles* will say *each one in your midst,*
> "The place is too strait for me; give place to me that I may dwell."
> And you will say in your heart, "Who has *brought up* these for me, seeing I am bereaved and *solitary,* an exile and driven forth? These, who has *brought them up?*"

In TJ 49:20, the "children of your bereavement" are identified as "the children of the people of your exiles." In TJ, these children no longer speak intimately in mother Zion's ear; rather, they speak to one another in her midst. In the Hebrew text, mother Zion's amazed response refers to acts of giving birth and raising. In the Aramaic, the word רבי ("bring up") is used to translate both terms. Thus Zion is not concerned with the question of how she could have given birth to children despite her barrenness. She is

---

21. The reference to "your children" in Isa 49:17 is translated "your builders." However, this change may reflect a different base text. The Qumran manuscript reads בוניך ("your builders"), a reading reflected in Aquila and the Vulgate as well.

only concerned with how she could have raised them. Similarly, the word "barren" is rendered as "alone," thereby desexualizing the portrait of Zion.

TJ to Isa 54:1 effects a similar desexualizing through a striking midrashic reading. Isaiah 54:1 states:

> Rejoice, barren one who has not given birth; burst forth in joy, shout gladly, you who did not writhe.
> For the children of the desolate one will be more than the children of her that is married, says YHWH.

TJ:

> Sing praises, O Jerusalem, who was *as* a barren woman that did not bear; break forth into a song of praise and rejoice, you who were *as* a woman that did not conceive.
> For more shall be the children of desolate *Jerusalem* than the *children of inhabited Rome*, says YHWH.

In this case, the de-personification of Jerusalem occurs through the insertion of the comparative particle כ־ ("as"). Zion is not a barren woman; she is *like* a barren woman. The second half of the verse deviates more dramatically from a literalist reading. "The children of her that is married" becomes "the children of inhabited Rome." This gloss relies on the targum's consistent replacement of forms of the verb בעל ("be master/husband") with forms of the verb יתב ("dwell").[22] For the targumist, references to God's espousal of/sexual intercourse with Zion are metaphoric references to the resettlement of the exiles. Consequently, "her that is married (בְּעוּלָה)" is read as a reference to the quintessentially inhabited city, Rome.[23] The pattern of desexualization continues in Isa 62:4–5, in the final haftarah of the cycle. Isaiah 62:4–5 states:

> You will no longer be called "Forsaken" and your land will no longer be called "Desolate."
> For you will be called "My delight is in her" and your land will be called "Espoused" (בְּעוּלָה)."
> For the Lord delights in you, and your land shall be married (בָּעֵל)
> For as a young man marries (יִבְעַל) a virgin, so shall your sons marry you (יִבְעָלוּךְ);
> And the joy of a bridegroom over a bride will your God rejoice over you.

---

22. See also Isa 54:1, 62:4 (twice), 62:5.

23. This emendation is also polemical. It states that Jerusalem will eventually supersede its conqueror, whereas the biblical verse compares Jerusalem's future to its own past.

The Targum renders:

> You shall no more be termed "Forsaken" and your land shall no more be termed "Desolate";
> But you shall be called, "Those who do my pleasure in her," and your land, "Inhabited";
> For there shall be pleasure before YHWH in you, and your land shall be inhabited.
> For just as a young man dwells (דמתיתב) with a virgin, so shall your sons settle (יתיתבון) in your midst;
> And just as a bridegroom rejoices with a bride, so your God rejoices over you.

In this pericope, the four occurrences of the root בעל are replaced with forms of the verb יתב. There is no semantic relationship between the two roots. The Hebrew root signifies "to be master," "authority," "owner," "husband," and "male sexual partner." The Aramaic root means "to sit" or "to dwell." By replacing forms of בעל with forms of יתב, TJ identifies a presumed metaphor and replaces it with an assumed referent. This replacement of the term of simultaneous mastery/authority and sexual intimacy with the term of habitation shifts the focus of the text. In the Hebrew, בְּעוּלָה (the passive participle of בעל) is the name of the redeemed Zion. The sign of redemption is marriage to God and sexual union, as well as submission to God's authority. In the targum, the name of the redeemed Zion is יתבא ("Inhabited"). The sign of redemption is the return of the exiles and the rehabitation of Jerusalem.

The targumist also emends the references to God delighting in Israel. "My delight is in her" is rendered "they that do my pleasure are in her." The second reference, "For the Lord delights in you" is rendered "For there shall be pleasure before the Lord in you." God no longer takes (erotic) delight in Israel. Rather, the first instance refers to the presence of those who do God's will. The second uses the prepositional phrase "from before" to distance the experience of pleasure from God and to de-personalize it. Finally, in 62:5b, the phrase "the joy of a bridegroom over a bride will your God rejoice over you" is transformed into a simile by the inclusion of the comparative particle כמא ("as"): "*just as* a bridegroom rejoices with a bride, so will your God rejoice over you." In TJ, God does not experience the joy of the bridegroom over a bride; instead, God rejoices in a way *similar to* the way that a bridegroom rejoices over his bride. Through these strategies of replacement and modification, the entire pericope is desexualized. Habitation, not multivalent mastery, is now the central trope of the relationships between God and Zion and between Zion and her "children."

The consistent replacement of בעל by יתב is particularly significant. As I argued in chapter 2, the term בעל is central to the lectionary sequence. Because its semantic range encompasses both political mastery and sexual intercourse, the term serves as a highly condensed expression of two of the central theological tenets of post-biblical Judaism. God is Israel's sovereign and God is Israel's lover. According to much of rabbinic theology, Israel's historical fate and destiny are largely determined by these two factors. Because it expresses both of these ideas simultaneously, the term בעל is a powerful and oversignified theological term. In the haftarah cycle specifically, the term brings together the two forms of consolation which are articulated by the cycle. Consolation will come as a result of the exercise of God's sovereign power. Consolation also lies in the fact of God's romantic love for Israel. By eliminating the double-edged term from the translation while retaining references to God's power over nature and history, the targum replaces the material for this double-edged consolation with a more monolithic expression of divine power.

Conclusion

TJ emends the constituent tropes of the theology of reconciliation and intimate relation that are articulated forcefully in the genres explored in the previous chapters. The contrast between TJ's treatment of the haftarot of consolation and their treatment in PRK and the poems of Kallir underscores the liturgical specificity of the lectionary theology of consolation, and contributes to the ongoing discussion of the nature and function of TJ itself. Although the midrashim in PRK and the poems of Kallir represent different interpretive approaches to the lectionary texts and articulate divergent theological ideas, their interpretations converge around the theology of consolation that I discussed in the previous chapters. Both genres develop the tropes of reconciliation and intimate relationship and argue for both their consolatory and redemptive power. The convergence around these themes can only be attributed to their shared seasonal and liturgical context. As I noted in chapter 4, the piyyutim overlap with but do not replicate rabbinic ideology, especially with regard to the status of the defunct temple and its cult. Nor is this romantic theology so ubiquitous as to render its appearance in the relevant midrashim of PRK and the relevant *kedushtot* of Kallir meaningless. While the trope of romantic love between God and Israel is not absent from the rest of rabbinic literature, it is by no means the dominant trope. Similarly, it does not dominate Kallir's piyyutim for the rest of the liturgical year. Rather, the convergence testifies to the liturgical specificity of these themes. The synagogue setting in the Tisha b'Av season became the locus for the articulation of this theology of consolation by the creators of the lectionary itself, the authors of the midrashim in PRK, and Kallir.

There are several possible explanations for TJ's divergence from this pattern. It is possible that TJ's rendering of the haftarot is a product of later layers of redaction and is not contemporaneous with the other texts explored here. Alternatively, it is possible that the contrast is a result of differing provenances. TJ might represent a Babylonian tradition while the lectionary cycle, PRK, and the poems of Kallir are all Palestinian. It is also possible, however, that TJ's divergence from these other texts supports the hypothesis that TJ was not composed primarily as a synagogue text, but rather was an academic text that came to be used in the synagogue setting.

The contrast between TJ's rendering of the haftarot and that of PRK and Kallir is also relevant to the ongoing attempts to define "popular" rabbinic theology. As I mentioned above, many scholars of targum attribute TJ's anti-anthropomorphic tendencies to its role as a text for "the masses." According to this position, TJ's deviations from the literal were designed to prevent laypeople from interpreting the anthropomorphic imagery of the text too concretely. The evidence of the lectionary cycle and the *kedushtot* of Kallir challenge this hypothesis. These texts, which are more clearly and closely linked to the exegesis of scripture in the synagogue, underscore precisely those anthropomorphic and anthropopathic tropes that TJ emends. Certainly for the creators of the lectionary cycle and Kallir, anthropopathism was a particularly powerful and appropriate trope for the synagogue audience. TJ's anti-anthropomorphism, then, should not be attributed solely or primarily to a concern for a popular audience, but rather to a theological stance on the part of its authors that would necessitate the emendation of the text in both academic and popular settings.

6

Conclusion: The Literature of the Tisha b'Av Season

In the preceding chapters, I have demonstrated that the lectionary cycle, the midrashim in PRK that comment on it, and the corresponding *kedushtot* of Eleazar Kallir constitute a corpus of Tisha b'Av literature that coheres around the articulation of a particular seasonal theology: Israel's history conforms to a narrative of sin-punishment-redemption in which the destructions of the temples represent punishment for the nation's sins. While redemption has not yet occurred, the present represents a period of reconciliation between God and Israel in which God expresses a love for Israel that is, by definition, ultimately redemptive. While the three genres are linked by this common theology, the particular articulations of this theology differ from genre to genre and are affected by the exegetical strategies and functions of the genres as well as by the different viewpoints of the authors. I have also demonstrated that TJ does not participate in the articulation of the seasonal theme and have suggested that this deviation might be due to a difference in provenance or *Sitz im Leben* as well as a difference in theological orientation.

The results of my analyses accord with much of the current research regarding the genres of homiletical midrash and piyyut, and the influence of the rabbis in fifth- to sixth-century Palestinian synagogue culture. In chapter 3 I noted that contemporary scholars no longer identify the homiletical midrashim as transcripts or even literary versions of oral sermons. Instead, scholars such as Richard Sarason and David Stern identify the homiletical midrashim as literary texts which are in some way connected to a preaching context.[1] In this study, I have developed this line of

---

1. See pp. 81–84.

thinking further by describing the interplay between the synagogue context and the midrashim in PRK. I have argued that while PRK is a literary text of the *beit midrash*, it is dependent on, and oriented toward, the public, synagogue form of the Bible as it is represented in the lectionary. It is not oriented toward the Bible in its academic, canonical form. This orientation toward the synagogal, lectionary context shapes the concerns and assertions of the midrashic composition. The midrash interprets its target texts through the lens of the Tisha b'Av season and its concerns, as well as through the lens of the theology articulated by the lectionary cycle itself. Within the context of the *beit midrash*, the Tisha b'Av season and its lectionary texts provide the opportunity and the impetus to expand on the theology of divine love that is otherwise primarily articulated around the exegesis of Song of Songs, and to more fully develop the theology of the redemptive power of that love.

This study also supports the identification of the piyyutim as texts that bridge the worlds of the synagogue and the *beit midrash*. Kallir's *kedushtot* for the Tisha b'Av season are strongly dependent on, and informed by, rabbinic exegetical traditions. At the same time, the poems' exegetical strategies are foreign to the academy, and some of the ideas that they communicate differ from those found in the lectionary cycle and the midrashim that comment on it. Unlike these texts, the *kedushtot* express a nostalgic longing for the temple and temple cult, and articulate a desire for their imminent restoration.

It is only with regard to TJ that my study suggests conclusions different from those of most contemporary scholars. While most contemporary scholars now agree that targum had a dual function, synagogue use is still regarded as the primary *raison d'être* of the targums. While my study certainly does not obviate claims regarding the use of the targum in the synagogue, it does suggest that TJ was not composed expressly for lectionary use. Comparison with Kallir's piyyutim and the midrashim in PRK underscores the fact that TJ's base text is the canonical Bible, not the synagogue Bible. Not only does TJ *not* comment on the texts in their lectionary order, it also ignores or emends those features that are present in the biblical text, but are particularly crucial to the message of the lectionary cycle. While TJ was certainly used in the synagogue, its target text is not the synagogue Bible, nor is its exposition of the meaning of the target texts informed by the synagogue context.

This study also contributes to the growing understanding of "popular" rabbinic Judaism. The observation that some rabbinic texts were composed for an imagined lay audience is not new. Many scholars have identified the targumim and homiletical midrashim as texts that were composed for "the masses." These judgments were based on evidence from the rabbinic literature that associated these genres with the synagogue and/or preaching as well as on intuitions regarding the nature of "popular" discourse.[2] Once these genres were identified as "popular," their content was identified as rabbinic popular theology and ideology. If the targumim were composed for a popular audience, then their theology must constitute what their authors wanted the public to hear. Thus, emendation of particularly strong anthropomorphisms and anthropopathisms was identified as a feature of rabbinic popular theology.

I use a more conservative method to identify texts composed for a general audience. I include in this category only texts whose structure and function are specific to the synagogue context: the lectionary itself and the piyyutim of Kallir. According to this method, the theology of these texts, not that of the targumim or homiletical midrash, constitutes rabbinic and, in the case of the piyyutim, semi-rabbinic popular theology. The features of this theology differ from those of the "popular" rabbinic theology identified, in particular, by targum scholars. When creating an expressly popular text—the lectionary—the rabbis select from among the most anthropomorphic and anthropopathic texts of Second Isaiah, suggesting that, in the eyes of the redactors, these were particularly appropriate and important "popular" tropes. The trope of God's romantic love for Israel also played a central role in this popular theology.

Text, Ritual, and Communal Experience

Having summarized the findings of the preceding chapters, I will conclude with a more synthetic discussion of the ritual experience of the Tisha b'Av season and the cultural messages that it engenders. It is, of course, impossible to gain access to the lived experience of fifth- to sixth-century Jews in Palestine. Here I am describing the potential power of participation in the seasonal ritual. The Tisha b'Av season makes the experience that I describe below possible and seems to encourage its enactment; however, it remains impossible to determine how the potential effects I identify here actually translated into lived experience for the synagogue community.

As I mentioned in chapter 1, the rabbinic literature demonstrates that certain dates in the Tisha b'Av season were invested with a range of meanings during, and probably prior to, the rabbinic period. The three weeks between the seventeenth of Tammuz and the ninth of Av are identified as a period of cosmic and supernatural malevolence and danger. The seventeenth of Tammuz and the ninth of Av are both identified with a range of catastrophes from Israel's past—an identification which depends on the

---

2. See pp. 81–84, 155–56.

inherently unlucky quality of the days. The fifteenth of Av (Tu b'Av), which falls during the first or second week of consolation, is identified in the rabbinic literature as a courtship and fertility festival which is only weakly connected to a biblical rationale. Finally, Rosh Hashanah, which marks the end of the cycle, is also invested with a variety of meanings ranging from the cosmic to the moral-theological. While many of these identifications are only attested in the rabbinic literature, it is quite probable that many of them predate the rise of rabbinic Judaism. The isolated references to the fertility festival of Tu b'Av and to the malevolence of the "three weeks," and the subordination of these traditions to the more dominant theological paradigm, suggest that the rabbis inherited rather than invented these traditions.[3] Through the creation of the Tisha b'Av season, the rabbis incorporate these various traditions into a coherent articulation of one of the master narratives of biblical and rabbinic Judaism: the narrative of sin-punishment-repentance-redemption. Within the Tisha b'Av season, as it is defined by the lectionary, the cosmic danger of the three weeks between the seventeenth of Tammuz and the ninth of Av is transformed into the covenantal danger of the sin segment of the sequence. The various misfortunes commemorated on Tisha b'Av and the autonomous malevolence of the day itself are subsumed into Lamentations' violent description of the destruction of the temple and Jerusalem and its quasi-demonic portrait of God's anger. The fertility themes of Tu b'Av are transposed onto the God-Israel relationship through the erotic thematics of the haftarot of consolation. Thus, the season is not a creation *de novo*, nor is it a tyrannical silencing of pre-rabbinic traditions. Rather, it represents an artful appropriation and incorporation of divergent seasonal traditions into a master narrative.

For both the redactors of the Hebrew Bible and the rabbinic sages, the historical-theological sequence of sin-punishment-repentance-redemption served as the central narrative for understanding Israel's past and future. However, it is not clear to what extent non-rabbinic or pre-rabbinic Jews in late antique Palestine had internalized this narrative. If, as Seth Schwartz suggests, particularist Jewish culture largely disintegrated in

---

3. The ubiquity of fertility festivals across cultures and the frequency of midsummer holidays of lament and mourning in Ancient Near Eastern cultures further support the hypothesis that at least some of these traditions pre-date the rabbinic movement. See J. Z. Smith, "Dying and Rising Gods," *Encyclopedia of Religion* (ed. Mircea Eliade; New York: Macmillan, 1987), 4:520–27; Raphael Kutscher, "The Cult of Dumuzi/Tammuz," in *Bar Ilan Studies in Assyriology Dedicated to Pinhas Artzi* (ed. Jacob Klein and Aaron Skaist; Ramat Gan: Bar Ilan University Press, 1990), 29–44; Noel Robertson, "The Ritual Background of the Dying God in Cyprus and Syro-Palestine," *Harvard Theological Review* 75 (1982): 313–59.

the few hundred years following the destruction of the second temple and the failed Bar Kochba revolt, then the assertion of this narrative in the public synagogue setting would have been a strong pedagogical move—a way to school the Jewish public in the central rabbinic understanding of its national history. If this narrative had continued to be widespread among Jews and central to their self-understanding in the centuries between the end of the biblical period and the rise of rabbinic influence, then its articulation in the Tisha b'Av season would be an opportunity to reiterate and affirm what all present believed to be true.

In either case, the particular version of the master narrative that is articulated through the literature and rituals of the Tisha b'Av season remains very powerful. First, the lectionary itself, and the interpretations of it in the piyyutim and midrashim, authorize and institutionalize a communal identification of the destructions as punishment for Israel's sins. By using biblical texts to articulate this assertion, the rabbinic creators of the lectionary cycle invest it with both biblical and communal authority. The "evidence" comes not only from the divinely authorized text, but also from the text that the community identifies as its own.

The Tisha b'Av season not only shapes the community's understanding of its history, it also has the power to shape the community's understanding of its location and identity within that history. The interaction of the texts and rituals of the season coalesce into a ritual drama that fosters identification between the worshiping community and Zion/Israel, whose story is recounted through the lectionary cycle. During the three weeks preceding Tisha b'Av, the members of the synagogue community are the addressees for the haftarot of rebuke. In becoming the audience for the prophetic rebuke, the synagogue community assumes the role of sinning Israel, which is addressed by the rebuking prophets. On the ninth of Av, the community participates in acts of self-mortification and penance that serve a dual ritual function. On one level, these acts are the rituals of mourning through which the community expresses grief over the catastrophes commemorated on Tisha b'Av. Within the lectionary drama, they are the actions that forge an identification between the worshiping community and suffering and lamenting Zion. Lamentations speaks of famine and starvation while the community fasts. The text speaks of the wearing of sackcloth, the wailing of lament, and sitting on the ground; the community mimics these acts of suffering, mourning and penance through the fast-day rituals. By doing as Zion does, the worshiping community once again plays the role of the protagonist of the lectionary cycle. In the context of this ritual drama, the reversal of the tropes of suffering and penance in the haftarot of consolation and in the piyyutim that interpret them not only responds to the experience of Zion in Lamentations, but also to the ritual experience of the worshiping community. In the synagogues where Kallir's *kedushtot* were recited, the first seasonally specific text of the weeks following Tisha b'Av would have been the *magen* that I analyzed in chapter 4. This poem exhorts its addressees to get up from their mourning, don clothing of glory and majesty, and go out and trample their enemies. It also assures them that their sins have been forgiven and that God's anger has abated. These exhortations would have been directly relevant to a community which had recently participated in the rituals of Tisha b'Av.

The identity with Zion/Israel that is fostered through the interaction of the texts and rituals of the season in turn fosters communal identification with both the journey from despair and anger to reconciliation and praise which is narrated by the haftarot of the season, and with the changing relationship between God and Israel that is described by them. Over the course of the cycle, the haftarot describe a surprising shift in the dynamics of power in the relationship between God and Israel. The haftarot of rebuke represent a period of destabilizing disobedience and rebuke; Lamentations describes a period of violence and alienation in which God is the omnipotent agent and Israel is the powerless victim. In the weeks following Tisha b'Av, God assumes the role of supplicant, doing whatever he can to console Israel. In the haftarot of consolation, as well as in Kallir's *kedushta* for the second week of consolation, Israel is in control; it determines the success or failure of the divine consolatory project. This surprising shift in the dynamic of power has implications for the significance of Rosh Hashanah. The rabbinic and post-rabbinic liturgies of Rosh Hashanah stress the acceptance of divine sovereignty. When Rosh Hashanah is read and/or experienced as the final stage of the Tisha b'Av season, this liturgical stance takes on a different nuance. It serves as a reinstatement of divine sovereignty which has only been made possible by the process of reconciliation that precedes it. This reconciliation is dependent not on Israel's submission to God's will, but on Israel's acceptance of God's attempts at consolation. Thus, the reaffirmation of divine power depends on the diminution of that power vis-à-vis the relationship with Israel that is implicit in the lectionary cycle. Thus, the Tisha b'Av cycle is not only about Tisha b'Av and the events that it commemorates; it also makes an argument about the larger relationship between God and Israel that is solemnified and celebrated on Rosh Hashanah.

The Propagation of Rabbinic Judaism in Late Antiquity

In the preceding section, I discussed what effects the complex of texts and rituals of the Tisha b'Av season might have had on the worshiping community. I will conclude by speculating further as to how the rabbinic creation of the Tisha b'Av season might have participated in the larger project of the rabbinization of Jews in late antique Palestine.

1) The privileging of the theological-historical understanding of the season articulated in the haftarot might have been tempered by the cosmic-mythic iconography of the synagogue and the stronger mythic valences of the piyyutim. The lectionary narrative offers a relatively monovocal interpretation of the significance of the Tisha b'Av season. However, when embedded in the surrounding texts and images of the synagogue, this monovocality might have given way to a more multi-layered representation of the season that articulated more strongly both its historical and cosmic valences.

2) As I mentioned in chapter 3, the inscriptional remains of the late antique synagogues suggest that late antique Jews saw their local communities as the human players in the covenantal relationship with God. The fostering of an identification between the worshiping community and the Zion/Israel of the lectionary texts might have brokered the distance between this view and the more nationalist view of the biblical and rabbinic literature.[4] Through the texts and rituals of the Tisha b'Av season, the worshiping community plays the role of Zion/Israel in the ritual drama of the season. This role-playing provides a means to maintain both ideologies of community simultaneously. The worshiping community, as it assumes the role of Israel, functions as the human partner in the covenantal relationship.

3) It is striking how little the haftarot and midrashim of the season focus on the temple and temple cult. The temple is a central topic in the rabbinic literature composed for a rabbinic audience and is also present in the liturgy—a rabbinic literature composed for the larger Jewish population. In light of this rabbinic concern for the temple, one might expect that the Tisha b'Av season would become the site for prolonged reflection on the demise of the temple and its cult. However, the temple is largely absent from the lectionary and from the midrashic reflections on the season.[5] In contrast, the piyyutim of the season, which do not originate in rabbinic circles, do invoke the temple and fantasize about its glorious restoration.[6] Even in synagogues which did not recite temple-focused piyyutim, the recitation of the haftarot would occur in a context heavily saturated with concern for the temple—both the iconography of the synagogue and the

---

4. The use of "congregation" in TJ might reflect a similar shift to the national focus. See Chilton, *Isaiah Targum*, xx.

5. This generalization largely holds for Lam R., and for Lam Z. as well.

6. See p. 136.

rabbinic liturgy include many references to the temple and its cult. Thus the relative absence of these topics from the haftarot would be countered by the prevalence of the temple in the synagogue setting and the surrounding liturgy. I cannot say definitively what the interaction of these various elements would have communicated. I can only speculate that the rabbinic choice to shift the focus of the season away from the temple testifies to ongoing anxiety about the place of the defunct temple in the synagogue community's understanding of itself and its history. The strong assertions regarding God's enduring presence and attention, as well as the institution of the lectionary and ritual enactment of repentance and reconciliation with God, argue that the absence of the temple is not synonymous with the absence of God and the impossibility of reconciliation. Perhaps paradoxically, the rabbinic creators of the Tisha b'Av season use the day of mourning for the destructions of the temples as an occasion to argue that the central functions of the temple—atonement and reconciliation—were still being fulfilled in the midst of the worshiping community.

Bibliography

Primary Sources

Aboth de Rabbi Natan: Edited from Manuscripts with an Introduction, Notes, and Appendices. Edited by Solomon Schechter. Vienna, 1887; repr. Hildesheim, 1979.

Biblia Hebraica Stuttgartensia. 2d ed. Edited by Karl Elliger and Wilhelm Rudolph. Stuttgart: Deutsche Bibel Gesellschaft, 1984.

Complete Abudarham. Jerusalem: Usha, 1958.

The Former Prophets According to Targum Jonathan. Vol. 2 of *The Bible in Aramaic, based on Old Manuscripts and Texts.* Edited by Alexander Sperber. Leiden: Brill, 1962.

Maḥzor Vitry. Edited by S. Hurwitz. Nurnberg: J. Bulka, 1923.

Mekilta de-Rabbi Ishmael: A Critical Edition on the Basis of the Manuscripts and Early Editions, with an English Translation, Introduction and Notes. Edited by Jacob Z. Lauterbach. Philadelphia: Jewish Publication Society, 1933–35.

Mekhilta de Rabbi Shimon ben Jochai al pi kitvei yad min hagenizah umimidrash haggadol. Edited by Jacob N. Epstein and Ezra Z. Melamed. Jerusalem: Mekitsei nirdamim, 1955.

Midrash Bereshit Rabba: Critical Edition with Notes and Commentary. Edited by Julius Theodor and Chanoch Albeck. Jerusalem: Wahrmann, 1965.

Midrash Eikhah Rabah. Edited by Solomon Buber. Vilna: Hildesheim 1889.

Midrash Haggadol on the Pentateuch. Jerusalem: Mossad HaRav Kook, 1967–75.

Midrash Pesikta Rabati. Edited by Meir Friedmann. Vienna: Friedmann and Guedemann, 1880; repr. Tel Aviv, 1963.

Midrash Rabbah. Edited by A. Mirkin. Tel Aviv: Yavneh, 1956–67.

Midrash Rabbah: Shir ha-shirim: midrash Hazit. Edited by Samson Dunski. Jerusalem: Devir, 1980.

Midrash Tanḥuma. Edited by Solomon Buber. Vilna: Romm, 1885; repr. Jerusalem: Ortsel, 1964.

Midrash Zuta. Edited by Solomon Buber. Vilna: Romm, 1925.

Pesiqta de Rav Kahana: According to an Oxford Manuscript, with Variants. Edited by Bernard Mandelbaum. New York: Jewish Theological Seminary, 1962.

Pesikta: Ve-hi agadat Erets Yisra'el meyuheset le-Rav Kahana. Edited by Solomon Buber. Lyck: Ḥevrat mekitse nirdamim, 1868.

Pirkei de-Rabbi Eliezer. Warsaw: Bomberg, 1852; repr. Jerusalem, 1963.

Seder Olam Rabba. Edited by Baer Ratner. Vilna: Romm, 1897.

Shishah Sidre Mishnah. Edited by Chanoch Albeck. Jerusalem: Mossad Bialik, 1952–58.

Talmud Bavli. Vilna, 1880–86. Repr. frequently.

Talmud Yerushalmi. Krotoshin, 1866. Repr. frequently.

Tosefta. Edited by Saul Lieberman. New York: Jewish Theological Seminary, 1955–73.

Treatise Soferim in *Seven Minor Treatises: Sefer Torah; Mezuzah; Tefillin; Zizit; Abadim; Kutim; Gerim. And Treatise Soferim.* Edited by Michael Higger. New York: Bloch, 1930.

Yalkut Shim'oni. Venice, 1566. Repr. frequently.

Works Consulted

Abrahamson, Barbara Elka. "Three Sermons of Rebuke: A Comparative Analysis of the Pesiqta De Rav Kahana and the Pesikta Rabbati." M.H.L. diss., Hebrew Union College-Jewish Institute of Religion, 1985.

Albrektson, Bertil. *Studies in the Text and Theology of the Book of Lamentations.* Lund: CWK Gleerup, 1963.

Alexander, Philip. "Jewish Aramaic Translations." Pages 217–54 in *Mikra: Text, Translation, Reading, and Interpretation of the Hebrew Bible in Ancient Judaism and Early Christianity.* Edited by Martin J. Mulder. Philadelphia: Fortress Press, 1988.

———. "The Rabbinic Lists of Forbidden Targumim." *Journal of Jewish Studies* 27 (1976): 177–91.

———. "The Targumim and the Rabbinic Rules for the Delivery of the Targum." Pages 14–28 in *Congress Volume: Salamanca, 1983.* Supplements to Vetus Testamentum 63. Edited by J. A. Emerton. Leiden: Brill, 1985.

Alon, Gedalia. *The Jews in Their Land in the Talmudic Age.* Translated by Gershon Levi. Cambridge: Harvard University Press, 1989.

Anderson, Bernhard. "Exodus Typology in Second Isaiah." Pages 177–95 in *Israel's Prophetic Heritage: Essays in Honor of James Muilenberg*. Edited by Bernhard W. Anderson and Walter Harrelson. New York: Harper and Row, 1962.

Anderson, Gary. *A Time to Mourn, A Time to Dance: The Expression of Grief and Joy in Israelite Religion*. University Park: Pennsylvania State University Press, 1991.

Aufrecht, Walter. "Some Observations on the *Überlieferungsgeschichte* of the Targums." Pages 77–88 in *Targum Studies I*. Edited by Paul Flesher. Atlanta: Scholars Press, 1992.

Auld, Graham. "Poetry, Prophecy, Hermeneutic: Recent Studes in Isaiah." *Scottish Journal of Theology* 33 (1980): 567–81.

Avi-Yonah, Michael. *Art in Ancient Palestine*. Jerusalem: Magnes Press, 1981.

———. *The Jews of Palestine: A Political History from the Bar Kokhba War to the Arab Conquest*. New York: Schocken, 1974.

Bacher, Wilhelm. *Die Proömien der alten jüdischen Homilie*. Leipzig: Hinrichs, 1913.

———. "Targum." Pages 135–36 in vol. 1 of *The Jewish Encyclopedia*. New York and London: Funk and Wagnalls, 1916.

Baeck, Leo. "Haggadah and Christian Doctrine." *Hebrew Union College Annual* 22 (1950–51): 549–60.

———. "Zwei Beispeiele midraschischer Predigt." *Monatschrift für Geschichte und Wissenschaft des Judentums* 69 (1925): 258–70.

Bakhtin, Mikhail. *The Dialogic Imagination*. Edited by Michael Holquist. Translated by Caryl Emerson and Michael Holquist. Austin: University of Texas Press, 1981.

Barr, James. *The Typology of Literalism in Ancient Biblical Translations*. Gottingen: Vandenhoeck & Ruprecht, 1979.

Bartal, Israel. "The Ingathering of Traditions: Zionism's Anthology Projects." *Prooftexts* 17 (1997): 77–93.

Barth, Lewis. "Literary Imagination and the Rabbinic Sermon: Some Observations." Pages 29–36 in *Proceedings of the Seventh World Congress of Jewish Studies*. Jerusalem: World Union for Jewish Studies, 1981.

———. "The 'Three of Rebuke and the Seven of Consolation': Sermons in the *Pesikta de Rav Kahana*." *Journal of Jewish Studies* 33 (1982): 503–15.

Bell, Catherine. *Ritual Theory, Ritual Practice*. New York: Oxford University Press, 1992.

Ben-Porat, Ziva. "The Poetics of Literary Allusion." *PTL: A Journal for Descriptive Poetics and Theory of Literature* 1 (1976): 110–11.

Bickermann, Elias. "Septuagint as Translation." *Proceedings of the American Academy for Jewish Research* 28 (1959): 1–40.

Biddle, Mark. "The Figure of Lady Jerusalem: Identification, Deification, and Personification of Cities in the Ancient Near East." Pages 173–94 in *The Biblical Canon in Comparative Perspectives*. Edited by K. Lawson Younger, Jr., William W. Hallo and Bernard F. Batto. Lewiston: Edwin Mellen, 1991.

Bird, Phyllis. "'To Play the Harlot': An Inquiry into an Old Testament Metaphor." Pages 75–94 in *Gender and Difference in Ancient Israel*. Edited by Peggy Day. Minneapolis: Fortress Press, 1989.

Black, Matthew. *An Aramaic Approach to the Gospels and Acts*. Oxford: Clarendon Press, 1967.

Blank, Sheldon. "Studies in Deutero-Isaiah." *Hebrew Union College Annual* 15 (1940): 1–46.

Bloch, Philipp. "Studien zur Aggadah." *Monatschrift fur Geschichte und Wissenschaft des Judentums* 31 (1885): 166–84.

Bokser, Baruch. "Rabbinic Responses to Catastrophe: From Continuity to Discontinuity." *Proceedings of the American Academy of Jewish Research* 50 (1983): 37–61.

Branham, Joan. "Vicarious Sacrality: Temple Space in Ancient Synagogues." Pages 319–45 in *Ancient Synagogues: Historical Analysis and Archaeological Discovery*. Vol. 2. Edited by Dan Urman and Paul Flesher. Leiden: Brill, 1995.

Braude, William G. and Israel J. Kapstein, eds. *Pesikta de-Rab Kahana: R. Kahana's Compilation of Discourses for Sabbaths and Festal Days*. Philadelphia: Jewish Publication Society, 1975.

Bregman, Marc. "Circular Proems and Proems Beginning with the Formula 'Zo hi shene'emrah beruah haq-qodesh.'" Pages 34–51 in *Studies in Aggadah, Targum and Jewish Liturgy in Memory of Joseph Heinemann*. Edited by Ezra Fleischer and Jakob Petuchowski. Jerusalem: Magnes Press, 1981 (Heb.).

———. "Midrash Rabbah and the Medieval Collector Mentality." *Prooftexts* 17 (1997): 63–76.

———. "The Triennial Haftarot and the Perorations of the Midrashic Homilies." *Journal of Jewish Studies* 32 (1981): 74–84.

Brock, Sebastian. "Aspects of Translation Technique in Antiquity." *Greek, Roman and Byzantine Studies* 20 (1979): 69–87.

Brown, Peter. *Society and the Holy in Late Antiquity*. Berkeley: University of California Press, 1982.

Buber, Martin and Franz Rosenzweig. *Scripture and Translation*. Translated by Lawrence Rosenwald with Everett Fox. Bloomington: Indiana University Press, 1994.

———. "The Reading of the Law and the Prophets in the Triennial Cycle." Parts 1, 2. *Jewish Quarterly Review* (1893) 4:420–68; (1894) 5:1–73.

Childs, Brevard S. *Introduction to the Old Testament as Scripture*. Philadelphia: Fortress Press, 1979.
Chilton, Bruce D. *The Glory of Israel: The Theology and Provenience of the Isaiah Targum*. Sheffield: JSOT Press, 1983.
———. *The Isaiah Targum*. Wilmington: Glazier, 1987.
Churgin, Pinchos. *Targum Jonathan to the Prophets*. New Haven: Yale University Press, 1927.
Clements, Ronald. "Beyond Tradition History: Deutero-Isaianic Development of First Isaiah's Themes." *Journal for the Study of the Old Testament* 31 (1985): 95–113.
Clifford, Richard. *Fair Spoken and Persuading: An Interpretation of Second Isaiah*. New York: Paulist Press, 1984.
Cohen, Abraham. *The Five Megilloth*. London: Soncino, 1946.
Cohen, Gerson. "The Song of Songs and the Jewish Religious Mentality." Pages 3–18 in idem, *Studies in the Variety of Rabbinic Cultures*. Philadelphia: Jewish Publication Society, 1991.
Cohen, Naomi. "Earliest Evidence of the Haftarah Cycle for the Sabbaths between *Tisha b'Av* and *Rosh Hashanah* in Philo." *Journal of Jewish Studies* 48 (1997): 225–49.
Cohen, Norman J. "Leviticus Rabba, Parashah 3: An Example of a Classic Rabbinic Homily." *Jewish Quarterly Review* 72 (1981): 18–31.
Cohen, Shaye J. D. "The Destruction: From Scripture to Midrash." *Prooftexts* 2 (1982): 18–39.
———. "The Place of the Rabbi in Jewish Society of the Second Century." Pages 157–73 in *The Galilee in Late Antiquity*. Edited by Lee I. Levine. New York: Jewish Theological Seminary, 1992.
———. "The Temple and the Synagogue." Pages 151–74 in *The Temple in Antiquity: Ancient Records and Modern Perspectives*. Edited by Truman G. Madsen. Provo, UT: Religious Studies Center, Brigham Young University, 1984.
Cook, Edward. "A New Perspective on the Language of Onqelos and Jonathan." Pages 142–57 in *The Aramaic Bible: Targums in Their Historical Context*. Edited by Derek R. G. Beattie and Martin J. McNamara. Sheffield: JSOT Press, 1994.
Crockett, Larrimore. "*Luke iv*: 16–30 and the Jewish Lectionary Cycle: A Word of Caution." *Journal of Jewish Studies* 17 (1966): 13–46.
Dahood, Mitchell. *Psalms III: 101–150*. Anchor Bible 17a. Garden City: Doubleday, 1964.
Davidson, Israel. *Maḥzor Yannai*. New York: Jewish Theological Seminary, 1919.
Dobbs-Allsopp, F. W. *Weep, O Daughter of Zion: A Study of the City-Lament Genre in the Hebrew Bible*. Rome: Editrice Pontificio Istituto Biblico, 1993.

Doty, William. *Mythography: The Study of Myths and Rituals.* Birmingham: University of Alabama Press, 1986.
Eaton, John. *Festal Drama in Deutero-Isaiah.* London: SPCK, 1979.
Elbaum, Yaakov. "*Yalqut Shim'oni* and the Medieval Midrashic Anthology." *Prooftexts* 17 (1997): 133–51.
Elbogen, Ismar. *Jewish Liturgy: A Comprehensive History.* Translated by Raymond P. Scheindlin. Philadelphia: Jewish Publication Society, 1993.
Elizur, Shulamit. "The Congregation in the Synagogue and the Ancient Qedushta." Pages 171–90 in *Knesset Ezra.* Edited by Shulamit Elizur et al. Jerusalem: Yad Izhak Ben-Zvi, 1994 (Heb.).
———. *Kedushah ve-shir: kedushta'ot le-shabtot ha-neḥamah le-Rabi El'azar bi-Rabi Kilir.* Jerusalem: Magnes Press, 1988.
———. *Ha-piyut ha-Ivri be-Erets Yisra'el uva-mizraḥ.* Jerusalem: Hebrew University Press, 1991.
———. *Piyute El'azar bi-Rabi Kilir ve-yaḥasam litsirato shel El'azar bi-Rabi Kilir.* Jerusalem: Hebrew University Press, 1981.
———. *Piyute R. Yehudah bi-Rabi Binyamin.* Jerusalem: Nirdamim Press, 1988.
Fine, Steven. *This Holy Place: On the Sanctity of the Synagogue During the Greco-Roman Period.* Notre Dame: University of Notre Dame Press, 1997.
Fishbane, Michael. "Arm of the Lord: Biblical Myth, Rabbinic Midrash, and the Mystery of History." Pages 271–92 in *Language, Theology, and the Bible: Essays in Honour of James Barr.* Edited by Samuel Balentine and John Barton. Oxford: Clarendon Press, 1994.
———. "Biblical Prophecy as a Religious Phenomenon." Pages 62–81 in *Jewish Spirituality.* Vol. 1, *From the Bible through the Middle Ages.* Edited by Arthur Green. New York: Crossroad, 1986.
———. *Garments of Torah: Essays in Biblical Hermeneutics.* Bloomington: Indiana University Press, 1989.
———. *JPS Bible Commentary: Haftarot.* Philadelphia: Jewish Publication Society, 2002.
———. "Substitutions for Sacrifice in Judaism." Pages 123–35 in idem, *The Exegetical Imagination: On Jewish Thought and Theology.* Cambridge: Harvard University Press, 1998.
Fitzgerald, Aloysius. "The Mythological Background for the Presentation of Jerusalem as a Queen and False Worship as Adultery in the OT." *Catholic Biblical Quarterly* 34 (1972): 403–16.
Fleischer, Ezra. *Hebrew Liturgical Poetry in the Middle Ages.* Jerusalem: Keter, 1975 (Heb.).
———. "Studies in the Problems Relating to the Liturgical Function of the Types of Early Piyyut." *Tarbiz* 40 (1970): 41–63 (Heb.).

———. "Le-fitron sheelat zemano u-makom peiloto shel R. El'azar bi-Rabi Kilir." *Tarbiz* 54 (1984): 387–427.

Flesher, Paul. "Translation and Exegetical Augmentation in the Targums." Pages 29–85 in *New Perspectives on Ancient Judaism III*. Edited by Jacob Neusner and Ernest S. Frerichs. Lanham: University Press of America, 1987.

Foerster, Gideon. "The Zodiac in Ancient Synagogues and its Place in Jewish Thought and Literature." *Eretz-Israel* 18 (1987): 380–91 (Heb.).

Fraade, Steven D. "Rabbinic Views on the Practice of Targum, and Multilingualism in the Jewish Galilee of the Third–Sixth Centuries." Pages 253–86 in *The Galilee in Late Antiquity*. Edited by Lee Levine. New York: Jewish Theological Seminary, 1992.

Freid, Natan. "Haftarah." Pages 1–31, 703–23 in vol. 10 of *Talmudic Encyclopedia*. Jerusalem: Talmudic Encyclopedia Publishing Company, 1947 (Heb.).

Frymer-Kensky, Tikva. *In the Wake of the Goddesses: Women, Culture, and the Biblical Transformation of Pagan Myth*. New York: Free Press, 1992.

Gaster, Theodor. *Myth, Legend, and Custom in Ancient Israel*. New York: Harper and Row, 1969.

———. *Thespis: Ritual, Myth, and Drama in the Ancient Near East*. New York: Doubleday, 1950.

Gaston, Lloyd. *No Stone on Another: Studies in the Significance of the Fall of Jerusalem in the Synoptic Gospels*. Leiden: Brill, 1970.

Ginzberg, Louis. *Ginze Shekhter*. New York: Jewish Theological Seminary, 1929.

Gitay, Yehoshua. *Prophecy and Persuasion: A Study of Isaiah 40–48*. Forum Theologiae Linguisticae 14. Bonn: Linguistica Biblica, 1981.

Glatzer, Nahum. "The Concept of Sacrifice in Post-biblical Judaism." Pages 48–57 in *idem, Essays in Jewish Thought*. University, AL: University Press, 1978.

Goldberg, Abraham. "On the Authority of the Chapters '*Vayehi baḥazi hallayla*' (Ex. XII, 29) and '*Shor o Kesev*' (Lev. XII, 27) in the Pesiqta," *Tarbiz* 38 (1968): 184–85.

———. Review of *Pesikta de Rav Kahana*, edited by Bernard Mandelbaum. *Kiryat Sefer* 43 (1967): 68–79 (Heb.).

Goldenberg, Robert. "Early Rabbinic Explanations of the Destruction of Jerusalem." *Journal of Jewish Studies* 33 (1982): 517–25.

Goldin, Judah. "Of Midrash and the Messianic Theme." Pages 359–78 in *Studies in Midrash and Related Literature*. Edited by Barry Eichler and Jeffrey Tigay. Philadelphia: Jewish Publication Society, 1988.

———. "Three Pillars of Simeon the Righteous." *Proceedings of the American Academy of Jewish Research* 27 (1958): 43–58.

Golomb, David M. "'A Liar, A Blasphemer, A Reviler': The Role of Biblical Ambiguity in the Palestinian Pentateuchal Targumim." Pages 135–46 in *Targum Studies I*. Edited by Paul Flesher. Atlanta: Scholars Press, 1992.

———. *A Grammar of Targum Neofiti*. Chico: Scholars Press, 1985.

Goodman, Martin. *State and Society in Roman Galilee, A.D. 132–212*. Totowa, NJ: Rowman & Allanheld, 1983.

Goodenough, Erwin. *Jewish Symbols in the Greco-Roman Period*. Princeton: Princeton University Press, 1953–68.

Gordis, Robert. "The Conclusion of the Book of Lamentations [5:22]." *Journal of Biblical Literature* 93 (1974): 289–93.

———. *The Song of Songs and Lamentations*. New York: Ktav, 1974.

Gordon, Robert. "Targum as Midrash: Contemporizing in the Targum to the Prophets." Pages 61–74 in *Proceedings of the Ninth World Congress of Jewish Studies*. Edited by Moshe Goshen-Gottstein. Jerusalem: World Union for Jewish Studies, 1985.

Goshen-Gottstein, Moshe. "Aspects of Targum Studies." Pages 61–74 in *idem, Proceedings of the Ninth World Congress of Jewish Studies*. Jerusalem: World Union for Jewish Studies, 1985.

Gottwald, Norman K. "Social Class and Ideology in Isaiah 40–55: An Eagletonian Reading." *Semeia* 59 (1992): 43–57.

———. *Studies in the Book of Lamentations*. London: SCM Press, 1962.

Green, Margaret W. "The Eridu Lament." *Journal of Cuneiform Studies* 30 (1978): 127–68.

———. "The Uruk Lament." *Journal of the American Oriental Society* 104 (1984) 253–79.

Greenberg, Moshe. *Ezekiel*. Anchor Bible 22–22a. New York: Doubleday, 1983, 1997.

Grimes, Ronald L. *Beginnings in Ritual Studies*. Washington: University Press of America 1982.

Grossberg, Daniel. *Centripetal and Centrifugal Structures in Biblical Poetry*. SBL Monograph Series 39. Atlanta: Scholars Press, 1989.

Gwaltney, W. C., Jr. "The Biblical Book of Lamentations in the Context of Near Eastern Lament Literature." Pages 242–65 in *Essential Papers on Israel and the Ancient Near East*. Edited by Frederick E. Greenspahn. New York: New York University Press, 1983.

Habermann, Abraham. *Ha-piyut: mahuto ve-hitpathuto*. Tel Aviv: Mifal hashikhpul, 1967.

———. *Toldot ha-piyut veha-shirah*. Ramat Gan: Masada, 1972.

Hachlili, Rachel. *Ancient Jewish Art and Archaeology in the Land of Israel*. Leiden: Brill, 1988.

Hammer, Reuven. "Galut va-sevel ha-shekhinah." Pages 20–29 in *Tura: Studies in Jewish Thought.* Edited by Meir Ayali. Tel Aviv: ha-Kibbuts ha-meuhad, 1989 (Heb.).

Hasan-Rokem, Galit. "Ha-meser ha-idiologi veha-meser ha-psikhologi be-ma'aseh bishne bene Zadok ha-cohen be-Ekhah Rabbah." In *Jerusalem Studies in Hebrew Literature* 3. Edited by Dan Miron. Jerusalem: Magnes Press, 1983.

Hays, Richard B. *Echoes of Scripture in the Letters of Paul.* New Haven: Yale University Press, 1989.

Heinemann. Joseph. "The Art of Composition in Midrash Leviticus Rabbah." *Hasifrut* 2 (1971): 808–834 (Heb.).

———. "Early Halakhah in the Palestinian Targumim." *Journal of Jewish Studies* 25 (1974): 114–22.

———. *Literature of the Synagogue.* With Jacob Petuchowski. New York: Behrman House, 1975.

———. "Mahzor ha-telat shanati ve-luah ha-shanah." *Tarbiz* 33 (1964): 362–68.

———. "Ha-petihtot be-midrashe ha-agadah: mekorotan ve-tafkidan." Pages 43–47 in *Papers of the Fourth World Congress of Jewish Studies.* Vol. 2. Jerusalem: World Union for Jewish Studies, 1965.

———. *Prayer in the Talmud: Forms and Patterns.* Berlin: de Gruyter, 1977.

———. "'The Priestly Blessing . . . Is Not Read.'" *Bar Ilan* 6 (1968): 33–41 (Heb.).

———. "The Proem in the Aggadic Midrashim: A Form-Critical Study." Pages 100–122 in *Studies in Aggadah and Jewish Folklore.* Scripta Hierosolymitana 22. Edited by Joseph Heinemann and Dov Noy. Jerusalem: Magnes Press, 1971.

———. "Profile of a Midrash." *Journal of the American Academy of Religion* 39 (1971): 141–50.

Hever, Hannan. "'Our Poetry is Like an Orange Grove': Anthologies of Hebrew Poetry in Erets Israel." *Prooftexts* 17 (1997): 199–225.

Hezser, Catherine. *The Social Structure of the Rabbinic Movement in Roman Palestine.* Tübingen: Mohr Siebeck, 1997.

Hillers, Delbert R. *Lamentations: A New Translation with Introduction and Commentary.* Anchor Bible 7a. Garden City: Doubleday, 1972.

Hoffman, Jeffrey. "The Bible in the Prayerbook: A Study in Intertextuality." Ph.D. diss., Jewish Theological Seminary, 1996.

Hoffman, Lawrence A. *Beyond the Text: A Holistic Approach to Liturgy.* Bloomington: Indiana University Press, 1987.

———. *The Canonization of the Synagogue Service.* Notre Dame: University of Notre Dame Press, 1979.

———. "Censoring In and Censoring Out: A Function of Liturgical Language." Pages 19–37 in *Ancient Synagogues: The State of Research*. Edited by Joseph Gutmann. Atlanta: Scholars Press, 1981.

———. "How Ritual Means: Ritual Circumcision in Rabbinic Culture and Today." *Studia Liturgica* 23 (1993): 78–97.

Hollander, John. *The Figure of Echo: A Mode of Allusion in Milton and After*. Berkeley: University of California Press, 1981.

Jacobsen, Thorkild. *Toward the Image of Tammuz*. Harvard Semitic Studies 21. Edited by W. L. Moran. Cambridge: Harvard University Press, 1970.

Jaffee, Martin S. "The Midrashic 'Proem': Towards the Description of Midrashic Exegesis." Pages 95–112 in *Approaches to Ancient Judaism*, vol. 4. Edited by William S. Green. Chico: Scholars Press, 1983.

Jakobson, Roman. "Grammatical Parallelism and its Russian Facet." *Language* 42 (1966): 399–429.

———. "Linguistics and Poetics." Pages 350–77 in *Style in Language*. Edited by T. A. Sebeok. Cambridge: MIT Press, 1966.

Jastrow, Marcus. *A Dictionary of the Targumim, the Talmud Babli and Yerushalmi, and the Midrashic Literature*. New York: Title Publishing, 1943.

Kahle, Paul. *Masoreten des Westens*. Stuttgart: Kohlhammer, 1927.

Kaiser, Barbara Bakke. "'Poet as Female Impersonator': The Image of Daughter Zion as Speaker in Biblical Poems of Suffering." *Journal of Religion* 67 (1987): 164–82.

Kasher, Rimon. "The Aramaic Targumim and their *Sitz im Leben*." Pages 75–88 in *Proceedings of the Ninth World Congress of Jewish Studies*. Edited by Moshe Goshen-Gottstein. Jerusalem: World Congress of Jewish Studies, 1988.

———. *Toseftot targum la-Nevi'im*. Jerusalem: World Union for Jewish Studies, 1996.

Kaufmann, Yehezkel. *History of the Religion of Israel*. Jerusalem and Tel Aviv: Bialik and Devir, 1937–56 (Heb.).

Kimelman, Reuven. "The Shema' Liturgy: From Covenant Ceremony to Coronation." Pages 12–25 in *Kenishta: Studies of the Synagogue World*. Edited by Joseph Tabory. Ramat Gan: Bar Ilan University Press, 2001.

Kirschner, Robert. "Apocalyptic and Rabbinic Responses to the Destruction of 70." *Harvard Theological Review* 78 (1985): 27–46.

Klein, Michael. *Anthropomorphisms and Anthropopathisms in the Targumim of the Pentateuch*. Jerusalem: Makor, 1982 (Heb.).

———. "Associative and Complementary Translations in the Targumim." *Eretz-Israel* 16 (1982): 134–40 (Heb.).

———. "Converse Translation: A Targumic Technique." *Biblica* 57 (1976): 515–37.

———. Four Notes on the Triennial Lectionary Cycle." *Journal of Jewish Studies* 32 (1981): 65–73.

———. "Not to be Translated in Public." *Journal of Jewish Studies* 39 (1988): 80–91.

———. "The Preposition *qdm* ('Before'): A Pseudo-Anti-Anthropomorphism in the Targums." *Journal of Theological Studies* 30 (1979): 502–7.

———. "Translation of Anthropomorphisms and Anthropopathisms in the Targumim." Pages 162–67 in *Congress Volume: Vienna 1980*. Leiden: Brill, 1981.

Knight, George A. F. *Deutero-Isaiah: A Theological Commentary on Isaiah 40–55*. New York: Abingdon Press, 1965.

Kraemer, David. *Reading the Rabbis: The Talmud as Literature*. New York: Oxford University Press, 1996.

———. *Responses to Suffering in Classical Rabbinic Literature*. New York: Oxford University Press, 1995.

Kramer, Samuel Noah, trans. "Lamentation over the Destruction of Sumer and Ur." Pages 611–19 in *Ancient Near Eastern Texts Relating to the Old Testament*. Edited by James Pritchard. Princeton: Princeton University Press, 1969.

———. "Lamentation over the Destruction of Ur." Pages 455–63 in *Ancient Near Eastern Texts Relating to the Old Testament*. Edited by James Pritchard. Princeton: Princeton University Press, 1969.

Kronfeld, Chana. "Allusion: An Israeli Perspective." *Prooftexts* 5 (1985): 137–63.

Kutscher, Edward. *A History of Aramaic*. Jerusalem: Academon, 1971.

Kutscher, Raphael. "The Cult of Dumuzi/Tammuz." Pages 29–44 in *Bar Ilan Studies in Assyriology Dedicated to Pinhas Artzi*. Edited by Jacob Klein and Aaron Skaist. Ramat Gan: Bar Ilan University Press, 1990.

———. *A History of the Hebrew Language*. Jerusalem: Magnes Press, 1982 (Heb.).

Lanahan, William. "The Speaking Voice in the Book of Lamentations." *Journal of Biblical Literature* 93 (1974): 41–49.

Leiman, Sid Z. *The Canonization of Hebrew Scripture: The Talmudic and Midrashic Evidence*. Hamden: The Connecticut Academy of Arts and Sciences, 1976.

Levine, Etan. *The Aramaic Version of the Bible: Contents and Context*. Berlin: de Gruyter, 1988.

Levine, Lee I. *The Ancient Synagogue: The First Thousand Years*. New Haven: Yale University Press, 2000.

———. *The Rabbinic Class of Roman Palestine in Late Antiquity*. New York: Jewish Theological Seminary, 1989.

———. "The Sages and the Synagogue in Late Antiquity: The Evidence of the Galilee." Pages 201–22 in *The Galilee in Late Antiquity*. Edited by Lee I. Levine. New York: Jewish Theological Seminary, 1992.

Lewin, Ellen Davis. "Arguing for Authority: A Rhetorical Study of Jeremiah 1:4–19 and 20:7–18." *Journal for the Study of the Old Testament* 32 (1985): 105–19.

Liebrich, Leon. "The Compilation of the Pesuke De-Zimra." *Proceedings of the American Academy for Jewish Research* 18 (1949): 255–67.

Linafelt, Tod. "Surviving Lamentations." *Horizons in Biblical Theology* 17 (1995): 45–61.

———. *Surviving Lamentations: Catastrophe, Lament, and Protest in the Afterlife of a Biblical Book*. Chicago: University of Chicago Press, 2000.

Mann, Jacob. *The Bible as Read and Preached in the Old Synagogue*. Cincinnati: Hebrew Union College, 1940–66.

———. "Changes in the Divine Service Due to Religious Persecution." *Hebrew Union College Annual* 4 (1927): 241–310.

Maori, Yeshayahu. "The Aramaic Targumim to the Torah and Rabbinic Exegesis." Pages 1–12 in *Proceedings of the Ninth World Congress of Jewish Studies*, Hebrew section. Edited by Moshe Goshen-Gottstein. Jerusalem: World Union for Jewish Studies, 1988.

Margoliot, Eleazar. "Ivrit ve-Aramit be-talmud u-midrash." *Leshonenu* 27 (1962–63): 20–33.

Maybaum, S. *Die ältesten Phasen in der Entwicklung der jüdischen Predigt*. Berlin: H. Itzkowski, 1901.

McDaniel, Thomas F. "The Alleged Sumerian Influence upon Lamentations." *Vetus Testamentum* 18 (1968): 198–209.

McFague, Sallie. *Metaphorical Theology: Models of God in Religious Language*. Philadelphia: Fortress Press, 1982.

McKenzie, John L. *Second Isaiah*. Anchor Bible 20. Garden City: Doubleday, 1968.

McNamara, Martin. *Targum and Testament: Aramaic Paraphrases of the Hebrew Bible: A Light on the New Testament*. Shannon: Irish University Press, 1972.

Melamed, Ezra Zion. *Bible Commentators*. Vol. 2. Jerusalem: Magnes Press, 1978 (Heb.).

Melugin, Roy. *The Formation of Isaiah 40–55*. Berlin: de Gruyter, 1976.

Menn, Esther. *Judah and Tamar (Genesis 38) in Ancient Jewish Exegesis: Studies in Literary Form and Hermeneutics*. Leiden: Brill, 1997.

Mettinger, Tryggve. *A Farewell to the Servant Songs: A Critical Examination of an Exegetical Axiom*. Lund: CWP Gleerup, 1982.

Mintz, Alan. *Hurban: Responses to Catastrophe in Hebrew Literature*. New York: Columbia University Press, 1984.

———. "The Rhetoric of Lamentations and the Representation of Catastrophe." *Prooftexts* 2 (1982): 1–17.
Mirsky, Aaron. "Earlier and Later Stages in the Poetry of Eleazar ha-Kallir." *Kiryat Sefer* 35 (1959): 237–39 (Heb.).
———. *Maḥtsavtan shel tsurot ha-piyut: tsemiḥatan ve-hitpatḥutan shel tsurot ha-shirah ha-Erets Yisre'elit ha-kedumah*. Jerusalem: Schocken, 1968.
———. *Ha-piyut: The Development of Post-biblical Poetry in Erets Yisrael and the Diaspora*. Jerusalem: Magnes Press, 1990 (Heb.).
———. *Reshit ha-piyut*. Jerusalem: Jewish Agency, 1965.
Moore, Michael S. "Human Suffering in Lamentations." *Revue Biblique* 90 (1983): 534–55.
Morris, Nathan. *The Jewish School: An Introduction to the History of Jewish Education*. New York: Jewish Education Committee Press, 1964.
Muilenberg, James. "Isaiah, Chapters 40–66." Pages 381–773 in *The Interpreter's Bible*. Vol. 5. Edited by George Buttrick. New York: Abingdon Press, 1956.
Muñoz-León, Domingo. "Memra in the Targum to Isaiah." Pages 135–42 in *Proceedings of the Ninth World Congress of Jewish Studies*. Edited by Moshe Goshen-Gottstein. Jerusalem: World Congress of Jewish Studies, 1986.
Naidoff, Bruce D. "The Rhetoric of Encouragement in Isaiah 40:12–31: A Form-Critical Study." *Zeitschrift für die Alttestamentliche Wissenschaft* 93 (1981): 62–76.
Neusner, Jacob. *Beyond Catastrophe: The Rabbis' Reading of Isaiah's Vision*. Atlanta: Scholars Press, 1996.
———. *From Tradition to Imitation: The Plan and Program of Pesiqta Rabbati and Pesiqta deRab Kahana*. Atlanta: Scholars Press, 1987.
———. "Judaism in a Time of Crisis: Four Responses to the Destruction of the Second Temple." *Judaism* 21 (1972): 313–27.
———. "Map Without Territory: Mishnah's System of Sacrifice and Sanctuary," Pages 133–53 in idem, *Method and Meaning in Ancient Judaism*. Missoula, MT: Scholars Press, 1979.
———, trans. *Pesiqta deRab Kahana: An Analytical Translation*. Atlanta: Scholars Press, 1987.
———. *Symbol and Theology in Early Judaism*. Minneapolis: Fortress Press, 1991.
Newsom, Carol A. "A Response to Norman Gottwald, 'Social Class and Ideology in Isaiah 40–55.'" *Semeia* 59 (1992): 73–78.
O'Connell, Robert H. *Concentricity and Continuity: The Literary Structure of Isaiah*. Sheffield: Sheffield Academic Press, 1994.
Pagis, Dan. *Ḥidush u-masoret be-shirat ha-ḥol ha-Ivrit: Sefarad ve-Italyah*. Jerusalem: Keter, 1976.

Rabinowitz, Zvi Meir. *Halakhah ve-agadah be-fiyutei Yanai: mekorot ha-payetan, le-shono u-tekufato.* Tel Aviv: Keren Aleksander Kahut, 1965.

Ransom, John C. *The New Criticism.* Westport: Greenwood Press, 1979.

Ratzaby, Yehuda. *Texts and Studies in Orient Liturgical Poetry.* Jerusalem: Misgav Yerushalayim, 1991 (Heb.).

Re, Lucia. "(De)Constructing the Canon: The Agon of the Anthologies on the Scene of Modern Italian Poetry." *Modern Language Review* 87 (1992): 585–602.

Reif, Stefan. "The Early History of Jewish Worship." Pages 109–36 in *The Making of Jewish and Christian Liturgy.* Edited by Paul F. Bradshaw and Lawrence A. Hoffman. Notre Dame: University of Notre Dame, 1991.

———. *Judaism and Hebrew Prayer: New Perspectives on Jewish Liturgical History.* Cambridge: Cambridge University Press, 1993.

Rendtorff, Rolf. *Canon and Theology: Overtures to an Old Testament Theology.* Edited and translated by Margaret Kohl. Minneapolis: Fortress Press, 1993.

Ribera, Josep. "Prophecy According to Targum Jonathan to the Prophets and the Palestinian Targum to the Pentateuch." Translated by Fiona Ritchie. Pages 61–74 in *Targum Studies I.* Edited by Paul Flesher. Atlanta: Scholars Press, 1992.

Robertson, Noel. "The Ritual Background of the Dying God in Cyprus and Syro-Palestine." *Harvard Theological Review* 75 (1982): 313–59.

Roskies, David. *Against the Apocalypse: Responses to Catastrophe in Modern Jewish Culture.* Cambridge: Harvard University Press, 1984.

———. "The Holocaust According to its Anthologists." *Prooftexts* 17 (January 1997): 95–113.

Safrai, Hanna. "Women in the Ancient Synagogue." Pages 39–49 in *Daughters of the King: Women and the Synagogue.* Edited by Susan Grossman and Rivka Haut. Philadelphia: Jewish Publication Society, 1992.

Safrai, Shmuel and Menachem Stern, eds. *The Jewish People in the First Century: Historical Geography, Political History, Social, Cultural and Religious Life and Institutions.* Philadelphia: Fortress Press, 1976.

Samely, Alexander. "The Background of Speech: Some Observations on the Representation of Targumic Exegesis." *Journal of Jewish Studies* 39 (1988): 251–60.

Sarason, Richard. "On the Use of Method in the Modern Study of Jewish Liturgy." Pages 97–172 in *Approaches to Ancient Judaism: Theory and Practice.* Edited by William Scott Green. Missoula, MT: Scholars Press, 1978.

———. "The *Petihtot* in Leviticus Rabba: 'Oral Homilies' or Redactional Constructions?" *Journal of Jewish Studies* 33 (1982): 557–67.

―――. "Toward a New Agendum for the Study of Rabbinic Midrashic Literature." Pages 55–73 in *Studies in Aggadah, Targum and Jewish Liturgy in Memory of Joseph Heinemann*. Edited by Ezra Fleischer and Jacob Petuchowski. Jerusalem: Magnes Press, 1981.

Sawyer, John. "Daughter of Zion and Servant of the Lord in Isaiah: A Comparison." *Journal for the Study of the Old Testament* 44 (1989): 89–107.

Schaefer, Peter. "Die Peticha-ein Proömium?" *Kairos* 12 (1970): 216–19.

Schirmann, Jefim. "Hebrew Liturgical Poetry." *Jewish Quarterly Review* 44 (1953): 123–61.

Schmitt, John J. "The Gender of Ancient Israel." *Journal for the Study of the Old Testament* 26 (1983): 115–25.

Schwartz, Seth. *Imperialism and Jewish Society, 200 B.C.E. to 640 C.E.* Princeton: Princeton University Press, 2001.

Shinan, Avigdor. *The Biblical Story as Reflected in Its Aramaic Translations.* Tel Aviv: ha-Kibbuts ha-meuhad, 1993 (Heb.).

―――. *The Embroidered Targum: The Aggadah in Targum Pseudo-Jonathan of the Pentateuch.* Jerusalem: Magnes Press, 1992 (Heb.).

―――. *The Aggadah in the Aramaic Targums to the Pentateuch.* Jerusalem: Makor, 1979 (Heb.).

―――. "The Aggadah of the Palestinian Targums of the Pentateuch and the Rabbinic Aggadah: Some Methodological Considerations." Pages 203–17 in *The Aramaic Bible*. Edited by Derek R. G. Beattie and Martin J. McNamara. Sheffield: JSOT Press, 1994.

―――. "The Aramaic Targum as a Mirror of Galilean Jewry." Pages 241–51 in *The Galilee in Late Antiquity*. Edited by Lee I. Levine. New York: Jewish Theological Seminary, 1992.

―――. "Hebrew and Aramaic in the Literature of the Synagogue." Pages 224–32 in *Tura: Studies in Jewish Thought*. Edited by Meir Ayali. Tel Aviv: ha-Kibbuts ha-meuhad, 1989 (Heb.).

―――. "Le-torat ha-petihta." *Jerusalem Studies in Hebrew Literature* 1 (1981): 133–43.

―――. "Sermons, Targums, and the Reading from Scriptures in the Ancient Synagogue." Pages 97–110 in *The Synagogue in Late Antiquity*. Edited by Lee I. Levine. Philadelphia: American Schools of Oriental Research, 1987.

Silberman, Lou. "A Theological Treatise on Forgiveness: Chapter Twenty-Three of *Pesiqta Derab Kahana*." Pages 95–107 in *Studies in Aggadah, Targum and Jewish Liturgy in Memory of Joseph Heinemann*. Edited by Ezra Fleischer and Jacob Petuchowski. Jerusalem: Magnes Press, 1981.

Smith, Jonathan Z. "Dying and Rising Gods." Pages 521–27 in vol. 4 of *The Encyclopedia of Religion*. Edited by Mircea Eliade. New York: Macmillan, 1987.

———. *Map is Not Territory: Studies in the History of Religions*. Leiden: Brill, 1978.

Smolar, Leivy and Moshe Aberbach. *Studies in Targum Jonathan to the Prophets*. New York: Ktav, 1983.

Sommer, Benjamin. *A Prophet Reads Scripture: Allusion in Isaiah 40–66*. Stanford: Stanford University Press, 1998.

Sperber, Alexander. *The Bible in Aramaic*. Leiden: Brill, 1973.

Spykerboer, Hendrik C. *The Structure and Composition of Deutero-Isaiah, with Special Reference to the Polemics Against Idolatry*. Meppel: Krips Repro B. V., 1977.

Stern, David. "The Anthological Imagination in Jewish Literature." *Prooftexts* 17 (1997): 1–7.

———. "Midrash and the Language of Exegesis." Pages 105–24 in *Midrash and Literature*. Edited by Geoffrey Hartman and Sanford Budick. New Haven: Yale University Press, 1986.

———. "Anthology and Polysemy in Classical Midrash." Pages 108-39 in *The Anthology in Jewish Literature*. Edited by David Stern. New York: Oxford University Press, 2004.

———. *Parables in Midrash: Narrative and Exegesis in Rabbinic Literature*. Cambridge: Harvard University Press, 1991.

Strack, Hermann L. and Günter Stemberger. *Introduction to the Talmud and Midrash*. Translated by M. Bockmuehl. Minneapolis: Fortress Press, 1992.

Swartz, Michael. "Sage, Priest, and Poet: Typologies of Religious Leadership in the Ancient Synagogue. Pages 101–17 in *Jews, Christians, and Polytheists in the Ancient Synagogue*. Edited by Steven Fine. New York: Routledge, 1999.

Tabory, Joseph. "The Prayer Book (Siddur) As an Anthology of Judaism." *Prooftexts* 17 (1997): 115–32.

Theodor, Julius. "Zur Composition der agadischen Homilien." *Monatschrift für Geschichte und Wissenschaft des Judentums* 28 (1879): 97–112.

Turner, Victor. *The Ritual Process: Structure and Anti-Structure*. Ithaca: Cornell University Press, 1969.

Van Zijl, J. B. *A Concordance to the Targum of Isaiah*. Missoula, MT: Scholars Press, 1979.

Walton, John H. *Ancient Israelite Literature in Its Cultural Context*. Grand Rapids, MI: Zondervan, 1989.

Weems, Renita J. *Battered Love: Marriage, Sex, and Violence in the Hebrew Prophets*. Minneapolis: Fortress Press, 1995.

Weinberger, Leon. *Jewish Hymnography: A Literary History*. London: Littman Library of Jewish Civilization, 1998.

Weiss, Meir. *The Bible from Within: The Method of Total Interpretation*. Jerusalem: Magnes Press, 1984.

Weiss, Zvi and Ehud Netzer. "The Sepphoris Synagogues: A New Look at Synagogue Art and Architecture in the Byzantine Period." Pages 199–227 in *Galilee Through the Centuries*. Edited by Eric Meyers. Winona Lake: Eisenbrauns, 1999.
Westermann, Claus. *Isaiah 40–66, A Commentary*. Translated by David M. G. Stalker. Philadelphia: Westminster Press, 1969.
———. *Lamentations: Issues and Interpretation*. Translated by Charles Muenchow. Minneapolis: Fortress Press, 1994.
———. *The Praise of God in the Psalms*. Translated by Keith R. Crim. Richmond: John Knox Press, 1965.
Whybray, Roger Norman. *Isaiah 40–66*. London: Oliphants, 1975.
Wilken, Robert L. *The Land Called Holy*. New Haven: Yale University Press, 1992.
Willey, Patricia Tull. *Remember the Former Things: The Recollection of Previous Texts in Second Isaiah*. SBL Dissertation Series 161. Atlanta: Scholars Press, 1997.
Wimsatt, W. K. *The Verbal Icon: Studies in the Meaning of Poetry*. Lexington: University of Kentucky Press, 1954.
Yahalom, Joseph. "Piyyut as Poetry." Pages 111–26 in *The Synagogue in Late Antiquity*. Edited by Lee I. Levine. Philadelphia: American Schools of Oriental Research, 1987.
———. *Poetic Language in the Early Piyyut*. Jerusalem: Magnes Press, 1985 (Heb.).
———. *Poetry and Society in Jewish Galilee of Late Antiquity*. Tel Aviv: ha-Kibbuts ha-meuhad, 1999 (Heb.).
York, Anthony. "The Dating of Targumic Literature." *Journal for the Study of Judaism* 5 (1974): 49–62.
———. "The Targum in the Synagogue and School." *Journal for the Study of Judaism* 10 (1979): 74–86.
Zeitlin, Solomon. "Origins of the Synagogue: A Study in the Development of Jewish Institutions." *Proceedings of the American Academy of Jewish Research* 2 (1930–31): 69–81.
Zulay, Menachem. "Lidmutah lashon ha-payetanim." *Melilah* 5 (1955): 63–82.
Zunz, Leopold. *Die gottesdienstlichen Vörtrage der Juden Historisch Entwickelt*. Berlin: Asher, 1832.
———. *Ha-derashot be-Yisra'el: hishtalshelutan ha-historit*. Edited by Hanoch Albeck. Jerusalem: Bialik, 1954.

Index of Texts Cited

Hebrew Bible
Genesis
  1:1–6:8, 19
  1–6, 19
  1:16, 99
  1:28, 102, 103n43
  6:4, 46n53
  12:1, 89
  16:3, 103n43
  21:1, 99
  21:6, 98, 100, 101
  21:7, 99, 99n36, 100, 100n40, 101
  26:1, 89
  28:7, 89
  30:3, 46n53
  32:27, 37n42
Exodus
  8:11, 34–35n35
  12:41, 131
Leviticus
  1:14, 146
  12:2, 46n53
  12:6, 146
  14:30, 146
  15:19, 46n53
  15:20, 46n53
  15:24, 46n53
  15:25, 46n53
  15:26, 46n53
  15:33, 46n53
  18:19, 46n53
  26:40–42, 35
Deuteronomy
  7:5, 37n42
  11:13–25, 11n29
  11:28, 11n29
  28:1, 33
  28:15, 33
  29:22, 94
1 Samuel
  2:22, 99n36
  8:19, 37n42
  12:22, 141, 150n84
  18, 71n97
2 Kings
  25:8–9, 29
Isaiah
  1:1, 20–21n8, 22–23
  1:1–20, 42
  1:1–26, 43
  1:1–27, 42–43
  1:2–5, 42
  1:4, 40
  1:5–9, 40n47, 42
  1:7–8, 50
  1:10–17, 45
  1:11–12, 45

Hebrew Bible, Isaiah, cont.
1:11–17, 40
1:13–15, 42
1:14, 22
1:19–20, 40n47
1:21, 20, 20n8, 42, 44
1:21–24, 42
1:21–31, 42
1:23, 40
1:24–25, 40n47
1:25, 50
1:25–26, 42
1:26, 44, 67, 68
1:26–28, 42
5, 140n63
5:7, 141
10:22, 37n42
10:30, 89–90, 90, 91
29:1, 96
33:10, 132
38:14, 146
40:1, 22, 55, 58, 59n77, 60, 64, 65, 66, 125, 128, 134, 136, 159–160
40:1–2, 60
40:1–23, 130n46, 159, 163
40:1–26, 60, 61, 62
40:2, 127, 160
40:3, 67, 162
40:3–4, 126n40
40:3–5, 60
40:5, 55, 160
40:7, 160
40:8, 160
40:9, 67, 90, 162
40:9–11, 60
40:10, 67, 161, 162
40:10–11, 54, 126, 160, 160n14, 161
40:12, 160
40:12–26, 60
40:13, 161
40:17, 160
40:22, 159, 162
40:23, 159
40:25, 160
40:26, 61, 63, 159
40:27, 60
40:27–28, 59n78
40:28, 60
40–55, 59
40:55, 64
40–66, 49n59, 52, 52n61, 64, 67, 156, 163
40:66, 62
41:2–4, 33n30
41:15, 70n93
42:5–6, 19
42:5–43:11, 19
42:9, 49n59
43:12, 49n59
43:14, 132
44:7–8, 49n59
44:26, 49n59
44:28, 33n30
45:1, 33n30
45:19, 49n59
45:21, 49n59
45:23, 49n59
46:10–11, 49n59
47:6, 33n30
48:3–5, 49n59
49:7, 55
49:14, 21, 22, 58, 62, 67, 139, 141, 141n69, 149, 150, 151–152n88, 153
49:14–15, 137
49:14–17, 61
49:14–51:3, 61, 63
49:15, 126, 141, 141n69, 150, 153
49:15–16, 61
49:16–20, 126
49:17, 164n21
49:17–22, 54
49:18, 56, 61, 62, 105, 126

49:19–20, 55
49:20–21, 164
49:21, 145–156, 146
49:22, 126, 163
49:22–23, 55
49:23, 55, 101, 163
49:25, 163
50:1, 126, 164
50:2, 67
50:4–11, 53n68
50:8, 70n93
51:2, 22
51:3, 54, 55
51:9, 59
51:11–12, 53n68
51:12, 21, 55, 59, 59n77, 64, 126
51:12–16, 64
51:12–52:6, 64–65
51:12–52:12, 24
51:16, 70n92
51:17, 55, 64
51:17–23, 53n68, 64
51:18, 163
51:20, 163
51:22, 127, 163
51:22–23, 163
51:23, 54, 126n41
52:1, 55, 56, 126, 163
52:1–2, 101
52:1–3, 64
52:2, 55, 124n35, 127, 132, 132n51, 153n54, 163
52:7, 54
52:7–9, 64, 90
52:8, 55
52:9, 55, 67, 163
52:10, 55
52:11, 53
52:11–12, 54, 64, 126
52:12, 127
52:12–53:12, 53n68

54:1, 54, 56, 59, 65, 67, 70n93, 90, 101, 135, 145, 146, 163, 164, 164n22
54:1–3, 54
54:1–9, 65–66
54:1–10, 24
54:2, 44
54:3, 163
54:4, 124n32, 127, 163
54:4–5, 70
54:5, 65, 66
54:5–6, 56
54:5–10, 126
54:6–8, 53n68, 65
54:7, 127, 150–151
54:9, 55
54:9–10, 66
54:10, 21
54:11, 21, 56, 59, 63, 90
54:11–12, 54, 127
54:11–13, 53n68, 63
54:11–55:5, 24
54:11–55:12, 63
54:12, 44
54:14–18, 63
55:1, 54, 55
55:1–2, 67
55:5, 55, 101
55:6–8, 63
55:8–11, 49
55:9–11, 63
55:10, 44, 55
55:12, 54, 64, 127
55:12–13, 63, 63n81, 70n92
55:13, 44
55–66, 57n75
56:9–57:13, 57n75
56–66, 66
57:16, 149
59:11, 146
59:17, 105, 106n51
60:1, 21, 55, 59, 66, 127
60:1–3, 66

Hebrew Bible, Isaiah, cont.
  60:1–22, 57n75, 66–67
  60:4, 54, 66, 104, 126, 163, 164
  60:4–9, 55
  60:4–12, 57n75
  60:5–16, 55, 101
  60:7, 54, 66
  60:8, 146, 147
  60:9, 54, 66, 163
  60:10–13, 44
  60:13, 66
  60:14, 66
  60:14–16, 54
  60:16, 66
  60:17, 56
  60:17–18, 57n75
  60:18, 54
  60:19–20, 57n75, 66
  60:21, 44, 57n75
  61, 71n98
  61:10, 21, 54, 56, 59, 67, 99, 99n36, 100, 100n40, 101, 102, 103, 104, 104nn44–45, 105, 105n46, 106n49, 107, 135
  61:10–11, 98, 107
  61:11, 44, 98
  61–63, 71n98
  62, 71n98
  62:1, 67
  62:2, 55, 67
  62:3, 56, 67
  62:3–5, 107
  62:4, 44, 56, 67, 68, 70n93, 101, 164n22
  62:4–5, 164
  62:4–6, 70, 71
  62:5, 54, 70n93, 105, 164n22
  62:6–7, 74
  62:8, 67
  62:9, 67
  62:9–10, 44
  62:10, 55, 59, 67
  62:11, 67, 126
  62:11–12, 90
  62:12, 67
  63:1, 71, 106, 107
  63:1–2, 56
  63:1–6, 71n98
  63:1–7, 107
  63:2, 105, 106, 107
  63:3, 71
  63:6, 68
  63:7, 68
  63:7–64:11, 71n98
  63:9, 68, 71–72
  66:10, 125, 135
  66:10–11, 135
  66:11, 125
  67:10, 124
  67:11, 124
  54:1b, 146
  62:5b, 166
Jeremiah
  1, 20–21n8, 22
  1:1, 20, 22, 83, 84, 90, 97
  1:1–2:4, 41
  1:1–2:28, 43
  1:2–3, 96
  1:3, 96
  1:4–7, 96
  1:5–6, 50
  1:10, 41, 43
  1:13–15, 50
  1:14–16, 40
  1:15, 41
  1:16, 40
  2:1, 138n59
  2:2–3, 41
  2:4, 20–21n8, 22
  2:4–28, 40, 41, 47
  2:5, 48
  2:12–13, 29
  2:15, 50
  2:20–26, 42
  2:23–25, 46, 47

2:24, 47, 48
3:22, 95
4:1–2, 41, 41n49
4:7, 89
9:9, 93n22, 94
13:16, 93
31:10, 93
31:11, 93
31:13, 96
31:37, 149
33:11, 105
39:12, 92
39–40, 92
40:1, 92, 92n20
40:4, 93n22
40:4–5, 92
40:5, 93
40:6, 92
48:28, 146
51:14, 37n42
52:12–13, 29

Ezekiel
7:16, 146
17, 140n63

Hosea
2–3, 70n95
2:14–23, 70n95
5:15, 95
11:11, 146, 147

Amos
3:8, 96
5:22, 37n42

Micah
4:13, 124n33

Nahum
2:8, 146

Zephaniah
3:11, 124n32

Zechariah
2:17, 132, 132n51
8:19, 135
9:9, 104

Psalms
31:3, 149
31:13, 139
48:12, 104
55:7, 146
60:7, 151
79:4, 139
85:7, 98, 99–100
91:6, 30
91:15, 151
92:19, 135n57
93, 106, 108
93:1, 105, 105n46, 106
94:19, 124, 125
104, 106, 108
104:1, 105
104:1–2, 108
113:9, 138n58, 144–146
118:24, 101, 102
121:3, 151
137:5, 141, 150, 151–152n88, 152, 153
147:2, 96, 135

Job
6:10, 125, 135n57
7:10, 124

Song of Songs, 147
1:4, 101, 102, 103, 103n43, 104n44
1:5, 140n65, 147n80
1:15, 146
2:5, 141n68
2:14, 140n62, 146, 148, 152
4:1, 146
4:8, 105, 124n31, 131–132, 132, 133n53
4:10, 105
4:12, 105
4:12–16, 140n63
5:1, 105, 140n63
5:2, 140n62, 141n66, 146, 147n80, 148
5:8, 141n68

Hebrew Bible, Song of Songs, cont.
  5:12, 146
  5:13, 140n63
  6:2, 140n63
  6:8, 148
  6:9, 140n62, 141n66, 146, 147n80, 148
  6:23, 140n63
  7:5, 140n64
Lamentations
  1, 20–21n8, 36, 37
  1:1, 22, 31, 42–43, 55, 126
  1:2, 31, 47, 48, 55, 126
  1:2–4, 53n68
  1:3, 47
  1:3–5, 31, 54
  1–4, 143n74
  1:4, 31, 55
  1:5, 31, 33, 33n31, 42, 55
  1:7–8, 55
  1:8, 46, 138n60
  1:8–9, 33n31, 42, 46
  1:8–10, 31, 55
  1:9, 55, 126
  1:10, 46, 55
  1:11, 54, 55
  1:11, 31
  1:12, 33, 55
  1:13, 55
  1:13–15, 33n32
  1:14, 33n31, 42
  1:15, 126n41
  1:16, 126
  1:16–17, 55
  1:17, 58, 126
  1:17–18, 33n32
  1:18, 31, 33n31, 42, 54, 55
  1:19, 31, 54
  1:21, 31, 55, 126
  2, 36, 37
  2:1, 31, 55, 124n35, 127
  2:1–2, 45, 54
  2:1–8, 33n32
  2:1–9, 127
  2:2–3, 37
  2:3–4, 55
  2:4, 31, 124n35, 151
  2:6, 140n63
  2:6–7, 31, 45, 54
  2:8, 31, 55, 124n35
  2:9, 31, 54
  2:10, 55, 124n35, 126, 127
  2:10–13, 31
  2:11, 139n61
  2:11–12, 31, 54
  2:13, 124n35
  2:14, 42
  2:15–16, 31, 55
  2:17, 33n32
  2:18, 31, 55, 124n35
  2:18–19, 74
  2:18–20, 74
  2:20, 33n32, 74
  2:20–21, 31, 54
  2:22, 31, 33n32, 55
  3, 35, 36, 37, 38, 39, 53n68, 98
  3:1–18, 33n32
  3:21, 36
  3:21–22, 34, 34n33, 68n88
  3:28–29, 55
  3:31–33, 34, 34n34
  3:38, 33n32
  3:42, 33n31, 42
  3:43, 56
  3:43–45, 33n32
  3:55–56, 34, 34n35
  3:58–59, 36
  3:58–64, 36
  4, 36, 37, 53n68
  4:1–2, 53n68, 56
  4:3–10, 31, 54
  4:11, 33n32, 55
  4:13, 33n31, 42, 53
  4:15, 31, 53, 54
  4:16, 33n32
  4:18, 31, 55

4:19, 55
4:22, 37, 124n35
5, 36, 37
5:3, 56
5:4, 55
5:4–5, 31, 54
5:7, 33n31, 42
5:9–10, 31
5:9–13, 54
5:16, 33n31, 42
5:18, 31, 54
5:19, 36n39
5:19–22, 39, 53n68
5:20, 139, 149, 150, 150n83, 153
5:21, 36–37
5:22, 37, 37n42, 139, 149, 150, 153
Daniel
   7:9, 105, 106n51
Nehemiah
   8:8, 157

Mishnah
Berachot, 116n10
   2:2, 25
Megillah, 116
   4:1–2, 17, 18
   4:4, 18
Taanit
   2:1–4, 117
   4:6, 29

Tosefta
Megillah
   3:10, 18
   3:22, 4n16
Yebamot
   8:4, 102n42

Jerusalem Talmud
Ketubot
   12:3 (35b), 94n29
Kilayim
   9:4 (32b), 94n29
Megillah
   3:7, 41n49
   4:1 (74d), 4, 18, 157
   4:5, 18n3
Sukkot
   4:1 (54c), 92n20
Taanit
   1:1 (64a), 92n20
   4:8 (69b), 94n27, 95n30

Babylonian Talmud
Avot de-Rabbi Natan
   12, 155
   34 (Version A), 95n33
Baba Batra
   15a, 41n48
Baba Metzia
   87a, 99n36
Makkot
   10b, 81–82n4
Megillah
   23a, 18
   27a, 18–19
   29a, 92n20
   31a–b, 23
   29b, 26n21
   31b, 18n2, 20n7, 23
   10b–11a, 81–82n4
Rosh Hashanah
   31a, 95n33
Sanhedrin
   11a, 49n58
   97a–99a, 57n75
Shabbat
   145b, 94n27
Soferim, 116n10
   1–10, 18n1

Babylonian Talmud, Soferim, cont.
  12:1, 41n49
  Sotah
    48b, 49n58
  Taanit
    29a, 29
  Yoma
    24a, 94n29
    54a, 94n27
    9b, 49n58

Midrash
  Deuteronomy Rabbah
    2:37, 100n40, 104n44, 105n46
  Esther Rabbah
    7:12, 150n85
  Exodus Rabbah
    1:23, 145
    15:17, 92n20
    23:5, 132n52, 133n53
  Genesis Rabbah, 81–82n4
    45:3, 102n42
    45:4, 148
    53:5, 145
    53:8, 100n38
    53:8–9, 99n36
    65:1, 153n54
    90:1, 148
    94:1, 148
  Lamentations Rabbah, 123n29,
    150, 175
    1, 145
    1:1, 150n84
    1:3, 29–30
    1:54, 151
    2:2, 57n74
    2:3, 151
    5:20, 149
    5:22, 150
    25, 95n33
  34, 91n19, 92nn20–21, 93n22,
    94nn26–29, 95n30
  Lamentations Zuta, 123n29,
    175n5
    1:21, 145n76
    1:28, 135
  Leviticus Rabbah, 81–82n4, 84,
    85–86
    1:1, 86
    10:2, 100n40
  Mekhilta de-Rabbi Ishmael
    Pisḥa
      14, 131
    Beshallaḥ
      2, 148
      7, 132
    Baḥodesh
      3, 148
  Midrash Hagadol
    Bereishit
      1:30, 105n46
    Lekh lekha
      16:3, 102n42, 103n43
    Vayera
      21:8, 99n36
    Tazria
      13:59, 95n33
  Midrash Psalms
    92:6, 135n57
    94:3, 150n85
    119:30, 150n83
    119:38, 135n57
  Numbers Rabbah
    4:2, 148
    7:10, 92n20, 133n53
    9:14, 148
    12:3, 30n28
    14:10, 148
  Pesikta de-Rav Kahana
    9–11, 91–93
    11, 84
    12, 84

Index of Texts Cited

13, 83
13:1, 88–90, 97
13:2, 88
13:3, 83
13:4, 83, 88
13:5, 83, 88
13:5–7, 88
13:6, 88
13:7, 84, 88
13:8, 84, 88
13:8–11, 88
13:9, 88
13:9–10, 96
13:9–11, 96, 97
13:10, 88, 93n22
13:11, 84, 88, 96
13:12, 83, 84, 88
13:13, 88
13:14, 88
13:15, 88, 96–97, 97
15, 20n8
15:7, 147n78
16:4, 100n40
17:2, 150n84
17:5, 151
20:1, 145
22, 97–98, 136
22:1, 98–99, 99, 99n36, 100–101, 100n38
22:1.1, 99
22:1.2, 100
22:1.3, 100
22:1.4, 100
22:1.5, 100
22:2, 101–104, 104n44
22:2.2, 101–102
22:3, 104
22:4, 104
22:5, 104, 107
113–22, 123n29
Pesikta Rabbati, 99n36
    1, 94n29

28, 151
28–37, 123n29
29, 92n21, 151
31, 150
31:3, 149
31:5, 151
31:6–7, 151n88
37, 100n40
38, 105n46
42, 100n38
43 (180), 145
Pirkei de-Rabbi Eleazar
    42, 99n36
    43, 99n36
    51, 99n36
Ruth Rabbah
    2:12 (6), 150n85
Seder Olam
    27, 94n27, 94n29
Sifre Deuteronomy
    161, 155
Song of Songs Rabbah, 132
    1:1, 100n40
    1:2, 100n40
    1:4, 102n42, 103n43, 104n44, 135
    4:10, 105n46
    5:2, 148
    6:9, 148
Song of Songs Zuta
    4:8, 131n48, 133n53
Yalkut Shimoni
    Bereishit
        16, 103n43
    Lekh lekha
        79, 102n42
    Vayera
        93, 99n36, 100n38
    Daniel
        1066, 94n29
    Ezekiel
        350, 95n33

Midrash, Yalkut Shimoni, cont.
  Isaiah
    505, 100n40, 104nn44–45
    506, 105n46
  Jeremiah
    257, 95n33
    281, 94nn26–29, 95n30
    327, 91n19, 92nn20–21, 93n22
  Psalms
    474, 94n29
    847, 105n46
  Song of Songs
    988, 105n46
  Yebamot
    6:6, 102–103, 102n42

General Index

A

abandonment trope, 34, 58, 61, 126, 141–44, 149–50, 162–63
Abudarham, 23–24, 58, 59n77, 115n6
allusions
    dove (image), 138, 140, 140n62, 144, 145, 146–49, 152
    Lamentations in Second Isaiah, 52–54, 52n64
    metalepsis, 122–23
    in midrash, 122–23
    readers' recognition of, 122, 130, 131, 134n56
    to Song of Songs, 130–31, 133–34
    to Zion, 144–45
amidah, 114, 115, 117, 137
a minori ad majus (*kal vaḥomer*), 99n36, 100, 101, 102, 103n43
Anatoth, 88, 89, 90
anthology, 25–26, 27, 28, 28n24, 31
anthropomorphisms, 142, 151, 158–59, 160–63, 160n14
Aramaic, 157–58, 164, 166
audience
    allusions recognized by, 122, 130, 131, 134n56
    anthropomorphisms understood by, 160–61
    Aramaic literacy of, 157–58, 164, 166
    communal lectionary readings, 9–10n26
    kedushtot understood by, 134n56
    for Targum Jonathan, 10, 170–71
    for Tisha b'Av ritual re-enactments, 36–37, 36n39, 173–74
Auerbach, Moshe, 159
Avi-Yonah, Michael, 3

B

Babylonia
    conquest by, 31, 32–33
    exile in, 53, 127, 132
    Greece associated with, 105, 106n51
    Nebuchadnezzar in, 29, 89, 92, 93n22, 96, 97
    Torah lectionary system in, 21
Bar Kokhba, 57n74, 173
barrenness, 102–3, 103n43, 108, 164–65
beit midrash, 8, 9, 10, 81–82, 157, 170
Ben-Porat, Ziva, 121, 122

birth of Isaac, 98–99, 99n36, 100–101, 100n38
Braude, William, 106n51
bridal references, midrash and piyyutim, 105, 105n46, 106, 106n49, 108, 109, 124n31, 131–34, 133n53
Buber, Solomon, 22, 80n2

C

catastrophe
    Lamentations on, 44, 54
    reversals in haftarot of consolation, 97
    on seventeenth of Tammuz, 29–31, 171–72
    the three weeks, 30–31, 30nn27–28, 76, 171–72
    on Tisha b'Av, 29–33
    See also destruction of the temples in Jerusalem
Chilton, Bruce, 159, 162
Cohen, Gerson, 130n47
Cohen, Shaye J. D., 28n25
community
    access to biblical texts, 17
    in 5th–6th century CE, 56 , 56–58, 56n73, 57nn74–75, 75
    laments of, 36–37, 36n39
    lectionary system of, 9–10n26
    synagogue and, 3–4, 7, 75, 109
    voice of, 117, 143
    worshipping, 72–73, 75, 175
consolation, haftarot of, 40, 51–52
    absence of temple and, 75
    dialogic arrangement of, 58–59, 66, 68–69, 72
    exile motif in, 96
    God's coming and going in, 162–63
    God's love for Israel as redemptive, 107
    messianism, 107
    optimism in, 90, 91
    reconciliation between God and Israel, 61–62, 72
    reliability of divine word, 49–50
    restoration in, 43–44, 70, 97
    Second Isaiah, 55, 58, 60–69, 125, 128, 134–36, 150–51, 159–60
    shame, 69–70
    structure of, 23–24, 24n16
    voice in, 59, 73
    worshipping community, 72–73
    See also Isaiah; Jerusalem; kedushtot; Lamentations; Zion
correspondence paradigm, 105–6, 107

D

davar aḥer, 91, 95, 96, 97
Dead Sea Scrolls, 57n74
destruction of the temples in Jerusalem
    divine anger, 32–33, 45
    in Lamentations, 28, 31–34, 43, 54, 55
    as punishment for Israel's sins, 173
    sexual imagery, 45–46, 46n55
    theology of, 11–12
    Tisha b'Av and, 28–31
    See also Jerusalem; Zion
dialogue, 58–59, 66, 68–69, 72, 139, 144, 152, 153
dove (image), 138, 140, 140n62, 144, 145, 146–49, 152

E

Edom, 106, 107
Elizur, Shulamit, 134n56, 152

espousal
    abuse and, 149–50
    God as husband, 70–72, 70n93, 70n95, 71nn96–97, 104, 105, 165
    Israel as bride, 105, 105n46, 106, 106n49, 108, 109, 131
    as metaphor for Exodus, 133
exile
    God's presence in, 32–33, 91–93, 92n20, 94–96, 95n31, 126, 131–32
    in Isaiah, 44, 44n51
    Land of Israel and, 94–95, 95n31
    planting imagery of, 140n63
    in PRK, 90, 91–92
    redemption, 57n75, 63
    restoration after, 36–37, 43–44, 54–55, 57, 57n75, 62–63, 70, 97
    return from, 60, 63, 127, 132, 136
    as sign of divine displeasure, 57–58, 58n76, 95
    the supernatural in, 94–95
    synagogue iconography and, 109

F

fertility
    barrenness, 102–3, 103n43, 108, 145–46, 164–65
    birth of Isaac, 98–99, 99n36, 100–101, 100n38
    festivals of, 172, 172n3
    infertility and marriage, 101–2
    motherhood, 144–46, 145n75, 164–65
    Sarah, 98–99, 99n36, 100–101, 100n40, 103n43
    Zion's restoration as, 145–46
First Isaiah
    destruction of the people, 51
    exile narrative in, 44, 44n51
    haftarot of rebuke and, 20, 20n8, 42–43, 44
    on Jerusalem, 42, 43
    Lamentations, parallels to, 42–43, 44
    messianism, 57n75
    Pesikta de-Rav Kahana on, 89–91
    reliability of divine word in, 49
    See also Second Isaiah
Fishbane, Michael, 151n87
Fleischer, Ezra, 114, 119, 134n56
Frymer-Kensky, Tikva, 71n97

G

garment texts, 105, 105n46, 106, 106nn48–50, 108, 123, 126, 127
God
    anthropomorphisms, 142, 151, 158–59, 160–63, 160n14
    consolation, 34–35, 43, 58–59, 59n77, 61–63, 65, 68
    divine movement, 160, 160n14, 161–63
    dressing texts, 105, 105n46, 106, 106nn48–50, 108, 127
    exhortations to, 73–74
    history controlled by, 33–34, 71, 105–6
    as husband, 70–72, 70n93, 70n95, 71nn96–97, 104, 105
    Israel's obedience to, 11–12, 33, 148–49
    memra and, 160, 160n16
    nature and, 63, 63n82, 64, 69
    presence in exile, 32–33, 91–93, 92n20, 94–96, 95n31, 126, 131–32
    reconstruction of temple and, 127, 136
    as redeemer, 62–63

redemption of Israel, 69–71, 69nn90–91, 71–72, 106–7
as shekhinah, 95, 95n33, 131, 158, 159, 159n13
in Targum Jonathan, 158, 159, 159n13
wrath of, 37
Zion and, 60, 66, 67
God-Israel relationship
  abandonment trope in, 34, 58, 61, 126, 141–44, 149–50, 162–63
  desexualization of, 164–66
  destruction of temples in Jerusalem, 32–33, 45
  eroticism in, 66, 140n63, 172
  as gardener-plant relationship, 63n81, 140, 140n63, 141
  God's presence in exile, 32–33, 91–93, 92n20, 94–96, 95n31, 126, 131–32
  interdependence in, 151–52
  Israel's singular status, 147–49
  love in, 68–69, 71–72, 101–4, 103n43, 108, 133–34, 139, 144–48, 163, 167
  nostalgia in, 141–42
  reconciliation in, 38–39, 61–62, 65–66, 72
  redemption and, 139, 144, 147–48
  rejection trope in, 149–50, 164
  romance in, 130–31, 139, 144, 147–48, 153, 163, 167
  semantic fields for, 142
  in Song of Songs, 130–32, 130n47
  Targum Jonathan on, 164
Gog and Magog, 105, 107
Goldberg, Abraham, 81n3
Goodenough, Erwin, 3n9
Gordis, Robert, 37n42
Gottwald, Norman, 52, 54

H

haftarot, 9n26, 18–21, 20nn6–8, 22, 31, 41n49
  See also consolation, haftarot of; rebuke, haftarot of; Torah and Torah readings
Hays, Richard, 52n64, 122
Heinemann, Joseph, 9, 84–87
Helios imagery, 4, 7
Hillers, Delbert, 38
Hollander, John, 122

I

impurity, 45–46, 53, 55–56, 126, 138, 138n60
Isaac, birth of, 98–99, 99n36, 100–101, 100n38
Israel
  as bat-gallim, 89–90
  as bride, 105, 105n46, 106, 106n49, 108, 109, 131
  destruction of enemies of, 126
  as dove, 148–49, 152
  female personification of, 32, 37, 45–46, 65, 70–71, 70n93, 70n95, 142, 163
  God as husband of, 70–72, 70n93, 70n95, 71nn96–97, 104, 105, 165
  God's presence in exile, 32–33, 91–93, 92n20, 94–96, 95n31, 126, 131–32
  Isaiah on destruction of, 51
  Jeremiah on sinfulness of, 41–42
  Lebanon as epithet for, 124, 124n31, 126
  obedience of, 11–12, 33, 148–49
  as orphan, 104, 104n45
  as plant, 140, 140n63
  reconciliation with God, 38–39, 61–66, 72, 139, 144
  rejoicing of, 63, 65, 67

sexual transgression, 42, 44, 46–47, 47n57

J

Jakobson, Roman, 118n15
Jeremiah, book of
  abandonment trope in, 149
  on God's presence in exile, 91–95, 92n20
  on God's rejection of Israel, 150
  haftarot of rebuke, 20, 41–42, 43, 87–88, 89, 90
  introduction of prophetic speech in, 88
  Jerusalem's siege in, 51
  Lamentations and, 41, 41n48, 43n50, 47
  Pesikta de-Rav Kahana's discussion of, 83, 89–93, 95–96
  planting images in, 43–44
  reliability of divine word in, 49–50
  sexual language of, 46–47
  sin-punishment-restoration narrative and, 43
Jeremiah (prophet)
  God's charge to, 43, 91–92
  imprisonment of, 92–93
  name interpreted, 88, 91, 93n22, 95, 95n32, 97
  return from exile of, 93
Jerusalem
  epithets for, 96, 96n35, 140n64
  exile from, 54
  female personification of, 32, 41, 42, 46, 90
  isolation of, 47–48, 126, 143, 143n74
  Jeremiah on, 51
  in Lamentations, 28, 31–34, 43, 54, 55
  in messianic perorations, 57n75, 96, 97
  rejoicing of, 100, 102, 104, 135
  in Second Isaiah, 55, 56, 57, 57n75
  sexual violation of, 46–48, 47n57
  See also destruction of the temples in Jerusalem; temple in Jerusalem; Zion
Jochebed, 145
Judah b. Barzilai of Barcelona (Rabbi), 115

K

Kallir, Eleazar
  allusion used by, 121–22, 130–34
  audience of, 8n22, 134n56
  on God's rejection of Israel, 150
  on haftarot of consolation, 21, 42
  on Jerusalem, 136
  Pesikta de-Rav Kahana and, 79–80n1
  poetic techniques of, 12
  rabbinic tradition and, 8
  romantic relationship between God and Israel, 147–48
  on temple cult, 136
  Torah lectionary system, 22
  See also allusions; *kedushtot*; rhyme
kal vaḥomer, 99n36, 100, 101, 102, 103n43
Kapstein, Israel, 106n51
Kaufmann, Yehezkel, 52n61, 54
kedushtot
  abandonment trope in, 141–44, 149–50
  amidah and, 114, 117, 137
  audience's understanding of, 134n56

dove imagery in, 138, 140, 140n62, 144, 145, 146–49, 152
fast day liturgies and, 117
Magen to Shabbat *Vatomar Tzion*, 137–39, 142–43
meḥayeh to Shabbat *Vatomar Tzion*, 139–40, 143–44
motherhood in, 144–46, 145n75
nostalgia for the temple in, 136, 170
poetic techniques of, 12
rhyme patterns, 120, 128, 142–44
seven weeks of consolation, 125–26
structure of, 119
theme words in, 134
voice in, 143
Zion in, 124, 124n33, 124n35 , 126, 127, 129, 130, 140n64, 141–44
See also allusions; *Magen* for *Kedushta* to Shabbat *Naḥamu*; piyyutim
ketev meriri, 30–31
Klein, Michael, 13n30, 158–59, 162

L

Lamentations
abandonment in, 149–50
catastrophes in, 44, 54
communal laments and, 36–37, 36n39, 72–73, 173
consequences of transgression, 40–41
consolation themes in, 35–36, 38
the covenant in, 34, 35–36, 37
despair in, 37–39
divine control of history in, 33–34, 58
exhortations in, 74
exile imagery in, 53–55, 96
impurity images in, 45–46, 53, 55–56, 126, 138, 138n60
Isaiah parallels to, 42–43, 44
Jeremiah and, 41, 41n48, 43n50, 47
on Jerusalem, 28, 31–34, 43, 54, 55
kedushtot themes and, 126, 127–28
optimism, 35–36, 38, 39, 73
placement of, 43n50
rebuke, haftarot of, 48
Second Isaiah and, 52–55, 52n61, 52n64, 53n68, 127
sexual allusion in, 45–46, 47n57
speakers in, 35–36, 72–73, 143n74
suffering as consequence of disobedience, 33
temple destruction and, 28, 28n25, 45
Tisha b'Av lectionary cycle, 31, 40–41, 43, 43n50, 51–52, 76–77
Zion in, 31–32, 55, 56, 126
Land of Israel, 94–95, 95n31
Lebanon, 124, 124n31, 126, 131–34
Levine, Lee, 2, 3
Leviticus Rabbah, 84–86, 86n13
Linafelt, Tod, 38
lion motifs, 96, 96n35, 97
liturgical poetry. *See* piyyutim

M

Magen for *Kedushta* to Shabbat *Naḥamu*
consolatory tropes in, 126–28
dove image in, 147
Lamentations' tropes of destruction and, 126
Lebanon image in, 123, 124, 130
Song of Songs allusion in, 130–32, 130n47

text of, 123–25
trope of return in, 147
Zion in, 124, 126, 127
Magen to Shabbat *Vatomar Tzion*, 137–39, 142–43
Maḥzor Vitry, 20n7, 23–24, 62, 73n100
malevolence, 30–31, 30nn27–28
Mandelbaum, Bernard, 79–80n1, 80, 80n2, 81n3
McKenzie, John, 71n98
McNamara, Martin, 158
meḥayeh to Shabbat *Vatomar Tzion*, 139–40, 140n62, 143–44, 145, 146–47
Mekhilta de-Rabbi Ishmael, 131, 132
memra, 160, 160n16
Menn, Esther, 13n30
messianism, 49, 56 , 56n73, 57nn74–75, 96–97, 107
metalepsis, 122–23
midrash
   atomistic approach to exegesis, 83, 84, 87, 90
   audience for, 134n56
   davar aher in, 91, 95, 96
   exegesis in, 83–84, 86
   gezerah shavah used in, 100
   on God's presence in exile, 91–93, 92n20
   on Jeremiah, 88, 91–93, 93n22, 95, 95n32
   messianic perorations in, 96
   metalepsis in, 122–23
   puns used in, 90, 94, 106, 132
   thematic coherence in, 85–87
   on Torah, 83–84
   See also allusions; Pesikta de-Rav Kahana; *petiḥtot*; piyyutim; Targum Jonathan
Mintz, Alan, 46
Mirsky, Aaron, 117n11

mother of seven sons narrative, 145

N, O

nature, God's influence on, 63, 63n82, 64, 69
Nebuchadnezzar, 29, 89, 92, 93n22, 96, 97
Nebuzaradan, 92, 93, 93n22
Netser, Ehud, 109
Neusner, Jacob, 4
Ninth of Av. *See* Tisha b'Av
nymphomania, 42, 47, 47n57

P, Q

Palestinian Jews, 1–4, 7–8, 21–22, 157
Pentateuch. *See* Torah and Torah readings
Pesikta de-Rav Kahana
   alternate names for, 21–22, 42
   audience for, 10
   as *beit midrash* product, 81–82, 170
   Buber edition of, 22, 151
   calendrical order of, 80–81, 80n2, 82
   consolation in, 59n77, 109–10
   on God's influence on nature, 63n82
   on haftarot of rebuke, 20, 20nn6–8, 21, 42
   kal vaḥomer, 99, 99n36, 100, 101, 102, 103n43
   messianic perorations in, 96–97
   origins of, 79–80, 79n1, 80n2
   paradigm of correspondence in, 105–6, 107
   petiḥtot as sermons, 9, 81–82, 81–82n4

public recitation of scripture and, 82
rebuke, haftarot of, 20, 20nn6–8, 88
temple in Jerusalem absent from, 109
Yannai on haftarot of rebuke and, 22
Pesikta de-Rav Kahana 13
    davar aher, 91, 95, 96, 97
    Isaiah 10:30 linked with Jeremiah 1:1, 90–91
    on Jer 1:1, 87–89
    messianic perorations in, 96–97
    petihta of, 89–90
    rebuke, punishment and consolation in narrative of rebuke, 88–89
Pesikta de-Rav Kahana 22
    birth of Isaac, 98–99, 99n36, 100–101, 100n38
    gezerah shavah used in, 100
    on Isaiah 61:10, 99–104
    Song of Songs in, 22, 105–7, 133
pesukei dezimra, 24, 24n16, 25
petihtot
    birth of Isaac, 98–99, 99n36, 100–101, 100n39
    davar aher, 91, 95, 96, 97
    Isa 61:10 as, 101–2
    poetics of, 89–91, 98–104
    as sermons, 9, 81–82, 81–82n4
    Sitz im Leben of, 81–83
    Zion's fertility, 145–46
Pirqoi b. Boboi, 115
piyyutim
    allusion in, 121–22
    as didactic, 117, 118n14
    divine address in, 117, 117n11
    kedushta genre, 114
    literary analysis of, 13n30
    manner of recitation, 114
    metalepsis, 122–23

midrashim compared to, 118
    origins of, 114–16, 116n9
    poetic function of, 118, 118n15
    prayer and, 5, 115, 117, 153–54
    rabbinic Judaism and, 5, 8n22
    research tools for, 13n30
    temple cult in, 175
    yotser genre, 114
    See also kedushtot
prayer
    amidah, 114, 115, 117, 137
    biblical verses in, 117–18
    pesukei dezimra, 24, 24n16, 25
    piyyutim as, 5, 115
    redemptive response to, 147–48, 153–54
    shema, 24, 25, 25n17, 114, 115
    See also kedushtot
proems. *See petihtot*
prophecy, reliability of, 48–50, 49, 49n59
Psalms
    on catastrophe, 30
    consolation themes in, 34
    garment texts in, 105, 105n46, 106
    on Jerusalem, 141, 150, 151–52n88, 152, 153
    in *kedushtot*, 139, 149, 150
    of rejoicing, 99–100, 99n37

R

rabbinic Judaism
    authority of, 1–2
    beit midrash and, 8, 9, 10, 81–82, 157, 170
    history and, 11–12, 33, 172–73
    images of the deity in, 4
    literature of, 9–10, 81–84, 155–56, 170–71
    liturgical poetry and, 8n22
    rituals in, 4–5

synagogues and, 3–6, 75, 75n103
temple in Jerusalem, 109–10
Tisha b'Av lectionary cycle and, 23–24
See also midrash; Pesikta de-Rav Kahana; *petiḥtot*; piyyutim

rebuke, haftarot of
consequences of transgression in, 40–41
God as omnipotent agent in, 174
Isaiah in, 20, 20n8, 42–43, 44, 63
Israel's role in, 174
Jeremiah in, 20, 41–42, 87–88, 89, 90
Lamentations and, 20, 20n28, 31, 40–41, 48, 50
Pesikta de-Rav Kahana and, 20, 20nn6–8, 88
sexual transgression in, 42, 44, 46–47, 47n57
sinfulness recounted in, 41–42
sin-punishment-redemption paradigm, 88

redemption
crowning imagery and, 125, 127
garment texts and, 105, 105n46, 106, 106nn48–50, 124, 126, 127
God's love for Israel, 71–72, 98, 101–4, 103n43, 105, 106–7, 108, 132
Isaac's birth and, 101
prayer and, 147–48, 153–54
romance as trope for, 101, 132
Torah obedience and, 148–49
of Zion, 67, 70–71

Rendtorff, Rolf, 63n82

rhyme patterns
in *kedushtot*, 120, 128–30, 142–44
meaning in, 120
words in, 120–21, 120n20, 120n22
Zion in, 129, 130, 142–44

romantic love, 101, 102, 104, 104n45, 132, 153, 163, 167
Rosh Hashanah, 24–25n16, 73, 117, 172, 174

S

Samau'al ibn Yahyā al-Maghribī, 115
Sarah (biblical matriarch), 98–99, 99n36, 100–101, 100n40, 103n43, 145
Sarason, Richard, 81–82n4, 169
Scheindlin, Raymond, 117–18
Schwartz, Seth, 2, 7, 74–75, 76, 109, 113n2, 172–73
Second Isaiah
anthropomorphic portrait of God, 161
consolation, haftarot of, and, 55, 58, 60–69, 125, 128, 134–36, 150–51, 159–60
exiles in, 53, 55, 64–65, 127
garment imagery in, 56, 105–6
God's omnipotence and, 62, 69, 69n90, 162–63
Jerusalem in, 55, 56, 57, 57n75
Lamentations and, 52–55, 52n61, 52n64, 53n68, 127
paradigm of correspondence in, 105–6, 107
reconciliation of God and Israel in, 57, 61–66
on restoration and redemption, 54, 55, 57, 57n75
Targum Jonathan to, 162–67
sermons, 9, 81–82, 81–82n4
seventeenth of Tammuz, 29–31, 171–72
seven weeks of consolation, 21, 23, 26, 41
sexual imagery, 42, 45–48, 47n57, 164–66

shekhinah, 95, 95n33, 131, 158, 159, 159n13
shema, 24, 25, 25n17, 114, 115
Shinan, Avigdor, 13n30
Sinaitic revelation, 17–18, 18n1
sin-punishment-repentance-redemption, 109, 172
sin-punishment-restoration narrative, 40, 43, 44, 76, 88, 96, 110
Sitz im Leben, 9, 13, 81, 114–16, 169
Smolar, Leivy, 159
Sommer, Benjamin, 52n61, 54
Song of Songs
  allusions to in piyyutim, 130–31
  bride imagery in, 105, 105n46, 124n31, 131–34, 133n53
  dove (image) in, 140, 140n62, 144, 145, 146–47
  God-Israel relationship in, 130n47
  in Pesikta de-Rav Kahana 22, 105–7, 133
  romance in, 130–31
speakers
  in kedushtot, 143, 143n72, 143n74
  in Lamentations, 72–73, 143n74
  on rejoicing, 63, 65, 67–68
  in Tisha b'Av lectionary cycle, 59–60, 59n77, 73
Stern, David, 25, 27, 28, 28n24, 81–84, 86–87, 86n13, 169
suckling children, 32, 99, 100, 135, 141
synagogues
  archaeological evidence for, 2–3
  art in, 3, 4, 5, 75–76, 109
  of Palestinian Jews, 3–4
  population attending, 7, 7n25, 9
  rabbinic Judaism and, 3–6, 75, 75n103
  representations of God in, 108–9
  rituals in, 4–5
  sanctity of, 7–8, 7n20

targumim in, 10, 155–56
temple in Jerusalem identified with, 7–8, 75, 109–10
Torah shrines in, 5, 109
See also kedushtot; piyyutim; prayer

T, U, V

Targum Jonathan
  anthropomorphisms in, 158–63, 160n14
  Aramaic of, 157–58, 164, 166
  audience for, 10, 170–71
  on barrenness, 164–65
  biblical text and, 170
  emendations of text, 164
  erotic trope emended in, 163
  gendered personifications of Israel in, 163–64
  interpretation of haftarah texts, 156
  Kallir poetry compared to, 167–68
  memra in, 160, 160n16
  Pesikta de-Rav Kahana compared to, 167–68
  problematic Hebrew elements in, 158
  romance in, 166
  Second Isaiah and, 162
  shekhinah in, 158, 159, 159n13
  as synagogue texts, 10
  Tisha b'Av lectionary cycle compared to, 167–68
  translation and, 12, 157–58
  YHWH, 158–59
  Zion desexualized in, 164–66
Targum Onkelos, 10
temple in Jerusalem
  destruction of, 28–29, 31, 34, 45–46, 46n55, 48, 97, 151
  exiles' return to, 132, 136

Lebanon as epithet for, 131–32
nostalgia for, 109–10, 136, 170
reconstruction of, 97, 127, 136
synagogues identified with, 7–8, 75, 109–10
towers as epithet for, 125, 125n37
Theodosian Code, 4
the three weeks, 30–31, 30nn27–28, 76, 171–72
Tisha b'Av
  communal participation in, 36–37, 36n39, 72–73, 173–74
  as day of doom, 29–33, 76
  ketev meriri, 30–31
  reversal trope in, 135–36
  seventeenth of Tammuz and, 29–31, 171–72
  seven weeks of consolation and, 21, 23, 26, 41
  theology of, 11–12
  Tu b'Av (fifteenth of Av) and, 172
  See also destruction of the temples in Jerusalem; Lamentations; temple in Jerusalem
Tisha b'Av lectionary cycle
  anthology genre, 25–26, 27, 28, 28n24
  catastrophes in, 29–33
  chronological scheme in, 48–49
  consolation in, 58–59, 59n77
  cosmology and, 76
  "daughter of Zion" in, 31–32, 45, 124n33, 124n35
  dialogic arrangement of, 58–59, 59n77, 66, 68–69
  Lamentations in, 31, 40–41, 43, 43n50, 51–52, 76–77
  origins of, 21–23
  planting imagery in, 43–44, 63n81, 140n63

power of exhortation in, 73–74, 90–91
redaction of, 23–24, 26, 27–28, 31
sacrifice trope in, 147, 147n78
shema and, 24, 25, 25n17
sin-punishment-restoration narrative in, 40, 43, 44, 76, 88, 110
synagogue identification with temple and, 7–8. 109–110, 75
temple absent from, 175
tripartite structure, 40
See also consolation, haftarot of; Isaiah; Jeremiah; rebuke, haftarot of; Second Isaiah
Torah and Torah readings
  communal schedules of, 9–10n26
  haftarot readings and, 18, 19–20
  lectionary systems of, 21–22
  midrashic exegesis of, 83–84
  Pentateuch and, 17, 18–19
  prophetic books' status compared to, 18–19
  rituals of, 18n2, 18n4, 116n9
  Sinaitic revelation and, 17–18, 18n1, 106
  strength as epithet for, 106
  in synagogue, 5
tosafists, 20–21n8, 22, 42
Tu b'Av (fifteenth of Av), 172

W, X, Y

Weems, Renita J., 47n57
Weiss, Zvi, 109
Westermann, Claus, 35, 36–37, 36n39, 38, 63nn81–82
Willey, Patricia Tull, 52–54, 52n64
Wimsatt, W. K., 120
Yannai, 21–22, 42
YHWH
  on children of Zion, 165

compassion of, 60, 61, 92 , 93, 141
divine movements of, 160, 161–62
in exile with Israel, 131
as Helios, 108
Israel's transgressions and, 60, 131
Jeremiah and, 93
love for Israel, 65, 101, 147
restoration and, 36–37, 57n75, 62, 63
as source of Israel's suffering, 33
in Targum Jonathan, 158–59
York, Anthony, 155

Z

Zion
children of, 163, 164, 165
consolation for, 58–59, 127
daughter of, 31–32, 45, 124, 124n33, 124n35
exiles return to, 60, 132, 136
female personification of, 32, 37, 45–46, 66, 142, 163–64
as garden, 140n63, 141
garment imagery, 124, 126
God's love for Israel, 104
isolation of, 47–48, 126, 143, 143n74
in *kedushtot*, 124, 124n33, 124n35, 126, 127, 129, 130, 140n64, 141–44
lamentations of, 74, 137–38, 141
moral corruption of, 46–48, 47n57, 138, 138n60
as mother, 135, 144–46, 145n75, 164–65
as mourning dove, 146–47
redemption of, 67, 70–71
rejoicing of, 100, 102, 104, 135
in rhyme patterns, 129, 130, 142–44
as rising from the dust, 55, 124n35, 127, 129, 132, 132n51, 153n54, 163
Targum Jonathan on, 164
worshipping community, 72–73
zodiac motifs, 7, 97, 108
Zunz, Leopold, 21, 22, 79n1, 80n2